BLACK IVORY

R. M. BALLANTYNE

1ˢᵗ WORLD
LIBRARY
Literary Society

Black Ivory

R. M. Ballantyne

© 1st World Library, 2007
PO Box 2211
Fairfield, IA 52556
www.1stworldlibrary.com
First Edition

LCCN: 2007934198

Softcover ISBN: 978-1-4218-9671-7
Hardcover ISBN: 978-1-4218-9771-4
eBook ISBN: 978-1-4218-9571-0

Purchase *"Black Ivory"*
as a traditional bound book at:
www.1stWorldLibrary.com/purchase.asp?ISBN=978-1-4218-9671-7

1st World Library is a literary, educational organization
dedicated to:

- Creating a free internet library of downloadable ebooks

- Hosting writing competitions and offering book publishing
scholarships.

**Interested in more 1st World Library books? contact:
literacy@1stworldlibrary.com**

Check us out at: www.1stworldlibrary.com

1st World Library Literary Society

Giving Back to the World

"If you want to work on the core problem, it's early school literacy."

- James Barksdale, former CEO of Netscape

"No skill is more crucial to the future of a child, or to a democratic and prosperous society, than literacy."

- Los Angeles Times

"Literacy... means far more than learning how to read and write... The aim is to transmit... knowledge and promote social participation."

- UNESCO

"Literacy is not a luxury, it is a right and a responsibility. If our world is to meet the challenges of the twenty-first century we must harness the energy and creativity of all our citizens."

- President Bill Clinton

"Parents should be encouraged to read to their children, and teachers should be equipped with all available techniques for teaching literacy, so the varying needs and capacities of individual kids can be taken into account."

- Hugh Mackay

In writing this book, my aim has been to give a true picture in outline of the Slave Trade as it exists at the present time on the east coast of Africa.

In order to do this I have selected from the most trustworthy sources what I believe to be the most telling points of "the trade," and have woven these together into a tale, the warp of which is composed of thick cords of fact; the woof of slight lines of fiction, just sufficient to hold the fabric together. Exaggeration has easily been avoided, because—as Dr Livingstone says in regard to the slave-trade—"exaggeration is impossible."

If the reader's taste should be offended by finding the tragic and comic elements in too close proximity I trust that he will bear in remembrance that "such is life," and that the writer who would be true to life must follow, not lead, nature.

I have to acknowledge myself indebted to Dr Ryan, late Bishop of Mauritius; to the Rev. Charles New, interpreter to the Livingstone Search Expedition; to Edward Hutchinson, Esquire, Lay Secretary to the Church Missionary Society, and others, for kindly furnishing me with information in connexion with the slave trade.

Besides examining the Parliamentary Blue-books which treat of this subject, I have read or consulted, among others, the various authoritative works to which reference is made in the foot-notes sprinkled throughout this book,—all of which works bear the strongest possible testimony to the fact that the horrible traffic in human beings is in all respects as bad at the present time on the east coast of Africa as it ever was on the west coast in the days of Wilberforce.

I began my tale in the hope that I might produce something to interest the young (perchance, also, the old) in a most momentous cause,—the total abolition of the African slave-trade. I close it with the prayer that God may make it a tooth in the file which shall eventually cut the chains of slavery, and set the black man free.

R.M. Ballantyne.

1873

CHAPTER ONE

SHOWS THAT A GOOD BEGINNING MAY SOMETIMES BE FOLLOWED BY A BAD ENDING

"Six feet water in the hold, sir!"

That would not have been a pleasant announcement to the captain of the 'Aurora' at any time, but its unpleasantness was vastly increased by the fact that it greeted him near the termination of what had been, up to that point of time, an exceedingly prosperous voyage.

"Are you sure, Davis?" asked the captain; "try again."

He gave the order under the influence of that feeling which is styled "hoping against hope," and himself accompanied the ship's carpenter to see it obeyed.

"Six feet two inches," was the result of this investigation.

The vessel, a large English brig, had sprung a leak, and was rolling heavily in a somewhat rough sea off the east coast of Africa. It was no consolation to her captain that the shores of the great continent were visible on his lee, because a tremendous surf roared along the whole line of coast, threatening destruction to any vessel that should venture to approach, and there was no harbour of refuge nigh.

"She's sinking fast, Mr Seadrift," said the captain to a stout frank-looking youth of about twenty summers, who leant against the bulwarks and gazed wistfully at the land; "the carpenter cannot find the leak, and the rate at which the water is rising shows that she cannot float long."

"What then do you propose to do?" inquired young Seadrift, with a troubled expression of countenance.

"Abandon her," replied the captain.

"Well, *you* may do so, captain, but I shall not forsake my father's ship as long as she can float. Why not beach her somewhere on the coast? By so doing we might save part of the cargo, and, at all events, shall have done the utmost that lay in our power."

"Look at the coast," returned the captain; "where would you beach her? No doubt there is smooth water inside the reef, but the channels through it, if there be any here, are so narrow that it would be almost certain death to make the attempt."

The youth turned away without replying. He was sorely perplexed. Just before leaving England his father had said to him, "Harold, my boy, here's your chance for paying a visit to the land you've read and talked so much about, and wished so often to travel through. I have chartered a brig, and shall send her out to Zanzibar with a cargo of beads, cotton cloth, brass wire, and such like: what say you to go as supercargo? Of course you won't be able to follow in the steps of Livingstone or Mungo Park, but while the brig is at Zanzibar you will have an opportunity of running across the channel, the island being only a few miles from the main, and having a short run up-country to see the niggers, and perchance have a slap at a hippopotamus. I'll line your pockets, so that you won't lack the sinews of war, without which travel either at home or abroad is but sorry work, and I shall only expect you to give a good account of ship and cargo on your return.—Come, is it fixed?"

Need we say that Harold leaped joyfully at the proposal? And now, here he was, called on to abandon the 'Aurora' to her fate, as we have said, near the end of a prosperous voyage. No wonder that he was perplexed.

The crew were fully aware of the state of matters. By the captain's orders they stood ready to lower the two largest boats, into which they had put much of their worldly goods and provisions as they could hold with safety.

"Port, port your helm," said the captain to the man at the wheel.

"Port it is, sir," replied the man at the wheel, who was one of those broad-shouldered, big-chested, loose-garmented, wide-trousered, bare-necked, free-and-easy, off-hand jovial tars who have done so much, in years gone by, to increase the wealth and prosperity of the British Empire, and who, although confessedly scarce, are considerately allowed to perish in hundreds annually on our shores for want of a little reasonable legislation. But cheer up, ye jolly tars! There is a glimmer of sunrise on your political horizon. It really does seem as if, in regard to you, there were at last "a good time coming."

"Port, port," repeated the captain, with a glance at the compass and the sky.

"Port it is, sir," again replied the jovial one.

"Steady! Lower away the boat, lads.—Now, Mr Seadrift," said the captain, turning with an air of decision to the young supercargo, "the time has come for you to make up your mind. The water is rising in the hold, and the ship is, as you see, settling fast down. I need not say to you that it is with the utmost regret I find it necessary to abandon her; but self-preservation and the duty I owe to my men render the step absolutely necessary. Do you intend to go with us?"

"No, captain, I don't," replied Harold Seadrift firmly. "I do not blame you for consulting your own safety, and doing what you believe to be your duty, but I have already said that I shall stick by the ship as long as she can float."

"Well, sir, I regret it but you must do as you think best," replied the captain, turning away—"Now, lads, jump in."

The men obeyed, but several of those who were last to quit the ship looked back and called to the free-and-easy man who still stood at the wheel—"Come along, Disco; we'll have to shove off directly."

"Shove off w'en you please," replied the man at the wheel, in a deep rich voice, whose tones were indicative of a sort of good-humoured contempt; "wot I means for to do is to stop where I am. It'll never be said of Disco Lillihammer that he forsook the owner's son in distress."

"But you'll go to the bottom, man, if you don't come."

"Well, wot if I do? I'd raither go to the bottom with a brave man, than remain at the top with a set o' fine fellers like *you*!"

Some of the men received this reply with a laugh, others frowned, and a few swore, while some of them looked

R. M. Ballantyne

regretfully at their self-willed shipmate; for it must not be supposed that *all* the tars who float upon the sea are of the bold, candid, open-handed type, though we really believe that a large proportion of them are so.

Be this as it may, the boats left the brig, and were soon far astern.

"Thank you, Lillihammer," said Harold, going up and grasping the horny hand of the self-sacrificing sea-dog. "This is very kind of you, though I fear it may cost you your life. But it is too late to talk of that; we must fix on some plan, and act at once."

"The werry thing, sir," said Disco quietly, "that wos runnin' in my own mind, 'cos it's werry clear that we hain't got too many minits to spare in confabilation."

"Well, what do you suggest?"

"Arter you, sir," said Disco, pulling his forelock; "you are capting now, an' ought to give orders."

"Then I think the best thing we can do," rejoined Harold, "is to make straight for the shore, search for an opening in the reef, run through, and beach the vessel on the sand. What say you?"

"As there's nothin' else left for us to do," replied Disco, "that's 'zactly wot I think too, an' the sooner we does it the better."

"Down with the helm, then," cried Harold, springing forward, "and I'll ease off the sheets."

In a few minutes the 'Aurora' was surging before a stiff

breeze towards the line of foam which indicated the outlying reef, and inside of which all was comparatively calm.

"If we only manage to get inside," said Harold, "we shall do well."

Disco made no reply. His whole attention was given to steering the brig, and running his eyes anxiously along the breakers, the sound of which increased to a thunderous roar as they drew near.

"There seems something like a channel yonder," said Harold, pointing anxiously to a particular spot in the reef.

"I see it, sir," was the curt reply.

A few minutes more of suspense, and the brig drove into the supposed channel, and struck with such violence that the foremast snapped off near the deck, and went over the side.

"God help us, we're lost!" exclaimed Harold, as a towering wave lifted the vessel up and hurled her like a plaything on the rocks.

"Stand by to jump, sir," cried Disco. Another breaker came roaring in at the moment, overwhelmed the brig, rolled her over on her beam-ends, and swept the two men out of her. They struggled gallantly to free themselves from the wreck, and, succeeding with difficulty, swam across the sheltered water to the shore, on which they finally landed.

Harold's first exclamation was one of thankfulness for their deliverance, to which Disco replied with a hearty "Amen!" and then turning round and surveying the coast, while he slowly thrust his hands into his wet trouser-pockets, wondered whereabouts in the world they had got to.

"To the east coast of Africa, to be sure," observed the young supercargo, with a slight smile, as he wrung the water out of the foot of his trousers, "the place we were bound for, you know."

"Werry good; so here we are—come to an anchor! Well, I only wish," he added, sitting down on a piece of driftwood, and rummaging in the pockets before referred to, as if in search of something—"I only wish I'd kep' on my weskit, 'cause all my 'baccy's there, and it would be a rael comfort to have a quid in the circumstances."

It was fortunate for the wrecked voyagers that the set of the current had carried portions of their vessel to the shore, at a considerable distance from the spot where they had landed, because a band of natives, armed with spears and bows and arrows, had watched the wreck from the neighbouring heights, and had hastened to that part of the coast on which they knew from experience the cargo would be likely to drift. The heads of the swimmers being but small specks in the distance, had escaped observation. Thus they had landed unseen. The spot was near the entrance to a small river or creek, which was partially concealed by the formation of the land and by mangrove trees.

Harold was the first to observe that they had not been cast on an uninhabited shore. While gazing round him, and casting about in his mind what was best to be done, he heard shouts, and hastening to a rocky point that hid part of the coast from his view looked cautiously over it and saw the natives. He beckoned to Disco, who joined him.

"They haven't a friendly look about 'em," observed the seaman, "and they're summat scant in the matter of clothin'."

"Appearances are often deceptive," returned his companion,

"but I so far agree with you that I think our wisest course will be to retire into the woods, and there consult as to our future proceedings, for it is quite certain that as we cannot live on sand and salt water, neither can we safely sleep in wet clothes or on the bare ground in a climate like this."

Hastening towards the entrance to the creek, the unfortunate pair entered the bushes, through which they pushed with some difficulty, until they gained a spot sufficiently secluded for their purpose, when they observed that they had passed through a belt of underwood, beyond which there appeared to be an open space. A few steps further and they came out on a sort of natural basin formed by the creek, in which floated a large boat of a peculiar construction, with very piratical-looking lateen sails. Their astonishment at this unexpected sight was increased by the fact that on the opposite bank of the creek there stood several men armed with muskets, which latter were immediately pointed at their breasts.

The first impulse of the shipwrecked friends was to spring back into the bushes—the second to advance and hold up their empty hands to show that they were unarmed.

"Hold on," exclaimed Disco, in a free and easy confidential tone; "we're friends, we are; shipwrecked mariners we is, so ground arms, my lads, an' make your minds easy."

One of the men made some remark to another, who, from his Oriental dress, was easily recognised by Harold as one of the Arab traders of the coast. His men appeared to be half-castes.

The Arab nodded gravely, and said something which induced his men to lower their muskets. Then with a wave of his hand he invited the strangers to come over the creek to him.

This was rendered possible by the breadth of the boat already

R. M. Ballantyne

mentioned being so great that, while one side touched the right bank of the creek, the other was within four or five feet of the left.

Without hesitation Harold Seadrift bounded lightly from the bank to the half-deck of the boat, and, stepping ashore, walked up to the Arab, closely followed by his companion.

"Do you speak English?" asked Harold.

The Arab shook his head and said, "Arabic, Portuguese."

Harold therefore shook *his* head;—then, with a hopeful look, said "French?" interrogatively.

The Arab repeated the shake of his head, but after a moments' thought said, "I know littil Engleesh; speak, where comes you?"

"We have been wrecked," began Harold (the Arab glanced gravely at his dripping clothes, as if to say, I had guessed as much), "and this man and I are the only survivors of the crew of our ship—at least the only two who swam on shore, the others went off in a boat."

"Come you from man-of-war?" asked the Arab, with a keen glance at the candid countenance of the youth.

"No, our vessel was a trader bound for Zanzibar. She now lies in fragments on the shore, and we have escaped with nothing but the clothes on our backs. Can you tell us whether there is a town or a village in the neighbourhood? for, as you see, we stand sadly in need of clothing, food, and shelter. We have no money, but we have good muscles and stout hearts, and could work our way well enough, I doubt not."

Young Seadrift said this modestly, but the remark was unnecessary, for it would have been quite obvious to a man of much less intelligence than the Arab that a youth who, although just entering on the age of manhood, was six feet high, deep-chested, broad-shouldered, and as lithe as a kitten, could not find any difficulty in working his way, while his companion, though a little older, was evidently quite as capable.

"There be no town, no village, for fifty miles from where you stand," replied the Arab.

"Indeed!" exclaimed Harold in surprise, for he had always supposed the East African coast to be rather populous.

"That's a blue look-out anyhow," observed Disco, "for it necessitates starvation, unless this good gentleman will hire us to work his craft. It ain't very ship-shape to be sure, but anything of a seagoin' craft comes more or less handy to an old salt."

The trader listened with the politeness and profound gravity that seems to be characteristic of Orientals, but by no sign or expression showed whether he understood what was said.

"*I* go to Zanzibar," said he, turning to Harold, "and will take you,—so you wish."

There was something sinister in the man's manner which Harold did not like, but as he was destitute, besides being in the Arab's power, and utterly ignorant of the country, he thought it best to put a good face on matters, and therefore thanked him for his kind offer, and assured him that on reaching Zanzibar he would be in a position to pay for his passage as well as that of his friend.

R. M. Ballantyne

"May I ask," continued Harold, "what your occupation is?"

"I am trader."

Harold thought he would venture another question:—

"In what sort of goods do you trade?"

"Ivory. Some be white, an' some be what your contrymans do call black."

"Black!" exclaimed Harold, in surprise.

"Yees, black," replied the trader. "White ivory do come from the elephant—hims tusk; Black Ivory do come,"—he smiled slightly at this point—"from the land everywheres. It bees our chef artikil of trade."

"Indeed! I never heard of it before."

"No?" replied the trader; "you shall see it much here. But I go talk with my mans. Wait."

Saying this, in a tone which savoured somewhat unpleasantly of command, the Arab went towards a small hut near to which his men were standing, and entered into conversation with them.

It was evident that they were ill pleased with what he said at first for there was a good deal of remonstrance in their tones, while they pointed frequently in a certain direction which seemed to indicate the coast-line; but by degrees their tones changed, and they laughed and chuckled a good deal, as if greatly tickled by the speech of the Arab, who, however, maintained a look of dignified gravity all the time.

"I don't like the looks o' them fellers," remarked Disco, after observing them in silence for some time. "They're a cut-throat set, I'm quite sure, an' if you'll take my advice, Mister Seadrift, we'll give 'em the slip, an' try to hunt up one o' the native villages. I shouldn't wonder, now, if that chap was a slave-trader."

"The same idea has occurred to myself, Disco," replied Harold, "and I would willingly leave him if I thought there was a town or village within twenty miles of us; but we are ignorant on that point and I have heard enough of the African climate to believe that it might cost us our lives if we were obliged to spend a night in the jungle without fire, food, or covering, and with nothing on but a wet flannel shirt and pair of canvas breeches. No, no, lad, we must not risk it. Besides, although some Arabs are slave-traders, it does not follow that all are. This fellow may turn out better than he looks."

Disco Lillihammer experienced some sensations of surprise on hearing his young friend's remarks on the climate, for he knew nothing whatever about that of Africa, having sailed chiefly in the Arctic Seas as a whaler,—and laboured under the delusion that no climate under the sun could in any degree affect his hardy and well-seasoned frame. He was too respectful, however, to let his thoughts be known.

Meanwhile the Arab returned.

"I sail this night," he said, "when moon go down. That not far before midnight. You mus keep by boat here—close. If you go this way or that the niggers kill you. They not come *here*; they know I is here. I go look after my goods and chattels—my Black Ivory."

"Mayn't we go with 'ee, mister—what's your name?"

R. M. Ballantyne

"My name?—Yoosoof," replied the Arab, in a tone and with a look which were meant to command respect.

"Well, Mister Yoosoof," continued Disco, "if we may make bold to ax leave for to go with 'ee, we could lend 'ee a helpin' hand, d'ye see, to carry yer goods an' chattels down to the boat."

"There is no need," said Yoosoof, waving his hand, and pointing to the hut before mentioned. "Go; you can rest till we sail. Sleep; you will need it. There is littil rice in hut—eat that, and make fire, dry youselfs."

So saying, the Arab left them by a path leading into the woods, along which his men, who were Portuguese half-castes, had preceded him.

"Make fire indeed!" exclaimed Disco, as he walked with his companion to the hut; "one would think, from the free-and-easy way in which he tells us to make it, that he's in the habit himself of striking it out o' the point o' his own nose, or some such convenient fashion."

"More likely to flash it out of his eyes, I should think," said Harold; "but, see here, the fellow knew what he was talking about. There is fire among these embers on the hearth."

"That's true," replied Disco, going down on his knees, and blowing them carefully.

In a few minutes a spark leaped into a flame, wood was heaped on, and the flame speedily became a rousing fire, before which they dried their garments, while a pot of rice was put on to boil.

Scarcely had they proceeded thus far in their preparations,

when two men, armed with muskets, were seen to approach, leading a negro girl between them. As they drew nearer, it was observable that the girl had a brass ring round her neck, to which a rope was attached.

"A slave!" exclaimed Disco vehemently, while the blood rushed to his face; "let's set her free!"

The indignant seaman had half sprung to his legs before Harold seized and pulled him forcibly back.

"Be quiet man," said Harold quickly. "If we *could* free her by fighting, I would help you, but we can't. Evidently we have got into a nest of slavers. Rashness will only bring about our own death. Be wise; bide your time, and we may live to do some good yet."

He stopped abruptly, for the new comers had reached the top of the winding path that led to the hut.

A look of intense surprise overspread the faces of the two men when they entered and saw the Englishmen sitting comfortably by the fire, and both, as if by instinct threw forward the muzzles of their muskets.

"Oh! come in, come in, make your minds easy," cried Disco, in a half-savage tone, despite the warning he had received; "we're all *friends* here—leastwise we can't help ourselves."

Fortunately for our mariner the men did not understand him, and before they could make up their minds what to think of it, or how to act Harold rose, and, with a polite bow, invited them to enter.

"Do you understand English?" he asked.

A frown, and a decided shake of the head from both men, was the reply. The poor negro girl cowered behind her keepers, as if she feared that violence were about to ensue.

Having tried French with a like result, Harold uttered the name, "Yoosoof," and pointed in the direction in which the trader had entered the woods.

The men looked intelligently at each other, and nodded.

Then Harold said "Zanzibar," and pointed in the direction in which he supposed that island lay.

Again the men glanced at each other, and nodded. Harold next said "Boat—dhow," and pointed towards the creek, which remark and sign were received as before.

"Good," he continued, slapping himself on the chest, and pointing to his companion, "*I* go to Zanzibar, *he* goes, *she* goes," (pointing to the girl), "*you* go, and Yoosoof goes—all in the dhow together to Zanzibar—to-night—when moon goes down. D'ee understand? Now then, come along and have some rice."

He finished up by slapping one of the men on the shoulder, and lifting the kettle off the fire, for the rice had already been cooked and only wanted warming.

The men looked once again at each other, nodded, laughed, and sat down on a log beside the fire, opposite to the Englishmen.

They were evidently much perplexed by the situation, and, not knowing what to make of it, were disposed in the meantime to be friendly.

While they were busy with the rice, Disco gazed in silent wonder, and with intense pity, at the slave-girl, who sat a little to one side of her guardians on a mat, her small hands folded together resting on one knee, her head drooping, and her eyes cast down. The enthusiastic tar found it very difficult to restrain his feelings. He had heard, of course, more or less about African slavery from shipmates, but he had never read about it, and had never seriously given his thoughts to it, although his native sense of freedom, justice, and fair-play had roused a feeling of indignation in his breast whenever the subject chanced to be discussed by him and his mates. But now, for the first time in his life, suddenly and unexpectedly, he was brought face to face with slavery. No wonder that he was deeply moved.

"Why, Mister Seadrift," he said, in the confidential tone of one who imparts a new discovery, "I do honestly confess to 'ee that I think that's a *pretty* girl!"

"I quite agree with you," replied Harold, smiling.

"Ay, but I mean *really* pretty, you know. I've always thought that all niggers had ugly flat noses an' thick blubber lips. But look at that one: her lips are scarce a bit thicker than those of many a good-looking lass in England, and they don't stick out at all, and her nose ain't flat a bit. It's quite as good as my Nancy's nose, an' that's sayin' a good deal, *I* tell 'ee. Moreover, she ain't black—she's brown."

It is but justice to Disco to say that he was right in his observations, and to explain that the various negro tribes in Africa differ very materially from each other; some of them, as we are told by Dr Livingstone, possessing little of what, in our eyes, seems the characteristic ugliness of the negro— such as thick lips, flat noses, protruding heels, etcetera,—but being in every sense handsome races of humanity.

The slave-girl whom Disco admired and pitied so much belonged to one of these tribes, and, as was afterwards ascertained, had been brought from the far interior. She appeared to be very young, nevertheless there was a settled expression of meek sorrow and suffering on her face; and though handsomely formed, she was extremely thin, no doubt from prolonged hardships on the journey down to the coast.

"Here, have somethin' to eat," exclaimed Disco, suddenly filling a tin plate with rice, and carrying it to the girl, who, however, shook her head without raising her eyes.

"You're not hungry, poor thing," said the seaman, in a disappointed tone; "you look as if you should be. Come, try it," he added, stooping, and patting her head.

The poor child looked up as if frightened, and shrank from the seaman's touch, but on glancing a second time in his honest face, she appeared to feel confidence in him. Nevertheless, she would not touch the rice until her guardians said something to her sternly, when she began to eat with an appetite that was eloquent.

"Come, now, tell us what your name is, lass," said Disco, when she had finished the rice.

Of course the girl shook her head, but appeared to wish to understand the question, while the Portuguese laughed and seemed amused with the Englishman's eccentricities.

"Look here, now," resumed the tar, slapping his own chest vigorously, "Disco, Disco, Disco, that's me—Disco. And this man," (patting his companion on the breast) "is Harold, Harold, that's him—Harold. Now, then," he added, pointing straight at the girl, "you—what's you name, eh?"

A gleam of intelligence shot from the girl's expressive eyes, and she displayed a double row of beautiful teeth as in a low soft voice she said—"Azinte."

"Azinte? come, that's not a bad name; why, it's a capital one. Just suited to 'ee. Well, Azinte, my poor girl," said Disco, with a fresh outburst of feeling, as he clenched his horny right hand and dashed it into the palm of his left, "if I only knew how to set you free just now, my dear, I'd do it—ay, if I was to be roasted alive for so doin'. I would!"

"You'll never set anybody free in this world," said Harold Seadrift, with some severity, "if you go on talking and acting as you have done to-day. If these men had not, by good fortune, been ignorant of our language, it's my opinion that they would have blown our brains out before this time. You should restrain yourself, man," he continued, gradually dropping into a remonstrative and then into an earnestly confidential tone; "we are utterly helpless just now. If you did succeed in freeing that girl at this moment, it would only be to let her fall into the hands of some other slave-owner. Besides, that would not set free all the other slaves, male and female, who are being dragged from the interior of Africa. You and I *may* perhaps do some small matter in the way of helping to free slaves, if we keep quiet and watch our opportunity, but we shall accomplish nothing if you give way to useless bursts of anger."

Poor Lillihammer was subdued.

"You're right Mister Seadrift, you're right, sir, and I'm a ass. I never *could* keep my feelings down. It's all along of my havin' bin made too much of by my mother, dear old woman, w'en I was a boy. But I'll make a effort, sir; I'll clap a stopper on 'em—bottle 'em up and screw 'em down tight, werry tight indeed."

Disco again sent his right fist into the palm of his left hand, with something like the sound of a pistol-shot to the no small surprise and alarm of the Portuguese, and, rising, went out to cool his heated brow in the open air.

CHAPTER TWO

YOOSOOF'S "BLACK IVORY"

When Yoosoof entered the woods, as before stated, for the purpose of looking after his property, he followed a narrow footpath for about half a mile, which led him to another part of the same creek, at the entrance of which we introduced him to the reader. Here, under the deep shadow of umbrageous trees, floated five large Arab boats, or dhows, similar to the one which has been already referred to. They were quite empty, and apparently unguarded, for when Yoosoof went down the bank and stood on a projecting rock which overlooked them, no one replied to his low-toned hail. Repeating it once, and still receiving no answer, he sat quietly down on the rocks, lighted a small pipe, and waited patiently.

The boats, as we have said, were empty, but there were some curious appliances in them, having the appearance of chains, and wristlets, and bars of iron running along and fixed to their decks, or rather to the flooring of their holds. Their long yards and sails were cleared and ready for hoisting.

After the lapse of ten or fifteen minutes, Yoosoof raised his head—for he had been meditating deeply, if one might judge from his attitude—and glanced in the direction of an opening in the bushes whence issued a silent and singular train of

R. M. Ballantyne

human beings. They were negroes, secured by the necks or wrists—men, women, and children,—and guarded by armed half-caste Portuguese. When a certain number of them, about a hundred or so, had issued from the wood, and crowded the banks of the creek, they were ordered to stand still, and the leader of the band advanced towards his master.

These were some of Yoosoof's "goods and chattels," his "cattle," his "black ivory."

"You have been long in coming, Moosa," said the Arab trader, as the man approached.

"I have," replied Moosa, somewhat gruffly, "but the road was rough and long, and the cattle were ill-conditioned, as you see."

The two men spoke in the Portuguese tongue, but as the natives and settlers on that coast speak a variety of languages and dialects, we have no alternative, good reader, but to render all into English.

"Make the more haste now," said Yoosoof; "get them shipped at once, for we sail when the moon goes down. Pick out the weakest among the lot, those most likely to die, and put them by themselves in the small dhow. If we *must* sacrifice some of our wares to these meddling dogs the English, we may as well give them the refuse."

Without remark, Moosa turned on his heel and proceeded to obey orders.

Truly, to one unaccustomed to such scenes, it would have appeared that all the negroes on the spot were "most likely to die," for a more wretched, starved set of human beings could scarcely be imagined. They had just terminated a journey on foot of several hundreds of miles, with insufficient food and under severe hardships. Nearly all of them were lean to a degree,—many so reduced that they resembled nothing but skeletons with a covering of black leather. Some of the children were very young, many of them mere infants, clinging to the backs of the poor mothers, who had carried them over mountain and plain, through swamp and jungle, in blistering sunshine and pelting rain for many weary days. But prolonged suffering had changed the nature of these little ones. They were as silent and almost as intelligently anxious as their seniors. There were no old pieces of merchandise there. Most were youthful or in the prime of life; a few were middle-aged.

Difficult though the task appeared to be, Moosa soon selected about fifty men and women and a few children, who were so fearfully emaciated that their chance of surviving appeared but small. These were cast loose and placed in a sitting posture in the hold of the smallest dhow, as close together as they could be packed.

Their removal from the bank made room for more to issue from the wood, which they did in a continuous stream. Batch after batch was cast loose and stowed away in the manner already described, until the holds of two of the large boats were filled, each being capable of containing about two hundred souls. This was so far satisfactory to Yoosoof, who had expended a good deal of money on the venture— satisfactory, even although he had lost a large proportion of the goods—four-fifths at least if not more, by death and otherwise, on the way down to the coast; but that was a matter of little consequence. The price of black ivory was up in the market just at that time, and the worthy merchant could stand a good deal of loss.

The embarkation was effected with wonderful celerity, and

R. M. Ballantyne

in comparative silence. Only the stern voices of the half-caste Portuguese were heard as they ordered the slaves to move, mingled with the occasional clank of a chain, but no sounds proceeded from the thoroughly subdued and worn-out slaves louder than a sigh or a half-suppressed wail, with now and then a shriek of pain when some of the weaker among them were quickened into activity by the lash.

When all had been embarked, two of the five boats still remained empty, but Yoosoof had a pretty good idea of the particular points along the coast where more "cattle" of a similar kind could be purchased. Therefore, after stationing some of his men, armed with muskets, to guard the boats, he returned with the remainder of them to the hut in which the Englishmen had been left.

There he found Azinte and her guardians. He seemed angry with the latter at first, but after a few minutes' thought appeared to recover his equanimity, and ordered the men to remove the ropes with which the girl was tethered; then bidding her follow him he left the hut without taking any notice of the Englishmen further than to say he would be back shortly before the time of sailing.

Yoosoof's motions were usually slow and his mien some-what dignified, but, when occasion required, he could throw off his Oriental dignity and step out with the activity of a monkey. It was so on this occasion, insomuch that Azinte was obliged occasionally to run in order to keep up with him. Proceeding about two miles in the woods along the shore without halt, he came out at length on the margin of a bay, at the head of which lay a small town. It was a sorry-looking place, composed of wretchedly built houses, most of which were thatched with the leaves of the cocoa-nut palm.

Nevertheless, such as it was, it possessed a mud fort, an

army of about thirty soldiers, composed of Portuguese convicts who had been sent there as a punishment for many crimes, a Governor, who was understood to be honourable, having been placed there by his Excellency the Governor-General at Mozambique, who had been himself appointed by His Most Faithful Majesty the King of Portugal.

It was in quest of this Governor that Yoosoof bent his rapid steps. Besides all the advantages above enumerated, the town drove a small trade in ivory, ebony, indigo, orchella weed, gum copal, cocoa-nut oil, and other articles of native produce, and a very large (though secret) trade in human bodies and—we had almost written—souls, but the worthy people who dwelt there could not fetter souls, although they could, and very often did, set them free.

Senhor Francisco Alfonso Toledo Bignoso Letotti, the Governor, was seated at the open window of his parlour, just before Yoosoof made his appearance, conversing lightly with his only daughter, the Senhorina Maraquita, a beautiful brunette of about eighteen summers, who had been brought up and educated in Portugal.

The Governor's wife had died a year before this time in Madrid, and the Senhorina had gone to live with her father on the east coast of Africa, at which place she had arrived just six weeks previous to the date of the opening of our tale.

Among the various boats and vessels at anchor in the bay, were seen the tapering masts of a British war-steamer. The Senhorina and her sire were engaged in a gossiping criticism of the officers of this vessel when Yoosoof was announced. Audience was immediately granted.

Entering the room, with Azinte close behind him, the Arab stopped abruptly on beholding Maraquita, and bowed gravely.

"Leave us, my child," said the Governor, in Portuguese; "I have business to transact with this man."

"And why may not I stay to assist you, father, in this wonderful man-mystery of transacting business?" asked Maraquita, with an arch smile.

"Whenever you men want to get rid of women you frighten them away with *business*! If you wish not to explain something to us, you shake your wise heads, and call it *business*! Is it not so?—Come, Arab," she added, turning with a sprightly air to Yoosoof, "you are a trader, I suppose; all Arabs are, I am told. Well, what sort of wares have you got to sell?"

Yoosoof smiled slightly as he stepped aside and pointed to Azinte.

The speaking countenance of the Portuguese girl changed as if by magic. She had seen little and thought little about slavery during the brief period of her residence on the coast, and had scarcely realised the fact that Sambo, with the thick lips—her father's gardener—or the black cook and house-maids, were slaves. It was the first entrance of a new idea with something like power into her mind when she saw a delicate, mild-looking, and pretty negro girl actually offered for sale.

Before she could bethink herself of any remark the door opened, and in walked, unannounced, a man on whose some-what handsome countenance villainy was clearly stamped.

"Ha! Marizano," exclaimed Senhor Letotti, rising, "you have thought better of it, I presume?"

"I have, and I agree to your arrangement," replied Marizano, in an off-hand, surly tone.

"There is nothing like necessity," returned the Governor, with a laugh. "'Twere better to enjoy a roving life for a short time with a lightish purse in one's pocket, than to attempt to keep a heavy purse with the addition of several ounces of lead in one's breast! How say you?"

Marizano smiled and shrugged his broad shoulders, but made no reply, for just then his attention had been attracted to the slave-girl.

"For sale?" he inquired of the Arab carelessly.

Yoosoof bowed his head slightly.

"How much?"

"Come, come, gentlemen," interposed the Governor, with a laugh and a glance at his daughter, "you can settle this matter elsewhere. Yoosoof has come here to talk with me on other matters.—Now, Maraquita dear, you had better retire for a short time."

When the Senhorina had somewhat unwillingly obeyed, the Governor turned to Yoosoof: "I presume you have no objection to Marizano's presence during our interview, seeing that he is almost as well acquainted with your affairs as yourself?"

As Yoosoof expressed no objection, the three drew their chairs together and sat down to a prolonged private and very interesting palaver.

We do not mean to try the reader's patience by dragging him through the whole of it; nevertheless, a small portion of what

R. M. Ballantyne

was said is essential to the development of our tale.

"Well, then, be it as you wish, Yoosoof," said the Governor, folding up a fresh cigarette; "you are one of the most active traders on the coast, and never fail to keep correct accounts with your Governor. You deserve encouragement but I fear that you run considerable risk."

"I know that; but those who make much must risk much."

"Bravo!" exclaimed Marizano, with hearty approval; "nevertheless those who risk most do not always make most. Contrast yourself with me, now. You risk your boats and cattle, and become rich. I risk my life, and behold! I am fleeced. I have little or nothing left, barely enough to buy yonder girl from you—though I *think* I have enough for that."

He pointed as he spoke to Azinte, who still stood on the spot where she had been left near the door.

"Tell me," resumed Senhor Letotti, "how do you propose to elude the English cruiser? for I know that her captain has got wind of your whereabouts, and is determined to watch the coast closely—and let me tell you, he is a vigorous, intelligent man."

"You tell me he has a number of captured slaves already in his ship?" said Yoosoof.

"Yes, some hundreds, I believe."

"He must go somewhere to land these, I presume?" rejoined the Arab.

Yoosoof referred here to the fact that when a British cruiser engaged in the suppression of the slave-trade on the east coast of Africa has captured a number of slaves, she is under the necessity of running to the Seychelles Islands, Aden, or some other British port of discharge, to land them there as free men, because, were she to set them free on any part of the coast of Africa, belonging either to Portugal or the Sultan of Zanzibar, they would certainly be recaptured and again enslaved. When therefore the cruisers are absent—it may be two or three weeks on this duty, the traders in human flesh of course make the most of their opportunity to run cargoes of slaves to those ports in Arabia and Persia where they always find a ready market.

On the present occasion Yoosoof conceived that the captain of the 'Firefly' might be obliged to take this course to get rid of the negroes already on board, who were of course consuming his provisions, besides being an extremely disagreeable cargo, many of them being diseased and covered with sores, owing to their cruel treatment on board the slave-dhows.

"He won't go, however, till he has hunted the coast north and south for you, so he assures me," said the Governor, with a laugh.

"Well, I must start to-night, therefore I shall give him a small pill to swallow which will take him out of the way," said Yoosoof, rising to leave the room.

"I wish you both success," said the Governor, as Marizano also rose to depart, "but I fear that you will find the Englishman very troublesome.—Adieu."

The Arab and the half-caste went out talking earnestly together, and followed by Azinte, and immediately afterwards the Senhorina Maraquita entered hurriedly.

"Father, you must buy that slave-girl for me. I want a pretty slave all to myself," she said, with unwonted vehemence.

"Impossible, my child," replied the Governor kindly, for he was very fond as well as proud of his daughter.

"Why impossible? Have you not enough of money?"

"Oh yes, plenty of that, but I fear she is already bespoken, and I should not like to interfere—"

"Bespoken! do you mean sold?" cried Maraquita, seizing her father's hands, "not sold to that man Marizano?"

"I think she must be by this time, for he's a prompt man of business, and not easily thwarted when he sets his mind to a thing."

The Senhorina clasped her hands before her eyes, and stood for a moment motionless, then rushing wildly from the room she passed into another apartment the windows of which commanded a view of a considerable part of the road which led from the house along the shore. There she saw the Arab and his friend walking leisurely along as if in earnest converse, while Azinte followed meekly behind.

The Senhorina stood gazing at them with clenched hands, in an agony of uncertainty as to what course she ought to pursue, and so wrapt up in her thoughts that she failed to observe a strapping young lieutenant of H.M.S. steamer 'Firefly,' who had entered the room and stood close to her side.

Now this same lieutenant happened to be wildly in love with Senhorina Maraquita. He had met her frequently at her father's table, where, in company with his captain, he was entertained with great hospitality, and on which occasions the captain was assisted by the Governor in his investigations into the slave-trade.

Lieutenant Lindsay had taken the romantic plunge with all the charming enthusiasm of inexperienced youth, and entertained the firm conviction that, if Senhorina Maraquita did not become "his," life would thenceforth be altogether unworthy of consideration; happiness would be a thing of the past, with which he should have nothing more to do, and death at the cannon's mouth, or otherwise, would be the only remaining gleam of comfort in his dingy future.

"Something distresses you, I fear," began the lieutenant, not a little perplexed to find the young lady in such a peculiar mood.

Maraquita started, glanced at him a moment, and then, with flashing eyes and heightened colour, pointed at the three figures on the road.

"Yes, Senhor," she said; "I am distressed—deeply so. Look! do you see yonder two men, and the girl walking behind them?"

"I do."

"Quick! fly after them and bring them hither—the Arab and the girl I mean—not the other man. Oh, be quick, else they will be out of sight and then she will be lost; quick, if you— if—if you really mean what you have so often told me."

Poor Lindsay! It was rather a sudden and severe test of fidelity to be sent forth to lay violent hands on a man and woman and bring them forcibly to the Governor's house, without any better reason than that a self-willed girl ordered him so to do; at the same time, he perceived that, if he did not act promptly, the retreating figures would soon turn into

R. M. Ballantyne

the town, and be hopelessly beyond his power of recognition.

"But—but—" he stammered, "if they won't come—?"

"They *must* come. Threaten my father's high displeasure.—
Quick, Senhor," cried the young lady in a commanding tone.

Lindsay flung open the casement and leapt through it as
being the shortest way out of the house, rushed with
undignified speed along the road, and overtook the Arab and
his friend as they were about to turn into one of the narrow
lanes of the town.

"Pardon me," said the lieutenant laying his hand on
Yoosoof's shoulder in his anxiety to make sure of him, "will
you be so good as to return with me to the Governor's
residence?"

"By whose orders?" demanded Yoosoof with a look of
surprise.

"The orders of the Senhorina Maraquita."

The Arab hesitated, looked somewhat perplexed, and said
something in Portuguese to Marizano, who pointed to the
slave-girl, and spoke with considerable vehemence.

Lindsay did not understand what was said, but, conjecturing
that the half-caste was proposing that Azinte should remain
with him, he said:—"The girl must return with you—if you
would not incur the Governor's displeasure."

Marizano, on having this explained to him, looked with
much ferocity at the lieutenant and spoke to Yoosoof in
wrathful tones, but the latter shook his head, and the former,
who disliked Marizano's appearance excessively, took not

the least notice of him.

"I do go," said Yoosoof, turning back. Motioning to Azinte to follow, he retraced his steps with the lieutenant and the slave—while Marizano strode into the town in a towering rage.

We need scarcely say that Maraquita, having got possession of Azinte, did not find it impossible to persuade her father to purchase her, and that Yoosoof, although sorry to disappoint Marizano, who was an important ally and assistant in the slave-trade, did not see his way to thwart the wishes of the Governor, whose power to interfere with his trade was very great indeed, and to whom he was under the necessity of paying head-money for every slave that was exported by him from that part of the coast.

Soon after Azinte had been thus happily rescued from the clutches of two of the greatest villains on the East African coast—where villains of the deepest dye are by no means uncommon—Lindsay met Captain Romer of the 'Firefly' on the beach, with his first lieutenant Mr Small, who, by the way, happened to be one of the largest men in his ship. The three officers had been invited to dine that day with the Governor, and as there seemed no particular occasion for their putting to sea that night, and a fresh supply of water had to be taken on board, the invitation had been accepted, all the more readily, too, that Captain Romer thought it afforded an opportunity for obtaining further information as to the movements of certain notorious slavers who were said to be thereabouts at that time. Lieutenant Lindsay had been sent ashore at an earlier part of the day, accompanied by one of the sailors who understood Portuguese, and who, being a remarkably intelligent man, might, it was thought, acquire some useful information from some of the people of the town.

R. M. Ballantyne

"Well, Mr Lindsay, has Jackson been of any use to you?" inquired the captain.

"Not yet," replied the lieutenant; "at least I know not what he may have done, not having met him since we parted on landing; but I have myself been so fortunate as to rescue a slave-girl under somewhat peculiar circumstances."

"Truly, a most romantic and gallant affair," said the captain, laughing, when Lindsay had related the incident, "and worthy of being mentioned in despatches; but I suspect, considering the part that the Senhorina Maraquita played in it and the fact that you only rescued the girl from one slaveholder in order to hand her over to another, the less that is said about the subject the better!—But here comes Jackson. Perhaps he may have learned something about the scoundrels we are in search of."

The seaman referred to approached and touched his cap.

"What news?" demanded the captain, who knew by the twinkle in Jack's eye that he had something interesting to report.

"I've diskivered all about it sir," replied the man, with an ill-suppressed chuckle.

"Indeed! come this way. Now, let's hear what you have to tell," said the captain, when at a sufficient distance from his boat to render the conversation quite private.

"Well, sir," began Jackson, "w'en I got up into the town, arter leavin' Mr Lindsay, who should I meet but a man as had bin a messmate o' mine aboard of that there Portuguese ship w'ere I picked up a smatterin' o' the lingo? Of course we hailed each other and hove-to for a spell, and then we made sail for a grog-shop, where we spliced the main-brace. After a deal o' tackin' and beatin' about, which enabled me to find out that he'd left the sea an' taken to business on his own account, which in them parts seems to mean loafin' about doin' little or nothin', I went slap into the subject that was uppermost in my mind, and says I to him, says I, they does a deal o' slavin' on this here coast, it appears—Black Ivory is a profitable trade, ain't it? W'y, sir, you should have seen the way he grinned and winked, and opened out on 'em.—'Black Ivory!' says he, 'w'y, Jackson, there's more slaves exported from these here parts annooally than would fill a good-sized city. I could tell you—but,' says he, pullin' up sudden, 'you won't split on me, messmate?' 'Honour bright,' says I, 'if ye don't call tellin' my captain splittin'.' 'Oh no,' says he, with a laugh, 'it's little I care what *he* knows, or does to the pirates—for that's their true name, and murderers to boot—but don't let it come to the Governor's ears, else I'm a ruined man.' I says I wouldn't and then he goes on to tell me all sorts of hanecdots about their doin's—that they does it with the full consent of the Governor, who gets head-money for every slave exported; that nearly all the Governors on the coast are birds of the same feather, and that the Governor-General himself, [See Consul McLeod's *Travels in Eastern Africa*, volume one page 306.] at Mozambique, winks at it and makes the subordinate Governors pay him tribute. Then he goes on to tell me more about the Governor of this here town, an' says that, though a kind-hearted man in the main, and very good to his domestic slaves, he encourages the export trade, because it brings him in a splendid revenue, which he has much need of, poor man, for like most, if not all, of the Governors on the coast, he do receive nothin' like a respectible salary from the Portuguese Government at home, and has to make it up by slave-tradin'." [See McLeod's *Travels*, volume one page 293.]

It must be explained here that British cruisers were, and still

R. M. Ballantyne

are, kept on the east coast of Africa, for the purpose of crushing only the *export* slave-trade. They claim no right to interfere with "domestic slavery," an institution which is still legal in the dominions of the Sultan of Zanzibar and in the so-called colonies of Portugal on that coast.

"But that is not the best of it, sir," continued Jackson, with a respectful smile, "after we'd had our jaw out I goes off along the road by the beach to think a bit what I'd best do, an' have a smoke—for that's wot usually sets my brain to work full-swing. Bein' hot I lay down in the lee of a bush to excogitate. You see, sir, my old messmate told me that there are two men here, the worst characters he ever know'd—ashore or afloat. One they calls Yoosoof—an Arab he is; the other Marizano—he's a slave-catcher, and an outlaw just now, havin' taken up arms and rebelled against the Portuguese authorities. Nevertheless these two men are secretly hand and glove with the Governor here, and at this moment there are said to be a lot o' slaves ready for shipment and only waitin' till the 'Firefly' is out of the way. More than this my friend could not tell, so that's w'y I went to excogitate.—I beg parding, sir, for being so long wi' my yarn, but I ain't got the knack o' cuttin' it short, sir, that's w'ere it is."

"Never mind, lad; go on to the end of it," replied the captain. "Did you excogitate anything more?"

"I can't say as I did, sir, but it was cooriously enough excogitated *for* me. W'en I was lying there looking through the bush at the bay, I sees two men comin' along, arm in arm. One of 'em was an Arab. W'en they was near I saw the Arab start; I thought he'd seen me, and didn't like me. No more did I like him or his comrade. However, I was wrong, for after whisperin' somethin' very earnest-like to his friend, who laughed very much; but said nothin', they came and sat down not far from the bush where I lay. Now, thinks I, it ain't pleasant to be an eavesdropper, but as I'm here to find out the secrets of villains, and as these two look uncommon like villains, I'll wait a bit; if they broach business as don't consarn me or her Majesty the Queen, I'll sneeze an' let 'em know I'm here, before they're properly under weigh; but if they speaks of wot I wants to know, I'll keep quiet. Well, sir, to my surprise, the Arab—he speaks in bad English, whereby I came to suppose the other was an Englishman, but, if he is, the climate must have spoiled him badly, for I never did see such a ruffian to look at. But he only laughed, and didn't speak, so I couldn't be sure. Well, to come to the pint, sir, the Arab said he'd got hold of two shipwrecked Englishmen, whom he meant to put on board of his dhow, at that time lyin' up a river not three miles off, and full of slaves, take 'em off the coast, seize 'em when asleep, and heave 'em overboard; the reason bein' that he was afraid, if they was left ashore here, they'd discover the town, which they are ignorant of at present, and give the alarm to our ship, sir, an' so prevent him gettin' clear off, which he means to attempt about midnight just after the moon goes down."

This unexpected information was very gratifying to Captain Romer, who immediately gave orders to get steam up and have everything in readiness to start the moment he should make his appearance on board, at the same time enjoining absolute silence on his lieutenants and Jackson, who all returned to the 'Firefly,' chuckling inwardly.

If they had known that the Arab's information, though partly true, was a *ruse*; that Jackson had indeed been observed by the keen-eyed Oriental, who had thereupon sat down purposely within earshot, and after a whispered hint to his companion, gave forth such information as would be likely to lead the British cruiser into his snares—speaking in bad English, under the natural impression that the sailor did not understand Portuguese, to the immense amusement of

R. M. Ballantyne

Marizano, who understood the *ruse*, though he did not understand a single word of what his companion said—had they known all this, we say, it is probable that they would have chuckled less, and—but why indulge in probabilities when facts are before us? The sequel will show that the best-laid plans may fail.

CHAPTER THREE

RELATES THE FURTHER ADVENTURES OF HAROLD AND DISCO, AND LIFTS THE CURTAIN A LITTLE HIGHER IN REGARD TO THE SLAVE-TRADE

So Captain Romer and his lieutenants went to dine with the worthy Governor Senhor Francisco Alfonso Toledo Bignoso Letotti, while Yoosoof returned to the creek to carry out his deep-laid plans.

In regard to the dinner, let it suffice to observe that it was good, and that the Governor was urbane, hospitable, communicative, and every way agreeable. It is probable that if he had been trained in another sphere and in different circumstances he might have been a better man. As things stood, he was unquestionably a pleasant one, and Captain Romer found it hard to believe that he was an underhand schemer.

Nothing could exceed the open way in which Senhor Letotti condemned the slave-trade, praised the English for their zeal in attempting to suppress it, explained that the King of Portugal and the Sultan of Zanzibar were equally anxious for its total extinction, and assured his guests that he would do everything that lay in his power to further their efforts to

R. M. Ballantyne

capture the guilty kidnappers, and to free the poor slaves!

"But, my dear sir," said he, at the conclusion of an emphatic declaration of sympathy, "the thing is exceedingly difficult. You are aware that Arab traders swarm upon the coast, that they are reckless men, who possess boats and money in abundance, that the trade is very profitable, and that, being to some extent real traders in ivory, palm-oil, indigo, and other kinds of native produce, these men have many *ruses* and methods—what you English call dodges—whereby they can deceive even the most sharp-sighted and energetic. The Arabs are smart smugglers of negroes—very much as your people who live in the Scottish land are smart smugglers of the dew of the mountain—what your great poet Burns speaks much of—I forget its name—it is not easy to put them down."

After dinner, Senhor Letotti led the officers into his garden, and showed them his fruit-trees and offices, also his domestic slaves, who looked healthy, well cared for, and really in some degree happy.

He did not, however, tell his guests that being naturally a humane man, his slaves were better treated than any other slaves in the town. He did not remind them that, being slaves, they were his property, his goods and chattels, and that he possessed the right and the power to flay them alive if so disposed. He did not explain that many in the town *were* so disposed; that cruelty grows and feeds upon itself; that there were ladies and gentlemen there who flogged their slaves—men, women, and children—nearly to the death; that one gentleman of an irascible disposition, when irritated by some slight oversight on the part of the unfortunate boy who acted as his valet, could find no relief to his feelings until he had welted him first into a condition of unutterable terror, and then into a state of insensibility. Neither did he inform them that a certain lady in the town, who seemed at most times to be possessed of a reasonably quiet spirit, was roused once to such a degree by a female slave that she caused her to be forcibly held, thrust a boiling hot egg into her mouth, skewered her lips together with a sail-needle, and then striking her cheeks, burst the egg, and let the scalding contents run down her throat. [See Consul McLeod's *Travels*, volume two page 32.]

No, nothing of all this did the amiable Governor Letotti so much as hint at. He would not for the world have shocked the sensibilities of his guests by the recital of such cruelties. To say truth, the worthy man himself did not like to speak or think of them. In this respect he resembled a certain class among ourselves, who, rather than submit to a little probing of their feelings for a few minutes, would prefer to miss the chance of making an intelligently indignant protest against slavery, and would allow the bodies and souls of their fellow-men to continue writhing in agony through all time.

It was much more gratifying to the feelings of Senhor Letotti to convey his guests to the drawing-room, and there gratify their palates with excellent coffee, while the graceful, and now clothed, Azinte brought a Spanish guitar to the Senhorina Maraquita, whose sweet voice soon charmed away all thoughts of the cruel side of slavery. But duty ere long stepped in to call the guests to other scenes.

"What a sweet girl the Senhorina is!" remarked Captain Romer, while on his way to the beach.

"Ay, and what a pretty girl Azinte is, black though she be," observed Lieutenant Small.

"Call her not black; she is brown—a brunette," said the captain.

"I wonder how *we* should feel," said Lindsay, "if the tables were turned, and *our* women and children, with our stoutest young men, were forcibly taken from us by thousands every year, and imported into Africa to grind the corn and hoe the fields of the black man. Poor Azinte!"

"Do you know anything of her history?" inquired Mr Small.

"A little. I had some conversation in French with the Senhorina just before we left—"

"Yes, I observed that," interrupted the captain, with a quiet smile.

"And," continued Lindsay, "she told me that she had discovered, through an interpreter, that the poor girl is married, and that her home is far away in the interior. She was caught, with many others, while out working in the fields one day several months ago, by a party of slave-traders, under an Arab named Yoosoof and carried off. Her husband was absent at the time; her infant boy was with its grandmother in their village, and she thinks may have escaped into the woods, but she has not seen any of them again since the day of her capture."

"It is a sad case," said the captain, "and yet bad though it be, it might be far worse, for Azinte's master and mistress are very kind, which is more than can be said of most slave-owners in this region."

In a few minutes the captain's gig was alongside the "Firefly," and soon afterwards that vessel quietly put to sea. Of course it was impossible that she should depart unobserved, but her commander took the precaution to run due south at first, exactly opposite to the direction of his true course, intending to make a wide sweep out to sea, and thus get unobserved to the northward of the place where the slaver's dhow was supposed to be lying, in time to intercept it.

Yoosoof, from a neighbouring height watched the manoeuvre, and thoroughly understood it. When the vessel had disappeared into the shades of night that brooded over the sea, he smiled calmly, and in a placid frame of mind betook himself to his lair in the creek beside the mangrove trees.

He found Harold Seadrift and Disco Lillihammer in the hut, somewhat impatient of his prolonged absence, and a dozen of his men looking rather suspiciously at the strangers.

"Is all ready, Moosa?" he inquired of a powerful man, half-Portuguese, half-negro in appearance, who met him outside the door of the hut.

"All ready," replied the half-caste, in a gruff tone of voice, "but what are you going to do with these English brutes?"

"Take them with us, of course," replied Yoosoof.

"For what end?"

"For our own safety. Why, don't you see, Moosa, that if we had set them free, they might have discovered the town and given information to the cruiser about us, which would have been awkward? We might now, indeed, set them free, for the cruiser is gone, but I still have good reason for wishing to take them with me. They think that we have but *one* boat in this creek, and I should like to make use of them for the purpose of propagating that false idea. I have had the good luck while in the town to find an opportunity of giving one of the sailors of the cruiser a little information as to my movements—some of it true, some of it false—which will perhaps do us a service."

The Arab smiled slightly as he said this.

"Do these men know our trade?" asked Moosa.

"I think they suspect it," answered Yoosoof.

"And what if they be not willing to go with us?" demanded Moosa.

"Can twelve men not manage two?" asked the Arab. Dark though the night had become by that time, there was sufficient light to gleam on the teeth that Moosa exposed on receiving this reply.

"Now, Moosa, we must be prompt," continued Yoosoof; "let some of you get round behind the Englishmen, and have the slave-chains handy. Keep your eye on me while I talk with them; if they are refractory, a nod shall be the signal."

Entering the hut Yoosoof informed Harold that it was now time to set sail.

"Good, we are ready," said Harold, rising, "but tell me one thing before my comrade and I agree to go with you,—tell us honestly if you are engaged in the slave-trade."

A slight smile curled the Arab's thin lip as he replied—"If I be a slave-trader, I cannot speak honestly, so you Engleesh think. But I do tell you—yes, I am."

"Then, I tell *you* honestly," said Harold, "that I won't go with you. I'll have nothing to do with slavers."

"Them's my sentiments to a tee," said Disco, with emphasis,

thumping his left palm as usual with his right fist, by way of sheating his remark home—to use his own words.

"But you will both perish on this uninhabited coast," said Yoosoof.

"So be it," replied Harold; "I had rather run the risk of starving than travel in company with slave-traders. Besides, I doubt the truth of what you say. There must be several villages not very far off, if my information in regard to the coast be not altogether wrong."

Yoosoof waited for no more. He nodded to Moosa, who instantly threw a noose round Harold's arms, and drew it tight. The same operation was performed for Disco, by a stout fellow who stood behind him, and almost before they realised what had occurred, they were seized by a number of men.

It must not be supposed that two able-bodied Englishmen quietly submitted at once to this sort of treatment. On the contrary, a struggle ensued that shook the walls of the little hut so violently as almost to bring it down upon the heads of the combatants. The instant that Harold felt the rough clasp of Moosa's arms, he bent himself forward with such force as to fling that worthy completely over his head, and lay him flat on the floor, but two of the other slavers seized Harold's arms, a third grasped him round the waist, and a fourth rapidly secured the ropes that had been thrown around him. Disco's mode of action, although somewhat different was quite as vigorous. On being grasped he uttered a deep roar of surprise and rage, and, raising his foot, struck out therewith at a man who advanced to seize him in front. The kick not only tumbled the man over a low bench and drove his head against the wall, but it caused the kicker himself to recoil on his foes behind with such force that they all fell on the floor

R. M. Ballantyne

together, when by their united weight the slavers managed to crush the unfortunate Disco, not, indeed, into submission, but into inaction.

His tongue, however, not being tied, continued to pour forth somewhat powerful epithets, until Harold very strongly advised him to cease.

"If you want to retain a whole skin," he said, "you had better keep a quiet tongue."

"P'raps you're right sir," said Disco, after a moment's consideration, "but it ain't easy to shut up in the succumstances."

After they had thoroughly secured the Englishmen, the traders led them down the bank of the creek to the spot where the dhow was moored. In the dark it appeared to Harold and his companion to be the same dhow, but this was not so. The boat by which they had crossed the creek had been removed up the water, and its place was now occupied by the dhow into which had been put the maimed and worn-out slaves of the band whose arrival we have described. The hold of the little vessel was very dark, nevertheless there was light enough to enable the Englishmen to guess that the rows of black objects just perceptible within it were slaves. If they had entertained any uncertainty on this point, the odour that saluted them as they passed to the stern would have quickly dispelled their doubts.

It was evident from the manner of the slavers that they did not now fear discovery, because they talked loudly as they pushed off and rowed away. Soon they were out of the creek, and the roar of breakers was heard. Much caution was displayed in guiding the dhow through these, for the channel was narrow, and darkness rendered its position almost indiscernible. At last the sail was hoisted, the boat bent over to a smart breeze, and held away in a north-easterly direction. As the night wore on this breeze became lighter, and, most of the crew being asleep, deep silence prevailed on board the slave-dhow, save that, ever and anon, a pitiful wail, as of a sick child, or a convulsive sob, issued from the hold.

Harold and Disco sat beside each other in the stern, with an armed half-caste on each side, and Yoosoof in front. Their thoughts were busy enough at first, but neither spoke to the other. As the night advanced both fell into an uneasy slumber.

When Harold awoke, the grey dawn was beginning to break in the east and there was sufficient light to render objects dimly visible. At first he scarcely recollected where he was, but the pain caused by the ropes that bound him soon refreshed his memory. Casting his eyes quickly towards the hold, his heart sank within him at the sight he there beheld. Yoosoof's Black Ivory was not of the best quality, but there was a good deal of it, which rendered judicious packing necessary. So many of his gang had become worthless as an article of trade, through suffering on the way down to the coast, that the boat could scarce contain them all. They were packed sitting on their haunches in rows each with his knees close to his chin, and all jammed so tightly together that none could rise up or lie down. Men, women, and little children sat in this position with an expression of indescribable hopelessness and apathy on their faces. The infants, of which there were several, lay motionless on their mothers' shrunken breasts. God help them! they were indeed utterly worthless as pieces of merchandise. The long journey and hard treatment had worn all of them to mere skin and bone, and many were suffering from bad sores caused by the slave-irons and the unmerciful application of the lash. No one knew better than Yoosoof that this was his "damaged stock"—hopelessly damaged, and he meant to make the best use he could of it.

The sun arose in all its splendour, and revealed more clearly to the horrified Englishmen all the wretchedness of the hold, but for a considerable time they did not speak. The circumstances in which they found themselves seemed to have bereft them of the faculty of speech. The morning advanced, and Yoosoof with his men, took a frugal breakfast, but they did not offer any to Harold or Disco. As these unfortunates had, however, supped heartily, they did not mind that. So much could not have been said for the slaves. They had received their last meal of uncooked rice and water, a very insufficient one, about thirty-six hours before, and as they watched the traders at breakfast, their glaring eyes told eloquently of their sufferings.

Had these been Yoosoof's valuable stock, his undamaged goods, he would have given them a sufficiency of food to have kept them up to condition as long as he possessed them; but being what they were, a very little drop of water and a few grains of raw rice at noon was deemed sufficient to prevent absolute starvation.

"How can you have the heart," said Harold at last turning to Yoosoof, "to treat these poor creatures so cruelly?"

Yoosoof shrugged his shoulders.

"My fader treat them so; I follow my fader's footsteps."

"But have you no pity for them? Don't you think they have hearts and feelings like ourselves?" returned Harold earnestly.

"No," replied the Arab coldly. "They have no feelings. Hard as the stone. They care not for mother, or child, or husband. Only brutes—cattle."

Harold was so disgusted with this reply that he relapsed into silence.

Towards the afternoon, while the dhow was running close in-shore, a vessel hove in sight on the horizon. A few minutes sufficed to show that it was a steamer. It was of course observed and closely watched by the slave-dealers as well as by Harold Seadrift and Disco Lillihammer, who became sanguinely hopeful that it might turn out to be a British man-of-war. Had they known that Yoosoof was equally anxious and hopeful on that point they would have been much surprised; but the wily Arab pretended to be greatly alarmed, and when the Union Jack became clearly visible his excitement increased. He gave some hurried orders to his men, who laughed sarcastically as they obeyed them.

"Yoosoof," said Harold, with a slight feeling of exultation, "your plans seem about to miscarry!"

"No, they not miscarry yet," replied the Arab, with a grim smile.

"Tell me, Yoosoof," resumed Harold, prompted by strong curiosity, "why have you carried us off bound in this fashion?"

Another smile, more grim than the former, crossed the Arab's visage as he replied—"Me carry you off 'cause that sheep," pointing to the steamer, "lie not two mile off, near to town of Governor Letotti, when I first met you. We not want you to let thems know 'bout us, so I carry you off, and I bind you 'cause you strong."

"Ha! that's plain and reasonable," returned Harold, scarce able to restrain a laugh at the man's cool impudence. "But it would appear that some one else has carried the news; so, you see, you have been outwitted after all."

"Perhaps. We shall see," replied the Arab, with something approaching to a chuckle.

Altering the course of the boat, Yoosoof now ran her somewhat off the shore, as if with a view to get round a headland that lay to the northward. This evidently drew the attention of the steamer—which was none other than the "Firefly"—for she at once altered her course and ran inshore, so as to intercept the dhow. Seeing this, Yoosoof turned back and made for the land at a place where there was a long line of breakers close to the shore. To run amongst these seemed to be equivalent to running on certain destruction, nevertheless the Arab held on, with compressed lips and a frowning brow. Yoosoof looked quite like a man who would rather throw away his life than gratify his enemy, and the Englishmen, who were fully alive to their danger, began to feel rather uneasy—which was a very pardonable sensation, when it is remembered that their arms being fast bound, rendered them utterly unable to help themselves in case of the boat capsizing.

The "Firefly" was by this time near enough to hold converse with the dhow through the medium of artillery. Soon a puff of white smoke burst from her bow, and a round-shot dropped a few yards astern of the boat.

"That's a broad hint, my lad, so you'd better give in," said Lillihammer, scarce able to suppress a look of triumph.

Yoosoof paid not the slightest attention to the remark, but held on his course.

"Surely you don't intend to risk the lives of these poor creatures in such a surf?" said Harold anxiously; "weak and worn as they are, their doom is sealed if we capsize."

Still the Arab paid no attention, but continued to gaze steadily at the breakers.

Harold, turning his eyes in the same direction, observed something like a narrow channel running through them. He was enough of a seaman to understand that only one who was skilled in such navigation could pass in safety.

"They're lowering a boat," said Disco, whose attention was engrossed by the manoeuvres of the "Firefly."

Soon the boat left the side of the vessel, which was compelled to check her speed for fear of running on the reef. Another gun was fired as she came round, and the shot dropped right in front of the dhow, sending a column of water high into the air. Still Yoosoof held on until close to the breakers, when, to the surprise of the Englishmen, he suddenly threw the boat's head into the wind.

"You can steer," he said sternly to Disco. "Come, take the helm an' go to your ship; or, if you choose, go on the breakers."

He laughed fiercely as he said this, and next moment plunged into the sea, followed by his crew.

Disco, speechless with amazement, rose up and sprang to the helm. Of course he could not use his bound hands, but one of his legs answered almost as well. He allowed the boat to come round until the sail filled on the other tack, and then looking back, saw the heads of the Arabs as they swam through the channel and made for the shore. In a few minutes they gained it, and, after uttering a shout of defiance, ran up into the bushes and disappeared.

Meanwhile the "Firefly's" boat made straight for the dhow, and was soon near enough to hail.

"Heave-to," cried an interpreter in Arabic.

"Speak your own mother tongue and I'll answer ye," replied Disco.

"Heave-to, or I'll sink you," shouted Mr Small, who was in charge.

"I'm just agoin' to do it, sir," replied Disco, running the dhow into the wind until the sail shook.

Another moment and the boat was alongside. "Jump aboard and handle the sail, lads; I can't help 'ee no further," said Disco.

The invitation was unnecessary. The moment the two boats touched, the blue-jackets swarmed on board, cutlass in hand, and took possession.

"Why, what!—where did *you* come from?" asked the lieutenant, looking in profound astonishment at Harold and his companion.

"We are Englishmen, as you see," replied Harold, unable to restrain a smile; "we have been wrecked and caught by the villains who have just escaped you."

"I see—well, no time for talking just now; cut them loose, Jackson. Make fast the sheet—now then."

In a few minutes the dhow ranged up alongside the "Firefly," and our heroes, with the poor slaves, were quickly transferred to the man-of-war's deck, where Harold told his tale to Captain Romer.

As we have already stated, there were a number of slaves on board the "Firefly," which had been rescued from various Arab dhows. The gang now received on board made their numbers so great that it became absolutely necessary to run to the nearest port to discharge them.

We have already remarked on the necessity that lies on our cruisers, when overladen with rescued slaves, to run to a distant port of discharge to land them; and on the readiness of the slave-traders to take advantage of their opportunity, and run north with full cargoes with impunity when some of the cruisers are absent; for it is not possible for a small fleet to guard upwards of a thousand miles of coast effectually, or even, in any degree, usefully. If we possessed a port of discharge—a British station and settlement—on the mainland of the east coast of Africa, this difficulty would not exist. As it is, although we place several men-of-war on a station, the evil will not be cured, for just in proportion as these are successful in making captures, will arise the necessity of their leaving the station for weeks at a time unguarded.

Thus it fell out on the occasion of which we write. The presence of the large slave-freight on board the man-of-war was intolerable. Captain Romer was compelled to hurry off to the Seychelles Islands. He sailed with the monsoon, but had to steam back against it. During this period another vessel, similarly freighted, had to run to discharge at Aden. The seas were thus comparatively clear of cruisers. The Arabs seized their opportunity, and a stream of dhows and larger vessels swept out from the various creeks and ports all along the East African coast, filled to overflowing with slaves.

Among these were the four large dhows of our friend

R. M. Ballantyne

Yoosoof. Having, as we have seen, made a slight sacrifice of damaged and unsaleable goods and chattels, in order to clear the way, he proceeded north, touching at various ports where he filled up his living cargo, and finally got clear off, not with goods damaged beyond repair, but with thousands of the sons and daughters of Africa in their youthful prime.

In the interior each man cost him about four yards of cotton cloth, worth a few pence; each woman three yards, and each child two yards, and of course in cases where he stole them, they cost him nothing. On the coast these would sell at from 8 pounds to 12 pounds each, and in Arabia at from 20 pounds to 40 pounds.

We mention this to show what strong inducement there was for Yoosoof to run a good deal of risk in carrying on this profitable and accursed traffic.

But you must not fancy, good reader, that what we have described is given as a specimen of the *extent* to which the slave-trade on that coast is carried. It is but as a specimen of the *manner* thereof. It is certainly within the mark to say that at least thirty thousand natives are annually carried away as slaves from the east coast of Africa.

Sir Bartle Frere, in addressing a meeting of the chief native inhabitants of Bombay in April 1873, said,—"Let me assure you, in conclusion, that what you have heard of the horrors of the slave-trade is in no way exaggerated. We have seen so much of the horrors which were going on that we can have no doubt that what you read in books, which are so often spoken of as containing exaggerations, is exaggerated in no respect. The evil is much greater than anything you can conceive. Among the poorer class of Africans there is nothing like security from fathers and mothers being put to death in order that their children may be captured;"—and, referring to the *east coast alone*, he says that—"thirty thousand, or more, human beings, are exported every year from Africa."

Dr Livingstone tells us that, on the average, about one out of every five captured human beings reaches the coast alive. The other four perish or are murdered on the way, so that the thirty thousand annually exported, as stated by Sir Bartle Frere, represents a loss of 150,000 human beings *annually* from the east coast alone, altogether irrespective of the enormous and constant flow of slaves to the north by way of the White Nile and Egypt.

Yoosoof's venture was therefore but a drop in the vast river of blood which is drained annually from poor Africa's veins—blood which flows at the present time as copiously and constantly as it ever did in the days of old—blood which cries aloud to God for vengeance, and for the flow of which *we*, as a nation, are far from blameless.

CHAPTER FOUR

IN WHICH OUR HEROES SEE STRANGE SIGHTS AT ZANZIBAR, AND RESOLVE UPON TAKING A BOLD STEP

Before proceeding to the Seychelles, the 'Firefly' touched at the island of Zanzibar, and there landed our hero Harold Seadrift and his comrade in misfortune, Disco Lillihammer.

Here, one brilliant afternoon, the two friends sat down under a palm-tree to hold what Disco called a palaver. The spot commanded a fine view of the town and harbour of Zanzibar.

We repeat that the afternoon was brilliant, but it is right to add that it required an African body and mind fully to appreciate the pleasures of it. The sun's rays were blistering, the heat was intense, and the air was stifling. Harold lay down and gasped, Disco followed his example, and sighed. After a few minutes spent in a species of imbecile contemplation of things in general, the latter raised himself to a sitting posture, and proceeded slowly to fill and light his pipe. Harold was no smoker, but he derived a certain dreamy enjoyment from gazing at Disco, and wondering how he could smoke in such hot weather.

"We'll get used to it I s'pose, like the eels," observed Disco, when the pipe was in full blast.

"Of course we shall," replied Harold; "and now that we have come to an anchor, let me explain the project which has been for some days maturing in my mind."

"All right; fire away, sir," said the sailor, blowing a long thin cloud from his lips.

"You are aware," said Harold, "that I came out here as supercargo of my father's vessel," (Disco nodded), "but you are not aware that my chief object in coming was to see a little of the world in general, and of the African part of it in particular. Since my arrival you and I have seen a few things, which have opened up my mind in regard to slavery; we have now been a fortnight in this town, and my father's agent has enlightened me still further on the subject, insomuch that I now feel within me an intense desire to make an excursion into the interior of Africa; indeed, I have resolved to do so, for the purpose of seeing its capabilities in a commercial point of view, of observing how the slave-trade is conducted at its fountain-head, and of enjoying a little of the scenery and the sport peculiar to this land of Ham."

"W'y, you speaks like a book, sir," said Disco, emitting a prolonged puff, "an' it ain't for the likes me to give an opinion on that there; but if I may make bold to ax, sir, how do you mean to travel—on the back of a elephant or a ry-noceris?—for it seems to me that there ain't much in the shape o' locomotives or 'busses hereabouts—not even cabs."

"I shall go in a canoe," replied Harold; "but my reason for broaching the subject just now is, that I may ask if you are willing to go with me."

"There's no occasion to ax that sir; I'm your man—north or

R. M. Ballantyne

south, east or west, it's all the same to me. I've bin born to roll about the world, and it matters little whether I rolls ashore or afloat—though I prefers the latter."

"Well, then, that's settled," said Harold, with a look of satisfaction; "I have already arranged with our agent here to advance me what I require in the way of funds, and shall hire men and canoes when we get down to the Zambesi—"

"The Zam-wot, sir?"

"The Zambesi; did you never hear of it before?"

"Never, nor don't know wot it is, sir."

"It is a river; one of the largest on the east coast, which has been well described by Dr Livingstone, that greatest of travellers, whose chief object in travelling is, as he himself says, to raise the negroes out of their present degraded condition, and free them from the curse of slavery."

"That's the man to *my* mind," said Disco emphatically; "good luck to him.—But w'en d'you mean to start for the Zambizzy, sir?"

"In a few days. It will take that time to get everything ready, and our money packed."

"Our money packed!" echoed the sailor, with a look of surprise, "w'y, wot d'ye mean!"

"Just what I say. The money current in the interior of Africa is rather cumbrous, being neither more nor less than goods. You'll never guess what sort—try."

"Rum," said Disco.

"No."

"Pipes and 'baccy."

Harold shook his head.

"Never could guess nothin'," said Disco, replacing the pipe, which he had removed for a few moments from his lips; "I gives it up."

"What would you say to cotton cloth, and thick brass wire, and glass beads, being the chief currency in Central Africa?" said Harold.

"You don't mean it, sir?"

"Indeed I do, and as these articles must be carried in large quantities, if we mean to travel far into the land, there will be more bales and coils than you and I could well carry in our waistcoat pockets."

"That's true, sir," replied Disco, looking earnestly at a couple of negro slaves who chanced to pass along the neighbouring footpath at that moment, singing carelessly. "Them poor critters don't seem to be so miserable after all."

"That is because the nigger is naturally a jolly, light-hearted fellow," said Harold, "and when his immediate and more pressing troubles are removed he accommodates himself to circumstances, and sings, as you hear. If these fellows were to annoy their masters and get a thrashing, you'd hear them sing in another key. The evils of most things don't show on the surface. You must get behind the scenes to understand them. You and I have already had one or two peeps behind the scenes."

R. M. Ballantyne

"We have indeed, sir," replied Disco, frowning, and closing his fists involuntarily, as he thought of Yoosoof and the dhow.

"Now, then," said Harold, rising, as Disco shook the ashes out of his little black pipe, and placed that beloved implement in the pocket of his coat, "let us return to the harbour, and see what chance there is of getting a passage to the Zambesi, in an honest trading dhow—if there is such a thing in Zanzibar."

On their way to the harbour they had to pass through the slave-market. This was not the first time they had visited the scene of this iniquitous traffic, but neither Harold nor Disco could accustom themselves to it. Every time they entered the market their feelings of indignation became so intense that it was with the utmost difficulty they could control them. When Disco saw handsome negro men and good-looking girls put up for public sale,—their mouths rudely opened, and their teeth examined by cool, calculating Arabs, just as if they had been domestic cattle—his spirit boiled within him, his fingers tingled, and he felt a terrible inclination to make a wild attack, single-handed, on the entire population of Zanzibar, though he might perish in the execution of vengeance and the relief of his feelings! We need scarcely add that his discretion saved him. They soon reached the small square in which the market was held. Here they saw a fine-looking young woman sold to a grave elderly Arab for a sum equal to about eight pounds sterling. Passing hastily on, they observed another "lot," a tall stalwart man, having his various "points" examined, and stopped to see the result. His owner, thinking, perhaps, that he seemed a little sluggish in his movements, raised his whip and caused it to fall upon his flank with such vigour that the poor fellow, taken by surprise, leaped high into the air, and uttered a yell of pain. The strength and activity of the man were unquestionable, and he soon found a purchaser.

But all the slaves were not fine-looking or stalwart like the two just referred to. Many of them were most miserable objects. Some stood, others were seated as if incapable of standing, so emaciated were they. Not a few were mere skeletons, with life and skin. Near the middle of the square, groups of children were arranged—some standing up to be inspected, others sitting down. These ranged from five years and upwards, but there was not one that betrayed the slightest tendency to mirth, and Disco came to the conclusion that negro children do not play, but afterwards discovered his mistake, finding that their exuberant jollity "at home" was not less than that of the children of other lands. These little slaves had long ago been terrified, and beaten, and starved into listless, apathetic and silent creatures.

Further on, a row of young women attracted their attention. They were ranged in a semicircle, all nearly in a state of nudity, waiting to be sold. A group of Arabs stood in front of them, conversing. One of these women looked such a picture of woe that Disco felt irresistibly impelled to stop. There were no tears in her eyes; the fountain appeared to have been dried up, but, apparently, without abating the grief which was stamped in deep lines on her young countenance, and which burst frequently from her breast in convulsive sobs. Our Englishmen were not only shocked but surprised at this woman's aspect, for their experience had hitherto gone to show that the slaves usually became callous under their sufferings. Whatever of humanity might have originally belonged to them seemed to have been entirely driven out of them by the cruelties and indignities they had so long suffered at the hands of their captors. [See Captain Sulivan's *Dhow-chasing in Zanzibar Waters*, page 252.]

"Wot's the matter with her, poor thing?" asked Disco of a

R. M. Ballantyne

half-caste Portuguese, dressed in something like the garb of a sailor.

"Oh, notting," answered the man in broken English, with a look of indifference, "she have lose her chile, dat all."

"Lost her child? how—wot d'ee mean?"

"Dey hab sole de chile," replied the man; "was good fat boy, 'bout two-yer ole. S'pose she hab carry him for months troo de woods, an' over de hills down to coast, an' tink she keep him altogether. But she mistake. One trader come here 'bout one hour past. He want boy—not want modder; so he buy de chile. Modder fight a littil at first, but de owner soon make her quiet. Oh, it notting at all. She cry a littil—soon forget her chile, an' get all right."

"Come, I can't stand this," exclaimed Harold, hastening away.

Disco said nothing, but to the amazement of the half-caste, he grasped him by the collar, and hurled him aside with a degree of force that caused him to stagger and fall with stunning violence to the ground. Disco then strode away after his friend, his face and eyes blazing with various emotions, among which towering indignation predominated.

In a few minutes they reached the harbour, and, while making inquiries as to the starting of trading dhows for the south, they succeeded in calming their feelings down to something like their ordinary condition.

The harbour was crowded with dhows of all shapes and sizes, most of them laden with slaves, some discharging cargoes for the Zanzibar market, others preparing to sail, under protection of a pass from the Sultan, for Lamoo, which is the northern limit of the Zanzibar dominions, and, therefore, of the so-called "domestic" slave-trade.

There would be something particularly humorous in the barefacedness of this august Sultan of Zanzibar, if it were connected with anything less horrible than slavery. For instance, there is something almost amusing in the fact that dhows were sailing every day for Lamoo with hundreds of slaves, although that small town was known to be very much overstocked at the time. It was also quite entertaining to know that the commanders of the French and English war-vessels lying in the harbour at the time were aware of this, and that the Sultan knew it, and that, in short, everybody knew it, but that nobody appeared to have the power to prevent it! Even the Sultan who granted the permits or passes to the owners of the dhows, although he *professed* to wish to check the slave-trade, could not prevent it. Wasn't that strange—wasn't it curious? The Sultan derived by far the largest portion of his revenue from the tax levied on the export of slaves—amounting to somewhere about 10,000 pounds a year—but *that* had nothing to do with it of course not, oh dear no! Then there was another very ludicrous phase of this oriental, not to say transcendental, potentate's barefacedness. He knew, and probably admitted, that about 2000, some say 4000, slaves a year were sufficient to meet the home-consumption of that commodity, and he also knew, but probably did not admit, that not fewer than 30,000 slaves were annually exported from Zanzibar to meet this requirement of 4000! These are very curious specimens of miscalculation which this barefaced Sultan seems to have fallen into. Perhaps he was a bad arithmetician. [See Captain Sulivan's *Dhow-chasing in Zanzibar Water*; page 111.] We have said that this state of things *was* so at the time of our story, but we may now add that it still *is* so in this year of grace 1873. Whether it shall continue to be so remains to be seen!

R. M. Ballantyne

Having spent some time in fruitless inquiry, Harold and Disco at last to their satisfaction, discovered an Arab dhow of known good character, which was on the point of starting for the Zambesi in the course of a few days, for the purpose of legitimate traffic. It therefore became necessary that our hero should make his purchases and preparations with all possible speed. In this he was entirely guided by his father's agent, a merchant of the town, who understood thoroughly what was necessary for the intended journey.

It is not needful here to enter into full details, suffice it to say that among the things purchased by Harold, and packed up in portable form, were a number of bales of common unbleached cotton, which is esteemed above everything by the natives of Africa as an article of dress—if we may dignify by the name of dress the little piece, about the size of a moderate petticoat, which is the only clothing of some, or the small scrap round the loins which is the sole covering of other, natives of the interior! There were also several coils of thick brass wire, which is much esteemed by them for making bracelets and anklets; and a large quantity of beads of various colours, shapes, and sizes. Of beads, we are told, between five and six hundred tons are annually manufactured in Great Britain for export to Africa.

Thus supplied, our two friends embarked in the dhow and set sail. Wind and weather were propitious. In few days they reached the mouths of the great river Zambesi, and landed at the port of Quillimane.

Only once on the voyage did they fall in with a British cruiser, which ordered them to lay-to and overhauled them, but on the papers and everything being found correct, they were permitted to pursue their voyage.

The mouths of the river Zambesi are numerous; extending

over more than ninety miles of the coast. On the banks of the northern mouth stands—it would be more appropriate to say festers—the dirty little Portuguese town of Quillimane. Its site is low, muddy, fever-haunted, and swarming with mosquitoes. No man in his senses would have built a village thereon were it not for the facilities afforded for slaving. At spring or flood tides the bar may be safely crossed by sailing vessels, but, being far from land, it is always dangerous for boats.

Here, then, Harold and Disco landed, and remained for some time for the purpose of engaging men. Appearing in the character of independent travellers, they were received with some degree of hospitality by the principal inhabitants. Had they gone there as simple and legitimate traders, every possible difficulty would have been thrown in their way, because the worthy people, from the Governor downwards, flourished,—or festered,—by means of the slave-trade, and legitimate commerce is everywhere found to be destructive to the slave-trade.

Dr Livingstone and others tell us that thousands upon thousands of negroes have, of late years, gone out from Quillimane into slavery under the convenient title of "free emigrants," their freedom being not quite equal to that of a carter's horse, for while that animal, although enslaved, is usually well fed, the human animal is kept on rather low diet lest his spirit should rouse him to deeds of desperate violence against his masters. All agricultural enterprise is also effectually discouraged here. When a man wants to visit his country farm he has to purchase a permit from the Governor. If he wishes to go up the river to the Portuguese towns of Senna or Tette, a pass must be purchased from the Governor. In fact it would weary the reader were we to enumerate the various modes in which every effort of man to act naturally, legitimately, or progressively, is hampered, unless his

R. M. Ballantyne

business be the buying and selling of human beings.

At first Harold experienced great difficulty in procuring men. The master of the trading dhow in which he sailed from Zanzibar intended to remain as short a time as possible at Quillimane, purposing to visit ports further south, and as Harold had made up his mind not to enter the Zambesi by the Quillimane mouth, but to proceed in the dhow to one of the southern mouths, he felt tempted to give up the idea of procuring men until he had gone further south.

"You see, Disco," said he, in a somewhat disconsolate tone, "it won't do to let this dhow start without us, because I want to get down to the East Luavo mouth of this river, that being the mouth which was lately discovered and entered by Dr Livingstone; but I'm not sure that we can procure men or canoes there, and our Arab skipper either can't or won't enlighten me."

"Ah!" observed Disco, with a knowing look, "he won't— that's where it is, sir. I've not a spark o' belief in that man, or in any Arab on the coast. He's a slaver in disguise, he is, an' so's every mother's son of 'em."

"Well," continued Harold, "if we must start without them and take our chance, we must; there is no escaping from the inevitable; nevertheless we must exert ourselves *to-day*, because the dhow does not sail till to-morrow evening, and there is no saying what luck may attend our efforts before that time. Perseverance, you know, is the only sure method of conquering difficulties."

"That's so," said Disco; "them's my sentiments 'xactly. Never say die—Stick at nothing—Nail yer colours to the mast: them's the mottoes that I goes in for—always s'posin' that you're in the right."

"But what if you're in the wrong, and the colours are nailed?" asked Harold, with a smile.

"W'y then, sir, of course I'd have to tear 'em down."

"So that perhaps, it would be better not to nail them at all, unless you're very sure—eh?"

"Oh, of *course*, sir," replied Disco, with solemn emphasis. "You don't suppose, sir, that I would nail 'em to the mast except I was sure, wery sure, that I wos right? But, as you wos a sayin', sir, about the gittin' of them 'ere men."

Disco had an easy way of changing a subject when he felt that he was getting out of his depth.

"Well, to return to that. The fact is, I would not mind the men, for it's likely that men of some sort will turn up somewhere, but I am very anxious about an interpreter. Without an interpreter we shall get on badly, I fear, for I can only speak French, besides a very little Latin and Greek, none of which languages will avail much among niggers."

Disco assumed a severely thoughtful expression of countenance.

"That's true," he said, placing his right fist argumentatively in his left palm, "and I'm afeard I can't help you there, sir. If it wos to steer a ship or pull a oar or man the fore-tops'l yard in a gale o' wind, or anything else in the seafarin' line, Disco Lillihammer's your man, but I couldn't come a furrin' lingo at no price. I knows nothin' but my mother tongue,— nevertheless, though I says it that shouldn't, I does profess to be somewhat of a dab at that. Once upon a time I spent six weeks in Dublin, an' havin' a quick ear for moosic, I soon managed to get up a strong dash o' the brogue; but p'raps that

R. M. Ballantyne

wouldn't go far with the niggers."

About two hours after the above conversation, while Harold Seadrift was walking on the beach, he observed his faithful ally in the distance grasping a short thickset man by the arm, and endeavouring to induce him to accompany him, with a degree of energy that fell little short of main force. The man was evidently unwilling.

As the pair drew nearer, Harold overheard Disco's persuasive voice:—"Come now, Antonio, don't be a fool; it's the best service you could enter. Good pay and hard work, and all the grub that's goin'—what could a man want more? It's true there's no grog, but we don't need that in a climate where you've only got to go out in the sun without yer hat an' you'll be as good as drunk in ten minutes, any day."

"No, no, not possibil," remonstrated the man, whose swarthy visage betrayed a mixture of cunning, fun, and annoyance. He was obviously a half-caste of the lowest type, but with more pretensions to wealth than many of his fellows, inasmuch as he wore, besides his loin-cloth, a white cotton shooting-coat, very much soiled, beneath the tails of which his thin black legs protruded ridiculously.

"Here you are, sir," cried Disco, as he came up; "here's the man for lingo: knows the native talkee, as well as Portuguese, English, Arabic, and anything else you like, as far as I know. Antonio's his name. Come, sir, try him with Greek, or somethin' o' that sort!"

Harold had much ado to restrain a smile, but, assuming a grave aspect, he addressed the man in French, while Disco listened with a look of profound respect and admiration.

"W'y, wot's wrong with 'ee, man," exclaimed Disco, on

observing the blank look of Antonio's countenance; "don't 'ee savay that?"

"I thought you understood Portuguese?" said Harold in English.

"So me do," replied Antonio quickly; "but dat no Portigeese— dat Spanaish, me 'spose."

"What *can* you speak, then?" demanded Harold sternly.

"Portigeese, Arbik, Fengleesh, an' two, tree, four, nigger lungwiches."

It was very obvious that, whatever Antonio spoke, he spoke nothing correctly, but that was of no importance so long as the man could make himself understood. Harold therefore asked if he would join his party as interpreter, but Antonio shook his head.

"Why not man—why not?" asked Harold impatiently, for he became anxious to secure him, just in proportion as he evinced disinclination to engage.

"Speak up, Antonio, don't be ashamed; you've no need to," said Disco. "The fact is, sir, Antonio tells me that he has just bin married, an' he don't want to leave his wife."

"Very natural," observed Harold. "How long is it since you were married?"

"Von veek since I did bought her."

"Bought her!" exclaimed Disco, with a broad grin; "may I ax wot ye paid for her?"

R. M. Ballantyne

"Paid!" exclaimed the man, starting and opening his eyes very wide, as if the contemplation of the vast sum were too much for him; "lat me zee—me pay me vife's pairyints sixteen yard ob cottin clothe, an' for me's hut four yard morer."

"Ye don't say that?" exclaimed Disco, with an extended grin. "Is she young an' good-lookin'?"

"Yonge!" replied Antonio; "yis, ver' yonge; not mush more dan baby, an' exiquitely bootiful."

"Then, my good feller," said Disco, with a laugh, "the sooner you leave her the better. A week is a long time, an' absence, you know, as the old song says, makes the heart grow fonder; besides, Mr Seadrift will give you enough to buy a dozen wives, if 'ee want 'em."

"Yes, I'll pay you well," said Harold; "that is, if you prove to be a good interpreter."

Antonio pricked up his ears at this.

"How mush vill 'oo gif?" he asked.

"Well, let me think; I shall probably be away three or four months. What would you say, Antonio, to twenty yards of cotton cloth a month, and a gun into the bargain at the end, if you do your work well?"

The pleased expression of Antonio's face could not have been greater had he been offered twenty pounds sterling a month. The reader may estimate the value of this magnificent offer when we say that a yard of cotton cloth was at that time sevenpence-halfpenny, so that Antonio's valuable services were obtained for about 12 shillings, 6 pence a month, and a gun which cost Harold less than twenty shillings in Zanzibar.

We may remark here that Antonio afterwards proved to be a stout, able, willing man, and a faithful servant, although a most arrant coward.

From this time Harold's difficulties in regard to men vanished. With Antonio's able assistance nine were procured, stout, young, able-bodied fellows they were, and all more or less naked. Two of these were half-caste brothers, named respectively Jose and Oliveira; two were half-wild negroes of the Somali tribe named Nakoda and Conda; three were negroes of the Makololo tribe, who had accompanied Dr Livingstone on his journey from the far interior of Africa to the East Coast, and were named respectively Jumbo, Zombo, and Masiko; and finally two, named Songolo and Mabruki, were free negroes of Quillimane. Thus the whole band, including Disco and the leader, formed a goodly company of twelve stout men.

Of course Harold armed them all with guns and knives. Himself and Disco carried Enfield rifles; besides which, Harold took with him a spare rifle of heavy calibre, carrying large balls, mingled with tin to harden them. This latter was intended for large game. Landing near the East Luavo mouth of the Zambesi, our hero was fortunate enough to procure two serviceable canoes, into which he transferred himself, his men, and his goods, and, bidding adieu to the Arab skipper of the dhow, commenced his journey into the interior of Africa.

R. M. Ballantyne

CHAPTER FIVE

IN WHICH THE TRAVELLERS ENJOY THEMSELVES EXTREMELY, AND DISCO LILLIHAMMER SEES SEVERAL ASTONISHING SIGHTS

Behold our travellers, then, fairly embarked on the waters of the great African river Zambesi, in two canoes, one of which is commanded by Harold Seadrift, the other by Disco Lillihammer.

Of course these enterprising chiefs were modest enough at first to allow two of the Makololo men, Jumbo and Zombo, to wield the steering-oars, but after a few days' practice they became sufficiently expert, as Disco said, to take the helm, except when strong currents rendered the navigation difficult, or when the weather became so "piping hot" that none but men clad in black skins could work.

We must however guard the reader here from supposing that it is always piping hot in Africa. There are occasional days when the air may be styled lukewarm, when the sky is serene, and when all nature seems joyful and enjoyable,— days in which a man opens his mouth wide and swallows down the atmosphere; when he *feels* his health and strength, and rejoices in them, and when, if he be not an infidel, he also feels a sensation of gratitude to the Giver of all good.

On such a day, soon after entering the East Luavo mouth of the Zambesi, the explorers, for such we may almost venture to style them, ascended the smooth stream close to the left bank, Harold leading, Disco following closely in his wake.

The men rowed gently, as if they enjoyed the sweet calm of early morning, and were unwilling to disturb the innumerable flocks of wild-fowl that chuckled among the reeds and sedges everywhere. Harold sat in the stern, leaning back, and only dipping the steering-oar lazily now and then to keep the canoe from running on the bank, or plunging into a forest of gigantic rushes. Disco, having resolved to solace himself with a whiff of his darling pipe, had resigned "the helm" to Jumbo, and laid himself in a position of comfort which admitted of his resting his head on the gunwale in such a manner that, out of the corners of his eyes, he could gaze down into the water.

The part of the river they had reached was so perfectly still that every cloud in the sky, every mangrove, root and spray, and every bending bulrush, was perfectly reproduced in the reflected world below. Plaintive cries of wild-fowl formed appropriate melody, to which chattering groups of monkeys and croaking bull-frogs contributed a fine tenor and bass.

"Hallo, Disco!" exclaimed Harold in a subdued key, looking over his shoulder.

"Ay, ay, sir?" sighed the seaman, without moving his position.

"Range up alongside; I want to speak to you."

"Ay, ay, sir.—Jumbo, you black-faced villain, d'ee hear that?

R. M. Ballantyne

give way and go 'longside."

Good-humoured Jumbo *spoke* very little English, but had come to understand a good deal during his travels with Dr Livingstone. He wrinkled his visage and showed his brilliant teeth on receiving the order. Muttering a word to the men, and giving a vigorous stroke, he shot up alongside of the leader's canoe.

"You seem comfortable," said Harold, with a laugh, as Disco's vast visage appeared at his elbow.

"I is."

"Isn't this jolly?" continued Harold.

"No, sir, 'taint."

"Why, what d'you mean?"

"I means that jolly ain't the word, by a long way, for to express the natur' o' my feelin's. There ain't no word as I knows on as 'ud come up to it. If I wor a fylosipher, now, I'd coin a word for the occasion. P'raps," continued Disco, drawing an unusually long whiff from his pipe, "p'raps, not bein' a fylosipher, I might nevertheless try to coin one. Wot's the Latin, now, for heaven?"

"Caelum," replied Harold.

"Sailum, eh? An' wot's the 'arth?"

"Terra."

"Terra? well now, wot rediklous names to give to 'em," said Disco, shaking his head gravely, "I can't see why the ancients couldn't ha' bin satisfied with the names that *we'd* given 'em. Hows'ever, that's neither here nor there. My notion o' the state o' things that we've got into here, as they now stand, is, that they are sailumterracious, which means heaven-upon-earth, d'ee see?"

As Disco pronounced the word with a powerful emphasis on the *u-m* part of it the sound was rather effective, and seemed to please him.

"Right; you're right, or nearly so," replied Harold; "but don't you think the word savours too much of perfection, seeing that breakfast would add to the pleasure of the present delightful state of things, and make them even more sailumterracious than they are?"

"No, sir, no; the word ain't too parfect," replied Disco, with a look of critical severity; "part of it is 'arth, and 'arth is imparfect, bein' susceptible of a many improvements, among which undoubtedly is breakfast, likewise dinner an' supper, to say nothin' of lunch an' tea, which is suitable only for babbies an' wimen; so I agrees with you, sir, that the state o' things will be sailumterraciouser if we goes ashore an' has breakfast."

He tapped the head of his very black little pipe on the edge of the canoe, and heaved a sigh of contentment as he watched the ash-ball that floated away on the stream; then, rousing himself, he seized the steering-oar and followed Harold into a small creek, which was pleasantly over-shadowed by the rich tropical foliage of that region.

While breakfast was being prepared by Antonio, whose talents as *chef-de-cuisine* were of the highest order, Harold took his rifle and rambled into the bush in search of game— any kind of game, for at that time he had had no experience

R. M. Ballantyne

whatever of the sport afforded by the woods of tropical Africa, and, having gathered only a few vague ideas from books, he went forth with all the pleasurable excitement and expectation that we may suppose peculiar to discoverers.

Disco Lillihammer having only consumed his first pipe of tobacco, and holding it to be a duty which he owed to himself to consume two before breakfast, remained at the camp-fire to smoke and chaff Antonio, whose good-nature was only equalled by his activity.

"Wot have 'ee got there?" inquired Disco, as Antonio poured a quantity of seed into a large pot.

"Dis? vy, hims be mapira," replied the interpreter, with a benignant smile. "Hims de cheef food ob dis konterie."

It must be remarked here that Antonio's English, having been acquired from all sorts of persons, in nearly every tropical part of the globe, was somewhat of a jumble, being a compound of the broken English spoken by individuals among the Germans, French, Portuguese, Arabs, and Negroes, with whom he had at various times associated, modified by his own ignorance, and seasoned with a dash of his own inventive fancy.

"Is it good?" asked Disco.

"Goot!" exclaimed Antonio. Being unable to find words to express himself, the enthusiastic cook placed his hand on the region which was destined ere long to become a receptacle for the mapira, and rolled his eyes upwards in rapture. "Hah! oo sall see behind long."

"Before long, you mean," observed the seaman.

"Dat all same ting, s'long's you onerstand him," replied Antonio complacently.—"Bring vatter now, Jumbo. Put him in careful. Not spill on de fire—zo—goot."

Jumbo filled up the kettle carefully, and a broad grin overspread his black visage, partly because he was easily tickled into a condition of risibility by the cool off-hand remarks of Disco Lillihammer, and partly because, having acquired his own small smattering of English from Dr Livingstone, he was intelligent enough to perceive that in regard to Antonio's language there was something peculiar.

"Now, go fitch noder kittle—queek."

"*Yis*, sar—zo—goot," replied Jumbo, mimicking the interpreter, and going off with a vociferous laugh at his little joke, in which he was joined by his sable clansmen, Masiko and Zombo.

"Hims got 'nuff of impoodidence," said the interpreter, as he bustled about his avocations.

"He's not the only one that's got more than enough impoodidence," said Disco, pushing a fine straw down the stem of his "cutty," to make it draw better. "I say, Tony," (our regardless seaman had already thus mutilated his name), "you seem to have plenty live stock in them parts."

"Plenty vat?" inquired the interpreter, with a perplexed expression.

"Why, plenty birds and beasts,—live stock we calls it, meanin' thereby livin' creeturs." He pointed towards an opening in the mangroves, through which were visible the neighbouring mud and sand flats, swarming with wild-fowl, and conspicuous among which were large flocks of pelicans, who seemed to be gorging themselves comfortably from an apparently inexhaustible supply of fish in the pools left by the receding tide.

"Ho, yis, me perceive; yis, plenty bird and beast—fishes too, and crawbs—look dare."

He pointed to a part of the sands nearest to their encampment which appeared to be alive with some small creatures.

"That's coorious," said Disco, removing his pipe, and regarding the phenomenon with some interest.

"No, 'taint koorous, it's crawbs," replied Antonio.

"Crabs, is it?" said Disco, rising and sauntering down to the sands; for he possessed an inquiring mind, with a special tendency to investigate the habits (pranks, as he called them) of the lower animals, which, in other circumstances, might have made him a naturalist.

Muttering to himself—he was fond of muttering to himself, it felt companionable,—"coorious, very coorious, quite 'stroanary," he crept stealthily to the edge of the mangroves, and there discovered that the sands were literally alive with myriads of minute crabs, which were actively engaged—it was supposed by those who ought to know best—in gathering their food. The moment the tide ebbed from any part of the sands, out came these crablets in swarms, and set to work, busy as bees, ploughing up the sand, and sifting it, apparently for food, until the whole flat was rendered rough by their incessant labours. Approaching cautiously, Disco observed that each crab, as he went along sidewise, gathered a round bit of moist sand at his mouth, which was quickly brushed away by one of his claws, and replaced by another, and another, as fast as they could be brushed aside.

"Eatin' sand they are!" muttered Disco in surprise; but presently the improbability of sand being very nutritious food, even for crabs, forced itself on him, and he muttered his conviction that they "was scrapin' for wittles."

Having watched the crabs a considerable time, and observed that they frequently interrupted their labours to dart suddenly into their holes and out again—for the purpose, he conjectured, of "havin' a drop o' summat to wet their whistles,"—Disco thrust the cutty into his vest pocket, and walked a little further out on the flat in the hope of discovering some new objects of interest. Nor was he disappointed. Besides finding that the pools left by the tide swarmed with varieties of little fish—many of them being "coorious,"—he was fortunate enough to witness a most surprising combat.

It happened thus:—Perceiving, a little to his right, some small creature hopping about on the sand near to a little pool, he turned aside to observe it more closely. On his drawing near, the creature jumped into the pool. Disco advanced to the edge, gazed intently into the water, and saw nothing except his own reflected image at the bottom. Presently the creature reappeared. It was a small fish—a familiar fish, too—which he had known in the pools of his native land by the name of blenny. As the blenny appeared to wish to approach the edge of the pool, Disco retired, and, placing a hand on each knee, stooped, in order to make himself as small as possible. He failed, the diminution in his height being fully counterbalanced by the latitudinal extension of his elbows!

Presently the blenny put its head out of the water, and looked about. We speak advisedly. The blenny is altogether a singular, an exceptional fish. It can, and does, look sidewise, upwards and downwards, with its protruding eyes, as

R. M. Ballantyne

knowingly, and with as much vivacity, as if it were a human being. This power in a fish has something of the same awesome effect on an observer that might possibly result were a horse to raise its head and smile at him.

Seeing that the coast was clear, for Disco stood as motionless as a mangrove tree, blenny hopped upon the dry land. The African blenny is a sort of amphibious animal, living nearly as much out of the water as in it. Indeed its busiest time, we are told, [See Dr Livingstone's Zambesi and its Tributaries, page 843.] is at low water, when, by means of its pectoral fins it crawls out on the sand and raises itself into something of a standing attitude, with its bright eyes keeping a sharp look-out for the light-coloured flies on which it feeds.

For several seconds Disco gazed at the fish, and the fish gazed around, even turning its head a little, as well as its eyes, on this side and on that. Presently a small fly, with that giddy heedlessness which characterises the race, alighted about two inches in front of blenny's nose. Instantly the fish leaped that vast space, alighted with its underset mouth just over the fly, which immediately rose into it and was entombed.

"Brayvo!" passed through Disco's brain, but no sound issued from his lips.

Presently another of the giddy ones alighted in front of blenny about a foot distant. This appeared to be much beyond his leaping powers, for, with a slow, stealthy motion, like a cat, he began deliberately to stalk his victim. The victim appeared to be blind, for it took no notice of the approaching monster. Blenny displayed marvellous powers of self-control, for he moved on steadily without accelerating his speed until within about two inches of his prey—then he leapt as before, and another fly was entombed.

"Well done!" exclaimed Disco, mentally, but still his lips and body were motionless as before.

At this point an enemy, in the shape of another blenny, appeared on the scene. It came up out of a small pool close at hand, and seemed to covet the first blenny's pool, and to set about taking possession of it as naturally as if it had been a human being; for, observing, no doubt, that its neighbour was busily engaged, it moved quietly in the direction of the coveted pool. Being a very little fish, it was not observed by Disco, but it was instantly noticed by the first blenny, which, being rather the smaller of the two, we shall style the Little one.

Suddenly Big Blenny threw off all disguise, bounded towards the pool, which was about a foot square, and plunged in. No mortal blenny could witness this unwarrantable invasion of its hearth and home without being stirred to indignant wrath. With eyes that seemed to flash fire, and dorsal fin bristling up with rage, Little Blenny made five tremendous leaps of full three inches each, and disappeared. Another moment and a miniature storm ruffled the pool: for a few seconds the heavings of the deep were awful; then, out jumped Big Blenny and tried to flee, but out jumped Little Blenny and caught him by the tail; round turned the big one and caught the other by the jaw.

"Hallo, Disco! breakfast's ready—where are you?" shouted Harold from the woods.

Disco replied not. It is a question whether he heard the hail at all, so engrossed was he in this remarkable fight.

"Brayvo!" he exclaimed aloud, when Little Blenny shook his big enemy off and rolled over him.

R. M. Ballantyne

"Cleverly done!" he shouted, when Big Blenny with a dart took refuge in the pool.

"I knowed it," he cried approvingly, when Little Blenny forced him a second time to evacuate the premises, "Go in an' win, little 'un," thought Disco.

Thus the battle raged furiously, now in the water, now on the sand, while the excited seaman danced round the combatants—both of whom appeared to have become deaf and blind with rage—and gave them strong encouragement, mingled with appropriate advice and applause. In fact Disco's delight would have been perfect, had the size of the belligerents admitted of his patting the little blenny on the back; but this of course was out of the question!

At last having struck, worried, bitten, and chased each other by land and sea for several minutes, these pugnacious creatures seized each other by their respective throats, like two bull-dogs, and fell exhausted on the sand.

"It's a draw!" exclaimed Disco, rather disappointed.

"No, 'tain't," he said, as Little Blenny, reviving, rose up and renewed the combat more furiously than ever; but it was soon ended, for Big Blenny suddenly turned and fled to his own pool. Little Blenny did not crow; he did not even appear to be elated. He evidently felt that he had been called on to perform a disagreeable but unavoidable duty, and deemed it quite unnecessary to wave banners, fire guns, or ring bells in celebration of his victory, as he dived back into his pool amid the ringing cheers of Disco Lillihammer.

"Upon my word, if you have not gone stark mad, you must have had a sunstroke," said Harold, coming forward, "what's the matter?"

"Too late! too late!" cried Disco, in a mingled tone of amusement and regret.

"D'ye think it is? Are you incurable already?" asked his friend.

"Too late to see the most a-stonishin' scrimmage I ever did behold in *my* life," said Disco.

The description of this scrimmage gave the worthy seaman a subject for conversation and food for meditation during the greater part of the time spent over the morning meal, and there is no saying how long he would have kept referring to and chuckling over it—to the great admiration and sympathy of the black fellows, who are, as a race, excessively fond of jocularity and fun—had not another of the denizens of the mangrove jungle diverted his attention and thoughts rather suddenly.

This was a small monkey, which, seated on a branch overhead, peered at the breakfast-party from among the leaves, with an expression of inquiry and of boundless astonishment that it is quite impossible to describe. Surprise of the most sprightly nature, if we may say so, sat enthroned on that small monkey's countenance, an expression which was enhanced by the creature's motions, for, not satisfied with taking a steady look at the intruders from the right side of a leaf, it thrust forward its little black head on the left side of it, and then under it, by way of variety; but no additional light seemed to result from these changes in the point of observation, for the surprise did not diminish.

In one of its intent stares it caught the eye of Disco. The seaman's jaws stopped, as if suddenly locked, and his eyes opened to their widest.

The monkey seemed to feel uneasily that it had attracted attention, for it showed the smallest possible glimpse of its teeth. The action, coupled with the leafy shadows which fell on its countenance, had the effect of a smile, which caused Disco to burst into a loud laugh and point upwards. To bound from its position to a safer retreat, and thence stare at Disco with deep indignation, and a threatening display of all its teeth and gums, in addition to its looks of surprise, was the work of a moment on the part of the small monkey, whereat Disco burst into a renewed roar of laughter, in which he was joined by the whole party.

"Are there many o' them fellows hereabouts?" inquired the seaman of Antonio.

"Ho, yis, lots ob 'em. T'ousands ebery whars; see, dare am morer."

He pointed to another part of the umbrageous canopy overhead, where the face of a still smaller monkey was visible, engaged, like the previous one, in an earnest scrutiny of the party, but with a melancholy, rather than a surprised, expression of visage.

"Wot a miserable, broken-hearted thing!" said Disco, grinning, in which act he was immediately copied by the melancholy monkey, though from different motives.

Disco was very fond of monkeys. All his life he had felt a desire to pat and fondle those shivering creatures which he had been accustomed to see on barrel-organs in his native land, and the same strong impulse came over him now.

"Wot a pity the creeturs smell so bad, and ain't cleanly," he remarked, gazing affectionately up among the leaves, "they'd make such capital pets; why, there's another."

This remark had reference to a third monkey, of large dimensions and fierce countenance, which at that moment rudely thrust the melancholy monkey aside, and took its place. The latter, with a humble air and action, took up a new position, somewhat nearer to the fire, where its sad countenance was more distinctly seen.

"Well, it does seem a particularly sorrowful monkey, that," said Harold, laughing, as he helped himself to another canful of tea.

"The most miserable objic' I ever did see," observed Disco.

The negroes looked at each other and laughed. They were accustomed to monkeys, and took little notice of them, but they were mightily tickled by Disco's amusement, for he had laid down his knife and fork, and shook a good deal with internal chuckling, as he gazed upwards.

"One would suppose, now," he said softly, "that it had recently seen its father and mother, and all its brothers and sisters, removed by a violent death, or sold into slavery."

"Ha! they never see that," said Harold; "the brutes may fight and kill, but they never *enslave* each other. It is the proud prerogative of man to do that."

"That's true, sir, worse luck, as Paddy says," rejoined Disco. "But look there: wot's them coorious things round the creetur's waist—a pair o' the werry smallest hands— and, hallo! a face no bigger than a button! I do believe that it's—"

Disco did not finish the sentence, but he was right. The small melancholy monkey was a mother!

R. M. Ballantyne

Probably that was the cause of its sorrow. It is a touching thought that anxiety for its tiny offspring perhaps had furrowed that monkey's visage with the wrinkles of premature old age. That danger threatened it on every side was obvious, for no sooner had it taken up its new position, after its unceremonious ejection by the fierce monkey, than the sprightly monkey, before referred to, conceived a plot which it immediately proceeded to carry into execution. Observing that the tail of the sad one hung down in a clear space below the branch on which it sat, the sprightly fellow quickly, but with intense caution and silence, crept towards it, and when within a yard or so sprang into the air and caught the tail!

A wild shriek, and what Disco styled a "scrimmage," ensued, during which the mother monkey gave chase to him of the lively visage, using her arms, legs, and tail promiscuously to grasp and hold on to branches, and leaving her extremely little one to look out for itself. This it seemed quite capable of doing, for no limpet ever stuck to a solid rock with greater tenacity than did that infant to the maternal waist throughout the chase. The hubbub appeared to startle the whole monkey race, revealing the fact that troops of other monkeys had, unobserved, been gazing at the strangers in silent wonder, since the time of their landing.

Pleasant however, though this state of things undeniably was, it could not be expected to last. Breakfast being concluded, it became necessary that Disco should tear himself from the spot which, having first solaced himself with a pipe, he did with a good grace, remarking, as he re-embarked and "took the helm" of his canoe, that he had got more powerful surprises that morning than he had ever before experienced in any previous twelvemonth of his life.

Before long he received many more surprises, especially one of a very different and much less pleasant nature, an account of which will be found in the next chapter.

R. M. Ballantyne

CHAPTER SIX

DESCRIBES SEVERAL NEW AND SURPRISING INCIDENTS, WHICH MUST BE READ TO BE FULLY APPRECIATED

To travel with one's mouth and eyes opened to nearly their utmost width in a state of surprised stupefaction, may be unavoidable, but it cannot be said to be either becoming or convenient. Attention in such a case is apt to be diverted from the business in hand, and flies have a tendency to immolate themselves in the throat.

Nevertheless, inconvenient though the condition was, our friend Disco Lillihammer was so afflicted with astonishment at what he heard and saw in this new land, that he was constantly engaged in swallowing flies and running his canoe among shallows and rushes, insomuch that he at last resigned the steering-oar until familiarity with present circumstances should tone him down to a safe condition of equanimity.

And no wonder that Disco was surprised; no wonder that his friend Harold Seadrift shared in his astonishment and delight, for they were at once, and for the first time in their lives, plunged into the very heart of jungle life in equatorial Africa! Those who have never wandered far from the comparatively tame regions of our temperate zone, can form but a faint conception of what it is to ramble in the tropics, and therefore can scarcely be expected to sympathise fully with the mental condition of our heroes as they ascended the Zambesi. Everything was so thoroughly strange; sights and sounds so vastly different from what they had been accustomed to see and hear, that it seemed as though they had landed on another planet. Trees, shrubs, flowers, birds, beasts, insects, and reptiles, all were unfamiliar, except indeed, one or two of the more conspicuous trees and animals, which had been so imprinted on their minds by means of nursery picture-books that, on first beholding them, Disco unconsciously paid these books the compliment of saying that the animals "wos uncommon like the picturs."

Disco's mental condition may be said, for the first two or three days, to have been one of gentle ever-flowing surprise, studded thickly with little bursts of keen astonishment.

The first part of the river ran between mangrove jungle, in regard to which he remarked that "them there trees had legs like crabs," in which observation he was not far wrong, for, when the tide was out, the roots of the mangroves rose high out of the mud, forming supports, as it were, for the trees to stand on.

But it was the luxuriance of the vegetation that made the most powerful impression on the travellers. It seemed as if the various groups and families of the vegetable kingdom had been warmed by the sun into a state of unwonted affection, for everything appeared to entertain the desire to twine round and embrace everything else. One magnificent screw-palm in particular was so overwhelmed by affectionate parasites that his natural shape was almost entirely concealed. Others of the trees were decked with orchilla weed. There were ferns so gigantic as to be almost

R. M. Ballantyne

worthy of being styled trees, and palm-bushes so sprawling as to suggest the idea of huge vegetable spiders. Bright yellow fruit gleamed among the graceful green leaves of the mangroves; wild date-palms gave variety to the scene, if that had been needed, which it was not, and masses of umbrageous plants with large yellow flowers grew along the banks, while, down among the underwood, giant roots rose in fantastic convolutions above ground, as if the earth were already too full, and there wasn't room for the whole of them. There was an antediluvian magnificence, a prehistoric snakiness, a sort of primeval running-to-seedness, which filled Harold and Disco with feelings of awe, and induced a strange, almost unnatural tendency to regard Adam and Eve as their contemporaries.

Animal life was not wanting in this paradise. Frequently did our seaman give vent to "Hallo!" "There they go!" "Look out for the little 'un wi' the long tail!" and similar expressions, referring of course to his favourite monkeys, which ever and anon peered out upon the strangers with looks of intensity, for whatever their expression might be—sadness, grief, interrogation, wrath, surprise—it was always in the super-lative degree. There were birds also, innumerable. One, styled the "king-hunter," sang wild exultant airs, as if it found king-hunting to be an extremely exhilarating occu-pation, though what sort of kings it hunted we cannot tell. Perhaps it was the king of beasts, perhaps the kingfisher, a bright specimen of which was frequently seen to dart out from the banks, but we profess ignorance on this point. There were fish-hawks also, magnificent fellows, which sat in regal dignity on the tops of the mangrove trees, and the glossy ibis, with others of the feathered tribe too numerous to mention.

Large animals also were there in abundance, though not so frequently seen as those which have been already mentioned.

Disco occasionally made known the fact that such, or something unusual, had transpired, by the sudden and violent exclamation of "What's that?" in a voice so loud that "that," whatever it might be, sometimes bolted or took to flight before any one else caught sight of it.

"Hallo!" he exclaimed, on one such occasion, as the canoes turned a bend of the river.

"What now?" demanded Harold, looking at his companion to observe the direction of his eyes.

"I'm a Dutchman," exclaimed Disco in a hoarse whisper that might have been heard half a mile off, "if it's not a zebra!"

"So it is; my rifle—look sharp!" said Harold eagerly.

The weapon was handed to him, but before it could be brought to bear, the beautiful striped creature had tossed its head, snorted, whisked its tail, kicked up its heels, and dashed into the jungle.

"Give way, lads; let's after him," shouted Disco, turning the canoe's bow to shore.

"Hold on," cried Harold; "you might as well go after a needle in a haystack, or a locomotive."

"So I might," admitted Disco, with a mortified air, resuming his course; "but it ain't in reason to expect a feller to keep quiet w'en he sees one o' the very picturs of his child'ood, so to speak, come alive an' kick up its heels like that."

Buffaloes were also seen in the grassy glades, but it proved difficult to come within range of them; also wart-hogs, and three different kinds of antelope.

R. M. Ballantyne

Of these last Harold shot several, and they were found to be excellent food.

Human beings were also observed, but those first encountered fled at the sight of the white men, as if they had met with their worst foes; and such was in very truth the case,—if we may regard the Portuguese half-castes of that coast as white men,—for these negroes were runaway slaves, who stood the chance of being shot, or drowned, or whipped to death, if recaptured.

Other animals they saw—some queer, some terrible, nearly all strange—and last, though not least, the hippopotamus.

When Disco first saw this ungainly monster he was bereft of speech for some minutes. The usual "Hallo!" stuck in his throat and well-nigh choked him. He could only gasp, and point.

"Ay, there goes a hippopotamus," said Harold, with the easy nonchalance of a man who had been to the Zoological Gardens, and knew all about it. Nevertheless it was quite plain that Harold was much excited, for he almost dropped his oar overboard in making a hasty grasp at his rifle. Before he could fire, the creature gaped wide, as if in laughter, and dived.

"Unfortunate!" said Harold, in a philosophically careless tone; "never mind, we shall see lots more of them."

"Ugliness embodied!" said Disco, heaving a deep sigh.

"But him's goot for eat," said Antonio, smacking his lips.

"Is he?" demanded Disco of Jumbo, whose enjoyment of the sailor's expressive looks was so great, that, whenever the latter opened his lips, the former looked back over his shoulder with a broad grin of expectation.

"Ho yis; de hiputmus am fust-rate grub for dis yer boy," replied the negro, rolling his red tongue inside his mouth suggestively.

"He never eats man, does he?" inquired Disco.

"Nevair," replied Antonio.

"He looks as if he might," returned the seaman; "anyhow, he's got a mouth big enough to do it. You're quite sure he don't, I 'spose?"

"Kite sure an' sartin; but me hab seen him tak mans," said Antonio.

"Tak mans, wot d'ee mean by that?"

"Tak him," repeated Antonio. "Go at him's canoe or boat—bump with him's head—dash in de timbers—capsize, so's man hab to swim shore—all as got clear ob de crokidils."

While Disco was meditating on this unpleasant trait of character in the hippopotamus, the specimen which they had just seen, or some other member of his family, having compassion, no doubt, on the seaman's ignorance, proceeded to illustrate its method of attack then and there by rising suddenly under the canoe with such force, that its head and shoulders shot high out of the water, into which it fell with a heavy splash. Harold's rifle being ready, he fired just as it was disappearing.

Whether he hit or not is uncertain, but next moment the enraged animal rose again under Disco's canoe, which it nearly lifted out of the water in its efforts to seize it in its mouth. Fortunately the canoe was too flat for its jaws to grip; the monster's blunt teeth were felt, as well as heard, to grind across the planks; and Disco being in the stern, which was raised highest, was almost thrown overboard by the jerk.

Rising about two yards off, the hippopotamus looked savagely at the canoe, and was about to dive again when Harold gave it a second shot. The large gun being fortunately ready, had been handed to him by one of the Makololo men. The heavy ball took effect behind the eye, and killed the animal almost instantaneously. The hippopotamus usually sinks when shot dead, but in this case they were so near that, before it had time to sink, Zombo, assisted by his friend Jumbo, made a line fast to it, and it was finally dragged to the shore. The landing, however, was much retarded by the crocodiles, which now showed themselves for the first time, and kept tugging and worrying the carcase much as a puppy tugs and worries a ladies' muff; affording Disco and his friend strong reason to congratulate themselves that the canoe had not been overturned.

The afternoon was pretty well advanced when the landing was accomplished on a small sandy island, and as the spot was suitable for encamping, they determined to remain there for the night, and feast.

There are many points of resemblance between savage and civilised festivities. Whether the performers be the black sons of Africa, or the white fathers of Europe, there is the same powerful tendency to eat too much, and the same display of good-fellowship; for it is an indisputable fact that feeding man is amiable, unless, indeed, he be dyspeptic. There are also, however, various points of difference. The savage, owing to the amount of fresh air and exercise which he is compelled to take, usually eats with greater appetite, and knows nothing of equine dreams or sleepless nights. On the whole, we incline to the belief that, despite his lack of refinement and ceremony, the savage has the best of it in this matter.

Disco Lillihammer's visage, during the progress of that feast, formed a study worthy of a physiognomist. Every new achievement, whether trifling or important, performed by the Makololo triad, Jumbo, Zombo, and Masiko—every fresh hippopotamus steak skewered and set up to roast by the half-caste brothers Jose and Oliveira—every lick bestowed on their greasy fingers by the Somali negroes Nakoda and Conda, and every sigh of intense satisfaction heaved by the so-called "freemen" of Quillimane, Songolo and Mabruki, was watched, commented on, and, if we may say so, reflected in the animated countenance of the stout seaman, with such variety of expression, and such an interesting compound of grin and wrinkle, that poor Jumbo, who gazed at him over hippopotamus ribs and steaks, and tried hard not to laugh, was at last compelled to turn away his eyes, in order that his mouth might have fair-play.

But wonderful, sumptuous, and every way satisfactory though that feast was, it bore no comparison whatever to another feast carried on at the same time by another party, about fifty yards off, where the carcase of the hippopotamus had been left half in and half out of the water—for, of course, being fully more than a ton in weight, only a small portion of the creature was appropriated by the canoe-men. The negroes paid no attention whatever to this other festive party; but in a short time Disco turned his head to one side, and said—"Wy, wot's that splashin' I hears goin' on over there?"

"I suspect it must be some beast or other that has got hold of the carcase," replied Harold, who was himself busy with a portion of the same.

R. M. Ballantyne

"Yis, dat am krokidils got 'im," said Antonio, with his mouth full—very full.

"You don't say so?" said Disco, washing down the steak with a brimming cup of tea.

No one appeared to think it worth while to asseverate the fact, for it was self-evident. Several crocodiles were supping, and in doing so they tore away at the carcase with such violence, and lashed the water so frequently with their powerful tails, as to render it clear that their feast necessitated laborious effort, and seemed less a recreation than a duty. Moreover, they sat at their meat like insatiable gourmands, so long into the night that supper became transmuted into breakfast, and Harold's rest was greatly disturbed thereby. He was too sleepy and lazy, however, to rise and drive them away.

Next morning the travellers started early, being anxious to pass, as quietly as possible, a small Portuguese town, near to which it was said a party of runaway slaves and rebels against the Government were engaged in making depredations.

When grey dawn was beginning to rise above the tree-tops, they left their encampment in profound silence, and rowed up stream as swiftly as possible. They had not advanced far, when, on turning a point covered with tall reeds, Zombo, who was bowman in the leading canoe, suddenly made a sign to the men to cease rowing.

"What's the matter?" whispered Harold.

The negro pointed through the reeds, and whispered the single word "Canoe."

By this time the other canoe had ranged up alongside, and

after a brief consultation between Harold and Disco, it was decided that they should push gently into the reeds, and wait till the strange canoe should pass; but a few seconds sufficed to show that the two men who paddled it did not intend to pass down the river, for they pushed straight out towards the deepest part of the stream. They were, however, carried down so swiftly by the current that they were brought quite near to the point of rushes where our travellers lay concealed—so near that their voices could be distinctly heard. They talked in Portuguese.

Antonio muttered a few words, and Harold observed that there was a good deal of excitement in the looks of his men.

"What's the matter?" he asked anxiously.

Antonio shook his head. "Dat nigger goin' to be drownded," he said; "bad nigger—obstropolous nigger, suppose."

"Wot!" exclaimed Disco in a whisper, "goin' to be drownded! wot d'ee mean?"

Antonio proceeded to explain that it was a custom amongst the Portuguese slave-owners there, when they found any of their slaves intractable or refractory, to hire some individuals who, for a small sum, would bind and carry off the incorrigible for the purpose of making away with him. One method of effecting this was to tie him in a sack and throw him into the river, the crocodiles making quite sure that the unfortunate being should never again be seen, either alive or dead. But before Antonio had finished his brief explanation he was interrupted by an exclamation from the horrified Englishmen, as they beheld the two men in the canoe raise something between them which for a moment appeared to struggle violently.

"Shove off! give way!" shouted Harold and Disco in the same breath, each thrusting with his paddle so vigorously that the two canoes shot out like arrows into the stream.

At the same instant there was a heavy plunge in the water beside the strange canoe, and the victim sank. Next moment one end of the sack rose to the surface. Both Harold and Disco made straight towards it, but it sank again, and the two murderers paddled to the shore, on which they drew up their canoe, intending to take to the bush, if necessary, for safety.

Once again the sack rose not more than three yards from Disco's canoe. The bold seaman knew that if it disappeared a third time there would be little chance of its rising again. He was prompt in action, and daring to recklessness. In one moment he had leaped overboard, dived, caught the sack in his powerful grasp, and bore it to the surface. The canoe had been steered for him. The instant he appeared, strong and ready hands laid hold of him and his burden, and dragged them both inboard.

"Cut the lashin's and give him air," cried Disco, endeavouring to find his clasp-knife; but one of the men quickly obeyed the order, and opened the sack.

A groan of horror and pity burst from the seaman when he beheld the almost insensible form of a powerful negro, whose back was lacerated with innumerable ragged cuts, and covered with clotted blood.

"Where are the—"

He stopped short on looking round, and, observing that the two men were standing on the shore, seized a double-barrelled gun. The stream had carried the canoe a considerable distance below the spot where the murder had been attempted, but they were still within range. Without a moment's hesitation Disco took deliberate aim at them and fired.

Fortunately for him and his party Disco was a bad shot—nevertheless the bullet struck so close to the feet of the two men that it drove the sand and pebbles into their faces. They turned at once and fled, but before they reached the cover of the bushes the second barrel was fired, and the bullet whistled close enough over their heads greatly to accelerate their flight.

The negroes opened their great round eyes, and appeared awe-struck at this prompt display of a thirst for vengeance on the part of one who had hitherto shown no other disposition than hilarity, fun, and good-humour.

Harold was greatly relieved to observe Disco's failure, for, if he had hit either of the fugitives, the consequences might have been very disastrous to their expedition.

On being partially revived and questioned, it turned out that the poor fellow had been whipped almost to death for refusing to be the executioner in whipping his own mother. This was a refinement in cruelty on the part of these professedly Christian Portuguese, which our travellers afterwards learned was by no means uncommon.

We are told by those who know that region well, and whose veracity is unquestionable, that the Portuguese on the east coast of Africa live in constant dread of their slaves rising against them. No wonder, considering the fiendish cruelties to which they subject them! In order to keep them in subjection they underfeed them, and if any of them venture to steal cocoa-nuts from the trees the owners thereof are at liberty to shoot them and throw them into the sea. Slaves being cheap there, and plentiful, are easily replaced, hence a cruel owner never hesitates. If a slave is refractory, and flogging only makes him worse, his master bids the overseer flog him until "he will require no more." Still further to keep them in subjection, the Portuguese then endeavour to eradicate from them all sympathy with each other, and all natural affection, by the following means. If a woman requires to be flogged, her brother or son is selected to do it. Fathers are made to flog their daughters, husbands their wives, and, if two young negroes of different sexes are observed to show any symptoms of growing attachment for each other, these two are chosen for each other's executioners. [See *Travels in Eastern Africa*, by Lyons McLeod, Esquire, FRGS, and late Her Britannic Majesty's Consul at Mozambique, volume one pages 274 to 277, and volume two page 27.]

The poor wretch whom we have just described as having been saved from death, to which he had been doomed for refusing to become the executioner of his own mother, was placed as tenderly and comfortably as circumstances would admit of in the bottom of the canoe, and then our travellers pushed on with all haste—anxious to pass the town before the two fugitives could give the alarm.

They were successful in this, probably because the two men may have hid themselves for some time in the jungle, under the impression that the exasperated Englishmen might be searching for them on shore.

Giving themselves time only to take a hurried meal in the middle of the day, our travellers rowed continuously till sunset when, deeming it probable that pursuit, if undertaken at all, must have been abandoned, they put ashore on the right bank of the river and encamped.

When the sufferer had been made as comfortable as circumstances would allow—for he was much weakened by loss of blood as well as agonised with pain—and after he had been refreshed with food and some warm tea, Harold questioned him, through the interpreter, as to his previous history.

At first the man was brusque in his manner, and inclined to be sulky, for a long course of cruelty had filled him with an intense hatred of white men. Indeed, an embittered and desperate spirit had begun to induce callous indifference to all men, whether white or black. But kind treatment, to which he was evidently unaccustomed, and generous diet, which was obviously new to him, had a softening influence, and when Harold poured a small glass of rum into his tea, and Antonio added a lump of sugar, and Disco pressed him tenderly to drink it off—which he did—the effect was very decided; the settled scowl on his face became unsettled, and gradually melting away, was replaced by a milder and more manly look. By degrees he became communicative, and, bit by bit, his story was drawn from him. It was brief, but very sorrowful.

His name, he said, was Chimbolo. He belonged to a tribe which lived far inland, beyond the Manganja country, which latter was a country of hills. He was not a Manganja man, but he had married a Manganja woman. One night he, with his wife and mother, was paying a visit to the village of his wife's relations, when a band of slave-hunters suddenly attacked the village. They were armed with guns, and at once began to murder the old people and capture the young. Resistance was useless. His relatives were armed only with bows and spears. Being taken by surprise, they all fled in terror, but were pursued and few escaped. His wife, he said—and a scowl of terrible ferocity crossed Chimbolo's face as he said it—was about to become a mother at the time. He seized her in his arms on the first alarm, and fled with her into the bush, where he concealed her, and then hurried back

R. M. Ballantyne

to aid his relations, but met them—old and young, strong and feeble—flying for their lives. It was not possible to rally them; he therefore joined in the flight. While running, a bullet grazed his head and stunned him. Presently he recovered and rose, but in a few minutes was overtaken and captured. A slave-stick was put on his neck, and, along with a number of Manganja men, women, and children, he was driven down to the coast, and sold, with a number of other men and women, among whom was his own mother, to a Portuguese merchant on the coast, near the East Luavo mouth of the Zambesi. There he was found to be of a rebellious spirit, and at last on positively refusing to lash his mother, his master ordered him to be whipped to death, but, changing his mind before the order had been quite carried out he ordered him to be bound hand and foot and taken away in a sack. As to his wife, he had never heard of her since that night which was about two years past. He knew that she had not been found, because he had not seen her amongst the other captives. If they had found her they would have been sure to carry her off, because—here Chimbolo's visage again grew diabolical—she was young, he said, and beautiful.

When all this had been translated into bad English by Antonio, Harold asked if Chimbolo thought it probable that his wife was still alive in the Manganja highlands. To this the former said that he thought it likely.

"W'y, then," said Disco, giving his right thigh a powerful slap, which was his favourite method of emphasising a remark, "wot d'ye say, sir, to lay our course for these same highlands, and try for to find out this poor critter?"

"Just what was running in my own mind, Disco," said Harold, musing over his supper. "It does not make much difference what part of this country we go to, being all new to us; and as Antonio tells me the Manganja highlands are up the Shire river, which was explored by Dr Livingstone not long ago, and is not distant many days' journey from this, I think we can't do better than go there. We shall have a good as well as a definite object in view."

"Wery good, sir; I'm agreeable," returned Disco, reaching forth his pewter plate; "another hunk o' that pottimus, Jumbo; it's better than salt-junk any day; and I say, Jumbo, don't grin so much, else ye'll enlarge yer pretty little mouth, which 'ud be a pity."

"Yis, saar," replied Jumbo, becoming very grave all of a sudden, but on receiving a nod and an expressive wink from the seaman, he exploded again, and rolled backward on the grass, in the performance of which act he capsized Zombo's can of tea, whereupon Zombo leaped upon him in wrath, and Masiko, as in duty bound, came to the rescue.

"Clap a stopper on yer noise, will 'ee?" cried Disco sternly, "else you'll be bringin' all the wild beasts in these parts down on us to see wot it's all about."

"That reminds me," said Harold, when quiet was restored, "that we must now organise ourselves into something of a fighting band—a company, as it were, of soldiers,—and take our regular spell of watching by night, for, from all that I hear of the disturbed state of the country just now, with these runaway slaves and rebels, it will be necessary to be on our guard. Of course," he added, smiling, "I suppose I must be captain of the company, and you, Disco, shall be lieutenant."

"Not at all," replied the seaman, shaking his head, and frowning at Jumbo, whose brilliant teeth at once responded to the glance, "not at all, none of your sodgerin' for me. I never could abide the lobsters. Fust-mate, sir, that's wot *I* am,

R. M. Ballantyne

if I'm to be expected to do my dooty."

"Well then, first-mate be it," rejoined Harold, "and Antonio shall be serjeant-major—"

"Bo's'n—bo's'n," suggested Disco; "keep up appearances wotiver ye do, an' don't let the memory of salt water go down."

"Very good," said Harold, laughing; "then you shall be boatswain, Antonio, as well as cook, and I will instruct you in the first part of your duty, which will be to keep watch for an hour while the rest of us sleep. My first-mate will teach you the whistling part of a boatswain's duty, if that should be required—"

"Ah, and the roar," interrupted Disco, "a bo's'n would be nothin' without his roar—"

At that moment the woods around them were filled with a tremendous and very unexpected roar, which caused the whole party to spring up, and induced the new bo's'n to utter a yell of terror that would have done credit to the whistle of the most violent bo's'n on the sea. Next moment the travellers were surrounded by a large and excited band of armed negroes.

CHAPTER SEVEN

ENEMIES ARE CHANGED INTO FRIENDS—
OUR TRAVELLERS PENETRATE INTO
THE INTERIOR OF THE LAND

To possess the power of looking perfectly calm and unconcerned when you are in reality considerably agitated and rather anxious, is extremely useful in any circumstances, but especially so when one happens to be in the midst of grinning, gesticulating, naked savages.

Our hero, Harold Seadrift possessed that power in an eminent degree, and his first-mate, Disco Lillihammer, was not a whit behind him. Although both had started abruptly to their legs at the first alarm, and drawn their respective revolvers, they no sooner found themselves surrounded by overwhelming numbers than they lowered their weapons, and, turning back to back, faced the intruders with calm countenances.

"Sit down, men, every one of you except Antonio," said Harold, in a quiet, but clear and decided voice.

His men, who, having left their guns in the canoe, were utterly helpless, quietly obeyed.

R. M. Ballantyne

"Who are you, and what do you want?" demanded Antonio, by Harold's order.

To this a tall negro, who was obviously the leader of the band, replied in the native tongue,—"It matters little who we are; you are in our power."

"Not quite," said Harold, slightly moving his revolver. "Tell him that he *may* overcome us, but before he does so my friend and I carry the lives of twelve of his men in our pistols."

The negro chief, who quite understood the powers of a revolver, replied—"Tell your master, that before he could fire two shots, he and his friend would have each twelve bullets in his body. But I have not time to palaver here. Who are you, and where are you going?"

"We are Englishmen, travelling to see the country," replied Harold.

The chief looked doubtfully at him, and seemed to waver, then suddenly making up his mind, he frowned and said sternly—"No; that is a lie. You are Portuguese scoundrels. You shall all die. You have robbed us of our liberty, our wives, our children, our homes; you have chained, and tortured, and flogged us!"—he gnashed his teeth at this point, and his followers grew excited. "Now we have got free, and you are caught. We will let you know what it is to be slaves."

As the negro chief stirred up his wrath by thus recounting his wrongs, and advanced a step, Harold begged Disco, in a low, urgent voice, not to raise his pistol. Then looking the savage full in the face, without showing a trace of anxiety, he said— "You are wrong. We are indeed Englishmen, and you know that the English detest slavery, and would, if they could, put a stop to it altogether."

"Yes, I know that," said the chief. "We have seen one Englishman here, and he has made us to know that not all men with white faces are devils—like the Portuguese and Arabs. But how am I to know you are English?"

Again the chief wavered a little, as if half-inclined to believe Harold's statement.

"Here is proof for you," said Harold, pointing to Chimbolo, who, being scarcely able to move, had remained all this time beside the fire leaning on his elbow and listening intently to the conversation. "See," he continued, "that is a slave. Look at him."

As he said this, Harold stepped quickly forward and removed the blanket, with which he had covered his lacerated back after dressing it.

A howl of execration burst from the band of negroes, who pointed their spears and guns at the travellers' breasts, and would have made a speedy end of the whole party if Antonio had not exclaimed "Speak, Chimbolo, speak!"

The slave looked up with animation, and told the rebels how his Portuguese owner had ordered him to be flogged to death, but changed his mind and doomed him to be drowned,—how that in the nick of time, these white men had rescued him, and had afterwards treated him with the greatest kindness.

Chimbolo did not say much, but what he did say was uttered with emphasis and feeling. This was enough. Those who would have been enemies were suddenly converted into warm friends, and the desperadoes, who would have torn their former masters, or any of their race, limb from limb, if they could have got hold of them, left our adventurers undisturbed in their bivouac, after wishing them a prosperous journey.

It was nevertheless deemed advisable to keep watch during the night. This was done faithfully and conscientiously as far as it went. Harold took the first hour by way of example. He sat over the fire, alternately gazing into its embers while he meditated of home, and round upon the dark forest while he thought of Africa. True to time, he called Disco, who, equally true to his sense of duty, turned out at once with a deep "Ay, ay, sir." The self-styled first-mate placed his back against a tree, and, endeavouring to believe it to be a capstan, or binnacle, or any other object appertaining to the sea, stared at the ghostly stems of the forest-trees until they began to dance hornpipes for his special gratification, or glowered at the shadows until they became instinct with life, and all but induced him to rouse the camp twenty times in the course of his hour's vigil. True to time also, like his predecessor, Disco roused Antonio and immediately turned in.

The vivacious *chef de cuisine* started up at once, took up his position at the foot of the tree which Disco had just left, leaned his back against it, and straightway went to sleep, in which condition he remained till morning, leaving the camp in unprotected felicity and blissful ignorance.

Fortunately for all parties, Disco awoke in time to catch him napping, and resolved to punish him. He crept stealthily round to the back of the tree against which the faithless man leaned, and reached gently round until his mouth was close to Antonio's cheek, then, collecting all the air that his vast lungs were capable of containing, he poured into Antonio's ear a cumulative roar that threw the camp and the denizens of the wilderness far and near into confusion, and almost drove the whole marrow in Antonio's body out at his heels. The stricken man sprang up as if earth had shot him forth, uttered a yell of terror such as seldom greets the ear, and rushed blindly forward. Repeating the roar, Disco plunged after him. Antonio tumbled over the fire, recovered himself, dashed on, and would certainly have plunged into the river, if not into the jaws of a crocodile, had not Jumbo caught him in his arms, in the midst of a chorus of laughter from the other men.

"How dare 'ee go to sleep on dooty?" demanded Disco, seizing the culprit by the collar, "eh! we might have bin all murdered by rebels or eaten by lions, or had our eyes picked out by gorillas, for all that *you* would have done to prevent it—eh?" giving him a shake.

"Oh, pardon, forgif. Nevair doot more again," exclaimed the breathless and trembling Antonio.

"You'd *better* not!" said Disco, giving him another shake and releasing him.

Having done so, he turned on his heel and bestowed a quiet look, in passing, on Jumbo, which of course threw that unfortunate man into convulsions.

After this little incident a hasty breakfast was taken, the canoes were launched, and the voyage was continued.

It is not necessary to trace the course of our explorers day by day as they ascended the Zambesi, or to recount all the adventures or misadventures that befell them on their journey into the interior. It is sufficient for the continuity of our tale to say that many days after leaving the coast they turned into the Shire river, which flows into the Zambesi about 150 miles from the coast.

R. M. Ballantyne

There are many fountain-heads of slavery in Africa. The region of the interior, which gives birth to the head-waters of the Shire river, is one of the chief of these. Here lies the great lake Nyassa, which was discovered and partly explored by Dr Livingstone, and hence flows a perennial stream of traffic to Kilwa, on the coast—which traffic, at the present time, consists almost exclusively of the two kinds of ivory, white and black, the former (elephants' tusks) being carried by the latter (slaves), by which means the slave-trade is rendered more profitable.

Towards this populous and fertile region, then, our adventurers directed their course, when they turned out of the great river Zambesi and began to ascend the Shire.

And here, at the very outset of this part of the journey, they met with a Portuguese settler, who did more to open their eyes to the blighting and withering influence of slavery on the land and on its people than anything they had yet seen.

Towards the afternoon of the first day on the Shire, they landed near the encampment of the settler referred to, who turned out to be a gentleman of a Portuguese town on the Zambesi.

Harold found, to his delight, that he could speak English fluently, and was, moreover, an exceedingly agreeable and well-informed man. He was out at the time on a hunting expedition, attended by a party of slaves.

Harold spent the evening in very pleasant intercourse with Senhor Gamba, and at a later hour than usual returned to his camp, where he entertained Disco with an account of his new acquaintance.

While thus engaged, he was startled by the most appalling

shrieks, which proceeded from the neighbouring encampment. Under the impression that something was wrong, both he and Disco leaped up and ran towards it. There, to his amazement and horror, Harold beheld his agreeable friend Senhor Gamba thrashing a young slave unmercifully with a whip of the most formidable character. Only a few lashes from it had been given when Harold ran up, but these were so powerful that the unhappy victim dropped down in a state of insensibility just as he reached the spot.

The Portuguese "gentleman" turned away from the prostrate slave with a scowl, but betrayed a slight touch of confusion on meeting the gaze of Harold Seadrift.

"Senhor!" exclaimed the latter sternly, with mingled remonstrance and rebuke in his tone, "how *can* you be so cruel? What has the boy done to merit such inhuman chastisement?"

"He has neglected my orders," answered the Portuguese, as though he resented the tone in which Harold spoke.

"But surely, surely," said Harold, "the punishment is far beyond the offence. I can scarcely believe the evidence of my own eyes and ears when they tell me that *you* have been guilty of this."

"Come," returned Senhor Gamba, softening into a smile, "you English cannot understand our case in this land. Because you do not keep slaves, you take the philanthropic, the religious view of the question. We who do keep slaves have a totally different experience. You cannot understand, you cannot sympathise with us."

"No, truly, we can *not* understand you," said Harold earnestly, "and God forbid that we should ever sympathise

R. M. Ballantyne

with you in this matter. We detest the gross injustice of slavery, and we abhor the fearful cruelties connected with it."

"That is because, as I said, you are not in our position," rejoined the Senhor, with a shrug of his shoulders. "It is easy for you to take the philanthropic view, which, however, I admit to be the best, for in the eyes of God all men are equal, and though the African be a degraded man, I know enough of him to be sure that he can be raised by kindness and religion into a position not very inferior to our own; but we who keep slaves cannot help ourselves we *must* act as we do."

"Why so?—is cruelty a necessity?" asked Harold.

"Yes, it is," replied the Senhor decidedly.

"Then the abolition of slavery is a needcessity too," growled Disco, who had hitherto looked on and listened in silent wonder, debating with himself as to the propriety of giving Senhor Gamba, then and there, a sound thrashing with his own whip!

"You see," continued the Portuguese, paying no attention to Disco's growl,—"You see, in order to live out here I must have slaves, and in order to keep slaves I must have a whip. My whip is no worse than any other whip that I know of. I don't justify it as right, I simply defend it as necessary. *Wherever slavery exists, discipline must of necessity be brutal.* If you keep slaves, and mean that they shall give you the labour of their bodies, and of their minds also, in so far as you permit them to have minds, you must degrade them by the whip and by all other means at your disposal until, like dogs, they become the unhesitating servants of your will, no matter what that will may be, and live for your pleasure only. It will never pay me to adopt your philanthropic, your religious views. I am here. I *must* be here. What am I to do?

Starve? No, not if I can help it. I do as others do—keep slaves and act as the master of slaves. I must use the whip. Perhaps you won't believe me," continued Senhor Gamba, with a sad smile, "but I speak truth when I say that I was tender-hearted when I first came to this country, for I had been well nurtured in Lisbon; but that soon passed away—it could not last. I was the laughing-stock of my companions. Just to explain my position, I will tell you a circumstance which happened soon after I came here. The Governor invited me to a party of pleasure. The party consisted of himself, his daughters, some officers, and others. We were to go in boats to a favourite island resort, several miles off. I took one of my slaves with me, a lad that I kept about my person. As we were going along, this lad fell into the river. He could not swim, and the tide was carrying him fast away to death. Dressed as I was, in full uniform, I plunged in after him and saved him. The wish alone to save the boy's life prompted me to risk my own. And for this I became the jest of the party; even the ladies tittered at my folly. Next evening the Governor had a large dinner-party. I was there. Having caught cold, I coughed slightly; this drew attention to me. Remarks were made, and the Governor alluded in scoffing terms to my exploit, which created much mirth. 'Were you drunk?' said one. 'Had you lost your senses, to risk your life for a brute of a negro?' said another. 'Rather than spoil my uniform, I would have knocked him on the head with a pole,' said a third; and it was a long time before what they termed my folly was forgotten or forgiven. You think I am worse than others. I am not; but I do not condescend to their hypocrisy. What I am now, I have been made by this country and its associates." [These words are not fictitious. The remarks of Senhor Gamba were actually spoken by a Portuguese slave-owner, and will be found in *The Story of the Universities' Mission to Central Africa*, pages 64-5-6.]

Senhor Gamba said this with the air of one who thinks that

he has nearly, if not quite, justified himself. "I am no worse than others," is an excuse for evil conduct, not altogether unknown in more highly favoured lands, and is often followed by the illogical conclusion, "therefore I am not to blame," but although Harold felt pity for his agreeable chance acquaintance, he could not admit that this explanation excused him, nor could he get over the shock which his feelings had sustained; it was, therefore, with comparatively little regret that he bade him adieu on the following morning, and pursued his onward way.

Everywhere along the Shire they met with a more or less hospitable reception from the natives, who regarded them with great favour, in consequence of their belonging to the same nation which had sent forth men to explore their country, defend them from the slave-dealer, and teach them about the true God. These men, of whom mention is made in another chapter, had, some time before this, been sent by the Church of England to the Manganja highlands, at the suggestion of Dr Livingstone, and laid, we believe, the foundation-stone of Christian civilisation in the interior of Africa, though God saw fit to arrest them in the raising of the superstructure.

Among other pieces of useful knowledge conveyed by them to the negroes of the Shire, was the fact that Englishmen are not cannibals, and that they have no special longings after black man steaks!

It may perchance surprise some readers to learn that black men ever entertain such a preposterous notion. Nevertheless, it is literally true. The slavers—Arabs and Portuguese—find it in their interest to instil this falsehood into the minds of the ignorant tribes of the interior, from whom the slaves are gathered, in order that their captives may entertain a salutary horror of Englishmen, so that if their dhows should be chased by our cruisers while creeping northward along the coast and run the risk of being taken, the slaves may willingly aid their captors in trying to escape. That the lesson has been well learnt and thoroughly believed is proved by the fact that when a dhow is obliged to run ashore to avoid capture, the slaves invariably take to the woods on the wings of terror, preferring, no doubt to be re-enslaved rather than to be roasted and eaten by white fiends. Indeed, so thoroughly has this been engrained into the native mind, that mothers frequently endeavour to overawe their refractory offspring by threatening to hand them over to the dreadful white monster who will eat them up if they don't behave!

R. M. Ballantyne

CHAPTER EIGHT

RELATES ADVENTURES IN THE SHIRE VALLEY, AND TOUCHES ON ONE OR TWO PHASES OF SLAVERY

Everything depends upon taste, as the monkey remarked when it took to nibbling the end of its own tail! If you like a thing, you take one view of it; if you don't like it, you take another view. Either view, if detailed, would be totally irreconcilable with the other.

The lower part of the river Shire, into which our travellers had now entered, is a vast swamp. There are at least two opinions in regard to that region. To do justice to those with whom we don't sympathise, we give our opponent's view first. Our opponent, observe, is an honest and competent man; he speaks truly; he only looks at it in another light from Harold Seadrift and Disco Lillihammer.

He says of the river Shire, "It drains a low and exceedingly fertile valley of from fifteen to twenty miles in breadth. Ranges of wooded hills bound this valley on both sides. After the first twenty miles you come to Mount Morambala, which rises with steep sides to 4000 feet in height. It is wooded to the top, and very beautiful. A small village peeps out about half-way up the mountain. It has a pure, bracing atmosphere, and is perched above mosquito range. The people on the summit have a very different climate and vegetation from those on the plains, and they live amidst luxuriant vegetation. There are many species of ferns, some so large as to deserve the name of trees. There are also lemon and orange trees growing wild, and birds and animals of all kinds." Thus far we agree with our opponent but listen to him as he goes on:—

"The view from Morambala is extensive, but cheerless past description. Swamp, swamp-reeking, festering, rotting, malaria-pregnant swamp, where poisonous vapours for several months in the year are ever bulging up and out into the air,— lies before you as far as the eye can reach, and farther. If you enter the river at the worst seasons of the year, the chances are you will take the worst type of fever. If, on the other hand, you enter it during the best season, when the swamps are fairly dried up, you have everything in your favour."

Now, our opponent gives a true statement of facts undoubtedly, but his view of them is not cheering.

Contrast them with the view of Disco Lillihammer. That sagacious seaman had entered the Shire neither in the "best" nor the "worst" of the season. He had chanced upon it some-where between the two.

"Git up your steam an' go 'longside," he said to Jumbo one afternoon, as the two canoes were proceeding quietly among magnificent giant-reeds, sedges, and bulrushes, which towered high above them—in some places overhung them.

"I say, Mister Harold, ain't it splendid?"

"Magnificent!" replied Harold with a look of quiet enthusiasm.

"I *does* enjoy a swamp," continued the seaman, allowing a thin cloud to trickle from his lips.

"So do I, Disco."

"There's such a many outs and ins an' roundabouts in it. And such powerful reflections o' them reeds in the quiet water. W'y, sir, I do declare w'en I looks through 'em in a dreamy sort of way for a long time I get to fancy they're palm-trees, an' that we're sailin' through a forest without no end to it; an' when I looks over the side an' sees every reed standin' on its other self, so to speak, an' follers the under one down till my eyes git lost in the blue sky an' clouds *below* us, I do sometimes feel as if we'd got into the middle of fairy-land,— was fairly afloat on the air, an' off on a voyage through the univarse! But it's them reflections as I like most. Every leaf, an' stalk, an' flag is just as good an' real *in* the water as out of it. An' just look at that there frog, sir, that one on the big leaf which has swelled hisself up as if he wanted to bust, with his head looking up hopefully to the—ah! he's down with a plop like lead, but he wos sittin' on his own image which wos as clear as his own self. Then there's so much variety, sir— that's where it is. You never know wot you're comin' to in them swamps. It may be a openin' like a pretty lake, with islands of reeds everywhere; or it may be a narrow bit like a canal, or a river; or a bit so close that you go scrapin' the gun'les on both sides. An' the life, too, is most amazin'. Never saw nothin' like it nowhere. All kinds, big an' little, plain an' pritty, queer an' 'orrible, swarms here to sitch an extent that I've got it into my head that this Shire valley must be the great original nursery of animated nature."

"It looks like it, Disco."

The last idea appeared to furnish food for reflection, as the two friends here relapsed into silence.

Although Disco's description was quaint, it could scarcely be styled exaggerated, for the swamp was absolutely alive with animal life. The principal occupant of these marshes is the elephant, and hundreds of these monster animals may be seen in one herd, feeding like cattle in a meadow. Owing to the almost impenetrable nature of the reedy jungle, however, it is impossible to follow them, and anxious though Disco was to kill one, he failed to obtain a single shot. Buffaloes and other large game were also numerous in this region, and in the water crocodiles and hippopotami sported about everywhere, while aquatic birds of every shape and size rendered the air vocal with their cries. Sometimes these feathered denizens of the swamp arose, when startled, in a dense cloud so vast that the mighty rush of their wings was almost thunderous in character.

The crocodiles were not only numerous but dangerous because of their audacity. They used to watch at the places where native women were in the habit of going down to the river for water, and not unfrequently succeeded in seizing a victim. This, however, only happened at those periods when the Shire was in flood, when fish were driven from their wonted haunts, and the crocodiles were reduced to a state of starvation and consequent ferocity.

One evening, while our travellers were proceeding slowly up stream, they observed the corpse of a negro boy floating past the canoe; just then a monstrous crocodile rushed at it with the speed of a greyhound, caught it and shook it as a terrier does a rat. Others dashed at the prey, each with his powerful tail causing the water to churn and froth as he tore off a piece. In a few seconds all was gone. [Livingstone's *Zambesi and its Tributaries*, page 452.] That same evening Zombo had a narrow escape. After dusk he ran down to the river to drink. He chanced to go to a spot where a crocodile was watching. It lay settled down in the mud with its head on a

R. M. Ballantyne

level with the water, so that in the feeble light it could not be seen. While Zombo was busy laving the water into his mouth it suddenly rushed at him and caught him by the hand. The limb of a bush was fortunately within reach, and he laid hold of it. There was a brief struggle. The crocodile tugged hard, but the man tugged harder; at the same time he uttered a yell which brought Jumbo to his side with an oar, a blow from which drove the hideous reptile away. Poor Zombo was too glad to have escaped with his life to care much about the torn hand, which rendered him *hors de combat* for some time after that.

Although Disco failed to get a shot at an elephant, his hopeful spirit was gratified by the catching of a baby elephant alive. It happened thus:—

One morning, not very long after Zombo's tussle with the crocodile, Disco's canoe, which chanced to be in advance, suddenly ran almost into the midst of a herd of elephants which were busy feeding on palm-nuts, of which they are very fond. Instantly the whole troop scattered and fled. Disco, taken completely by surprise, omitted his wonted "Hallo!" as he made an awkward plunge at his rifle, but before he could bring it to bear, the animals were over the bank of the river and lost in the dense jungle. But a fine little elephant, at that period of life which, in human beings, might be styled the toddling age, was observed to stumble while attempting to follow its mother up the bank. It fell and rolled backwards.

"Give way for your lives!" roared Disco.

The boat shot its bow on the bank, and the seaman flew rather than leaped upon the baby elephant!

The instant it was laid hold of it began to scream with

incessant and piercing energy after the fashion of a pig.

"Queek! come in canoe! Modder come back for 'im," cried Jumbo in some anxiety.

Disco at once appreciated the danger of the enraged mother returning to the rescue, but, resolved not to resign his advantage, he seized the vicious little creature by the proboscis and dragged it by main force to the canoe, into which he tumbled, hauled the proboscis inboard, as though it had been the bite of a cable, and held on.

"Shove off! shove off! and give way, lads! Look alive!"

The order was promptly obeyed, and in a few minutes the baby was dragged into the boat and secured.

This prize, however, was found to be more of a nuisance than an amusement and it was soon decided that it must be disposed of. Accordingly, that very night, much to the regret of the men who wanted to make a meal of it, Disco led his baby squealing into the jungle and set it free with a hearty slap on the flank, and an earnest recommendation to make all sail after its venerable mother, which it did forthwith, cocking its ears and tail, and shrieking as it went.

Two days after this event they made a brief halt at a poor village where they were hospitably received by the chief, who was much gratified by the liberal quantity of calico with which the travellers paid for their entertainment. Here they met with a Portuguese half-caste who was reputed one of the greatest monsters of cruelty in that part of the country. He was, however, not much more villainous in aspect than many other half-castes whom they saw. He was on his way to the coast in a canoe manned by slaves. If Harold and Disco had known that this was his last journey to the coast they would have regarded him with greater interest. As it was, having learned his history from the chief through their interpreter, they turned from him with loathing.

As this half-caste's career illustrates the depths to which humanity may fall in the hot-bed of slavery, as well as, to some extent, the state of things existing under Portuguese rule on the east coast of Africa, we give the particulars briefly.

Instead of the whip, this man used the gun, which he facetiously styled his "minister of justice," and, in mere wantonness, he was known to have committed murder again and again, yet no steps were taken by the authorities to restrain, much less to punish him. Men heard of his murders, but they shrugged their shoulders and did nothing. It was only a wild beast of a negro that was killed, they said, and what was that! They seemed to think less of it than if he had shot a hippopotamus. One of his murders was painfully notorious, even to its minutest particulars. Over the female slaves employed in a house and adjacent lands there is usually placed a head-woman, a slave also, chosen for such an office for her blind fidelity to her master. This man had one such woman, one who had ever been faithful to him and his interests, who had never provoked him by disobedience or ill-conduct, and against whom, therefore, he could have no cause of complaint. One day when half drunk he was lying on a couch in his house; his forewoman entered and made herself busy with some domestic work. As her master lay watching her, his savage disposition found vent in a characteristic joke: "Woman," said he, "I think I will shoot you." The woman turned round and said, "Master, I am your slave; you can do what you will with me. You can kill me if you like; I can do nothing. But don't kill me, master, for if you do, who is there to look after your other women? they will all run away from you."

She did not mean to irritate her master, but instantly the man's brutal egotism was aroused. The savage jest became a fearful reality, and he shouted with rage:—

"Say you that! say you that! fetch me my gun. I will see if my women will run away after I have killed you."

Trained to implicit obedience, the poor woman did as she was bid. She brought the gun and handed him powder and ball. At his command she knelt down before him, and the wretch fired at her breast. In his drunken rage he missed his mark—the ball went through her shoulder. She besought him to spare her. Deaf to her entreaties, he ordered her to fetch more powder and ball. Though wounded and in agony, she obeyed him. Again the gun was loaded, again levelled and fired, and the woman fell dead at his feet. [The above narrative is quoted almost *verbatim* from *The Story of the Universities' Mission to Central Africa*, pages 78 and 79, the author of which vouches for its accuracy.]

The facts of this case were known far and wide. The Portuguese Governor was acquainted with them, as well as the ministers of justice, but no one put forth a hand to punish the monster, or to protect his slaves.

But vengeance overtook him at last. On his way down the Zambesi he shot one of his men. The others, roused to irresistible fury, sprang upon him and strangled him.

Then, indeed, the Governor and Magistrates were roused to administer "justice!" They had allowed this fiend to murder slaves at his will, but no sooner had the slaves turned on and killed their master than ceaseless energy and resolution were displayed in punishing those who slew him. Soldiers were sent out in all directions; some of the canoe-men were shot down like wild beasts, the rest were recaptured and publicly whipped to death!

Reader, this is "domestic slavery." This is what Portugal and Zanzibar claim the right to practise. This is what Great Britain has for many years declined to interfere with. This is the curse with which Africa is blighted at the present day in some of her fairest lands, and this is what Portugal has decreed shall not terminate in what she calls her African dominions for some years to come. In other words, it has been coolly decreed by that weakest of all the European nations, that slavery, murder, injustice, and every other conceivable and unmentionable vice and villainy shall still, for some considerable time, continue to be practised on the men, women, and children of Africa!

Higher up the Shire river, the travellers saw symptoms of recent distress among the people, which caused them much concern. Chimbolo, in particular, was rendered very anxious by the account given of the famine which prevailed still farther up the river, and the numerous deaths that had taken place in consequence.

The cause of the distress was a common one, and easily explained. Slave-dealers had induced the Ajawa, a warlike tribe, to declare war against the people of the Manganja highlands. The Ajawa had done this before, and were but too ready to do it again. They invaded the land, captured many of the young people, and slew the aged. Those who escaped to the jungle found on their return that their crops were destroyed. Little seed remained in their possession, and before that was planted and grown, famine began to reduce the ranks, already thinned by war.

Indications of this sad state of things became more numerous as the travellers advanced. Few natives appeared to greet them on the banks of the river as they went along, and these few resembled living skeletons. In many places they found dead bodies lying on the ground in various stages of decomposition, and everywhere they beheld an aspect of settled unutterable despair on the faces of the scattered remnant of the bereaved and starving people.

It was impossible, in the circumstances, for Harold Seadrift to give these wretched people more than very slight relief. He gave them as much of his stock of provisions as he could spare, and was glad when the necessity of continuing the journey on foot relieved him from such mournful scenes by taking him away from the river's bank.

Hiring a party of the strongest men that he could find among them, he at length left his canoes, made up his goods, food, and camp-equipage into bundles of a shape and size suitable to being carried on the heads of men, and started on foot for the Manganja highlands.

"Seems to me, sir," observed Disco, as they plodded along together on the first morning of the land journey—"seems to me, sir, that Chimbolo don't stand much chance of findin' his wife alive."

"Poor fellow," replied Harold, glancing back at the object of their remarks, "I fear not."

Chimbolo had by that time recovered much of his natural vigour, and although not yet able to carry a man's load, was nevertheless quite capable of following the party. He walked in silence, with his eyes on the ground, a few paces behind Antonio, who was a step or two in rear of his leader, and who, in virtue of his position as "bo's'n" to the party, was privileged to walk hampered by no greater burden than his gun.

"We must keep up his sperrits, tho', poor chap," said Disco, in the hoarse whisper with which he was wont to convey secret remarks, and which was much more fitted to attract attention than his ordinary voice. "It 'ud never do to let his sperrits down; 'cause w'y? he's weak, an' if he know'd that his wife was dead, or took off as a slave, he'd never be able to go along with us, and we couldn't leave him to starve here, you know."

"Certainly not, Disco," returned Harold. "Besides, his wife *may* be alive, for all we know to the contrary.—How far did he say the village was from where we landed, Antonio?"

"'Bout two, t'ree days," answered the bo's'n.

That night the party encamped beside the ruins of a small hamlet where charred sticks and fragments of an African household's goods and chattels lay scattered on the ground.

Chimbolo sat down here on the ground, and, resting his chin on his knees, gazed in silence at the ruin around him.

"Come, cheer up, old fellow," cried Disco, with rather an awkward effort at heartiness, as he slapped the negro gently on the shoulder; "tell him, Antonio, not to let his heart go down. Didn't he say that what-dee-call-the-place—his village—was a strong place, and could be easily held by a few brave men?"

"True," replied Chimbolo, through the interpreter, "but the Manganja men are not very brave."

"Well, well, never mind," rejoined the sympathetic tar, repeating his pat on the back, "there's no sayin'. P'raps they got courage w'en it came to the scratch. P'raps it never came to the scratch at all up there. Mayhap you'll find 'em all right after all. Come, never say die s'long as there's a shot in the locker. That's a good motto for 'ee, Chimbolo, and ought to keep up your heart even tho' ye *are* a nigger, 'cause it wos inwented by the great Nelson, and shouted by him, or his bo's'n, just before he got knocked over at the glorious battle of Trafalgar. Tell him that, Antonio."

Whether Antonio told him all that, is extremely doubtful, although he complied at once with the order, for Antonio never by any chance declined at least to attempt the duties of his station, but the only effect of his speech was that Chimbolo shook his head and continued to stare at the ruins.

Next morning they started early, and towards evening drew near to Zomba.

The country through which, during the previous two days, they had travelled, was very beautiful, and as wild as even Disco could desire—and, by the way, it was no small degree of wildness that could slake the thirst for the marvellous which had been awakened in the breast of our tar, by his recent experiences in Africa. It was, he said—and said truly—a real out-and-out wilderness. There were villages everywhere, no doubt but these were so thickly concealed by trees and jungle that they were not easily seen, and most of them were at that time almost depopulated. The grass was higher than the heads of the travellers, and the vegetation everywhere was rankly luxuriant. Here and there open glades allowed the eye to penetrate into otherwise impenetrable bush. Elsewhere, large trees abounded in the midst of overwhelmingly affectionate parasites, whose gnarled lower limbs and twining tendrils and pendant foliage gave a softness to the landscape, which contrasted well with the wild passes and rugged rocks of the middle distance, and the towering mountains which rose, range beyond range, in the far distance.

But as the party approached the neighbourhood of Zomba mountains, few of them were disposed to give much heed to the beauties of nature. All being interested in Chimbolo, they became more or less anxious as to news that awaited him.

On turning a spur of one of the mountains which had hitherto barred their vision, they found themselves suddenly face to face with a small band of Manganja men, whose woe-begone countenances told too eloquently that the hand of the destroyer had been heavy upon them.

Of course they were questioned by Chimbolo, and the replies they gave him were such as to confirm the fears he had previously entertained.

The Ajawa, they said, had, just the day before, burnt their villages, stolen or destroyed their property, killed many of their kinsmen, and carried off their wives and children for slaves. They themselves had escaped, and were now on their way to visit their chief, who was at that time on the banks of the Zambesi, to beg of him to return, in order that he might bewitch the guns of the Ajawa, and so render them harmless!

"Has a woman of your tribe, named Marunga, been slain or captured?" asked Chimbolo eagerly.

To this the men replied that they could not tell. Marunga, they said, was known well to them by name and sight. They did not think she was among the captives, but could not tell what had become of her, as the village where she and her little boy lived had been burnt, and all who had not been killed or captured had taken to the bush. Marunga's husband, they added, was a man named Chimbolo—not a Manganja man, but a friend of the tribe—who had been taken by the slavers, under command of a Portuguese half-caste named Marizano, about two years before that time.

Chimbolo winced as though he had been stung when Marizano's name was mentioned, and a dark frown contracted his brows when he told the Manganja men that *he* was Chimbolo, and that he was even then in search of Marunga and her little boy.

When all this had been explained to Harold Seadrift he told the men that it was a pity to waste time in travelling such a long way to see their chief, who could not, even if he wished, bewitch the guns of the Ajawa, and advised them to turn back and guide him and his men to the place where the attack had been made on the Manganja, so that a search might be made in the bush for those of the people who had escaped.

This was agreed to, and the whole party proceeded on their way with increased speed, Chimbolo and Harold hoping they might yet find that Marunga had escaped, and Disco earnestly desiring that they might only fall in with the Ajawa and have a brush with them, in which case he assured the negroes he would show them a way of bewitching their guns that would beat their chief's bewitchment all to sticks and stivers!

The village in which Marunga had dwelt was soon reached. It was, as they had been told by their new friends, a heap of still smouldering ashes; but it was not altogether destitute of signs of life. A dog was observed to slink away into the bush as they approached.

The moment Chimbolo observed it he darted into the bush after it.

"Hallo!" exclaimed Disco in surprise; "that nigger seems to have took a sudden fancy to the cur?—Eh, Antonio, wot's the reason of that, think 'ee?"

"Dunno; s'pose where dog be mans be?"

"Ah! or womans," suggested Disco.

"Or womans," assented Antonio.

Just then they heard Chimbolo's shout, which was instantly followed by a succession of female shrieks. These latter were repeated several times, and sounded as though the fugitives were scattering.

"Hims find a nest of womins!" exclaimed Jumbo, throwing down his load and dashing away into the bush.

Every individual of the party followed his example, not excepting Harold and Disco, the latter of whom was caught by the leg, the moment he left the track, by a wait-a-bit thorn—most appropriately so-called, because its powerful spikes are always ready to seize and detain the unwary passer-by. In the present instance it checked the seaman's career for a few seconds, and rent his nether garments sadly; while Harold, profiting by his friend's misfortune, leaped over the bush, and passed on. Disco quickly extricated himself, and followed.

They were not left far behind, and overtook their comrades just as they emerged on an open space, or glade, at the extremity of which a sight met their eyes that filled them with astonishment, for there a troop of women and one or two boys were seen walking towards them, with Chimbolo in front, having a child on his left shoulder, and performing a sort of insane war-dance round one of the women.

"He's catched her!" exclaimed Disco, with excited looks, just as if Chimbolo had been angling unsuccessfully for a considerable time, and had hooked a stupendous fish at last.

And Disco was right. A few of the poor creatures who were so recently burnt out of their homes, and had lost most of those dearest to them, had ventured, as if drawn by an irresistible spell, to return with timid steps to the scene of their former happiness, but only to have their worst fears confirmed. Their homes, their protectors, their children, their hopes, all were gone at one fell swoop. Only one among them—one who, having managed to save her only child, had none to mourn over, and no one to hope to meet with—only one returned to a joyful meeting. We need scarcely say that this was Marunga.

The fact was instantly made plain to the travellers by the wild manner in which Chimbolo shouted her name, pointed to her, and danced round her, while he showed all his glistening teeth and as much of the whites of his eyes as was consistent with these members remaining in their orbits.

Really it was quite touching, in spite of its being ludicrous, the way in which the poor fellow poured forth his joy like a very child,—which he was in everything except years; and Harold could not help remembering, and recalling to Disco's memory, Yoosoof's observations touching the hardness of negroes' hearts, and their want of natural affection, on the morning when his dhow was captured by the boat of the "Firefly."

The way in which, ever and anon, Chimbolo kissed his poor but now happy wife, was wondrously similar to the mode in which white men perform that little operation, except that there was more of an unrefined smack in it. The tears which *would* hop over his sable cheeks now and then sparkled to the full as brightly as European tears, and were perhaps somewhat bigger; and the pride with which he regarded his little son, holding him in both hands out at arms'-length, was only excelled by the joy and the tremendous laugh with which he received a kick on the nose from that undutiful son's black little toes.

But Yoosoof never chanced to be present when such exhibitions of negro feeling and susceptibility took place. How could he, seeing that men and women and children—if black—fled from him, and such as he, in abject terror? Neither did Yoosoof ever chance to be present when women sat down beside their blackened hearths, as they did that night, and quietly wept as though their hearts would burst at the memory of little voices and manly tones—not silent in death, but worse than that—gone, gone *for ever*! Doubtless they felt though they never heard of, and could not in words express, the sentiment—

"Oh for the touch of a vanished hand,
And the sound of a voice that is still."

Yoosoof knew not of, and cared nothing for, such feelings as these. We ask again, how could he? His only experience of the negro was when cowering before him as a slave, or when yelling in agony under his terrible lash, or when brutalised and rendered utterly apathetic by inhuman cruelty.

Harold learned, that night on further conversation with the Manganja men, that a raid had recently been made into those regions by more than one band of slavers, sent out to capture men and women by the Portuguese half-castes of the towns of Senna and Tette, on the Zambesi, and that they had been carrying the inhabitants out of the country at the rate of about two hundred a week.

This however was but a small speck, so to speak, of the mighty work of kidnapping human beings that was going on—that is *still* going on in those regions. Yoosoof would have smiled—he never laughed—if you had mentioned such a number as being large.

But in truth he cared nothing about such facts, except in so far as they represented a large amount of profit accrueing to himself.

The result of Harold Seadrift's cogitations on these matters was that he resolved to pass through as much of the land as he could within a reasonable time, and agreed to accompany Chimbolo on a visit to his tribe, which dwelt at some distance to the north of the Manganja highlands.

CHAPTER NINE

IN WHICH A SAVAGE CHIEF
ASTONISHES A SAVAGE ANIMAL

There is something exceedingly pleasant in the act of watching—ourselves unseen—the proceedings of some one whose aims and ends appear to be very mysterious. There is such a wide field of speculation opened up in which to expatiate, such a vast amount of curious, we had almost said romantic, expectation created; all the more if the individual whom we observe be a savage, clothed in an unfamiliar and very scanty garb, and surrounded by scenery and circumstances which, albeit strange to us, are evidently by no means new to him.

Let us—you and me, reader,—quitting for a time the sad subject of slavery, and leaping, as we are privileged to do, far ahead of our explorers Harold Seadrift and his company, into the region of Central Africa; let you and me take up a position in a clump of trees by the banks of yonder stream, and watch the proceedings of that negro—negro chief let me say, for he looks like one,—who is engaged in some mysterious enterprise under the shade of a huge baobab tree.

The chief is a fine, stately, well-developed specimen of African manhood. He is clothed in black tights manufactured in nature's loom, in addition to which he wears round his loins a small scrap of artificial cotton cloth. If an enthusiastic member of the Royal Academy were in search of a model which should combine the strength of Hercules with the grace of Apollo, he could not find a better than the man before us, for, you will observe, the more objectionable points about *our* ideal of the negro are not very prominent in him. His lips are not thicker than the lips of many a roast-beef-loving John Bull. His nose is not flat, and his heels do not protrude unnecessarily. True, his hair is woolly, but that is scarcely a blemish. It might almost be regarded as the crisp and curly hair that surrounds a manly skull. His skin is black—no doubt about that, but then it is *intensely* black and glossy, suggestive of black satin, and having no savour of that dirtiness which is inseparably connected with whitey-brown. Tribes in Africa differ materially in many respects, physically and mentally, just as do the various tribes of Europe.

This chief, as we have hinted, is a "savage;" that is to say, he differs in many habits and points from "civilised" people. Among other peculiarities, he clothes himself and his family in the fashion that is best suited to the warm climate in which he dwells. This display of wisdom is, as you know, some-what rare among civilised people, as any one may perceive who observes how these over-clothe the upper parts of their children, and leave their tender little lower limbs exposed to the rigours of northern latitudes, while, as if to make up for this inconsistency by an inconsistent counterpoise, they swathe their own tough and mature limbs in thick flannel from head to foot.

It is however simple justice to civilised people to add here that a few of them, such as a portion of the Scottish Highlanders, are consistent inasmuch as the men clothe themselves similarly to the children.

R. M. Ballantyne

Moreover, our chief, being a savage, takes daily a sufficient amount of fresh air and exercise, which nine-tenths of civilised men refrain from doing, on the economic and wise principle, apparently, that engrossing and unnatural devotion to the acquisition of wealth, fame, or knowledge, will enable them at last to spend a few paralytic years in the enjoyment of their gains. No doubt civilised people have the trifling little drawback of innumerable ills, to which they say (erroneously, we think) that flesh is heir, and for the cure of which much of their wealth is spent in supporting an army of doctors. Savages know nothing of indigestion, and in Central Africa they have no medical men.

There is yet another difference which we may point out: savages have no literature. They cannot read or write therefore, and have no permanent records of the deeds of their forefathers. Neither have they any religion worthy of the name. This is indeed a serious evil, one which civilised people of course deplore, yet, strange to say, one which consistency prevents some civilised people from remedying in the case of African savages, for it would be absurdly inconsistent in Arab Mohammedans to teach the negroes letters and the doctrines of their faith with one hand, while with the other they lashed them to death or dragged them into perpetual slavery; and it would be equally inconsistent in Portuguese Christians to teach the negroes to read "Whatsoever ye would that men should do unto you, do ye even so to them," while "domestic slavery" is, in their so-called African territories, claimed as a right and the traffic connected with it sanctioned.

Yes, there are many points of difference between civilised people and savages, and we think it right to point this out very clearly, good reader, because the man at whom you and I are looking just now is a savage.

Of course, being capable of reading this book, you are too old to require to be told that there is nothing of our *nursery* savage about him. That peculiar abortion was born and bred in the nursery, and dwells only there, and was never heard of beyond civilised lands—although something not unlike him, alas! may be seen here and there among the lanes and purlieus where our drunkards and profligates resort. No; our savage chief does not roar, or glare, or chatter, or devour his food in its blood like the giant of the famous Jack. He carries himself like a man, and a remarkably handsome man too, with his body firm and upright, and his head bent a little forward, with his eyes fixed on the ground, as if in meditation, while he walks along.

But a truce to digressive explanation. Let us follow him.

Reaching the banks of the river, he stops, and, standing in an attitude worthy of Apollo, though he is not aware that we are looking at him, gazes first up the stream and then down. This done, he looks across, after which he tries to penetrate the depths of the water with his eye.

As no visible result follows, he wisely gives up staring and wishing, and apparently resolves to attain his ends by action. Felling a small tree, about as thick as his thigh, with an iron hatchet he cuts off it a length of about six feet. Into one end of this he drives a sharp-pointed hard-wood spike, several inches long, and to the other end attaches a stout rope made of the fibrous husk of the cocoa-nut. The point of the spike he appears to anoint—probably a charm of some kind,—and then suspends the curious instrument over a forked stick at a considerable height from the ground, to which he fastens the other end of the rope. This done, he walks quietly away with an air of as much self-satisfaction as if he had just performed a generous deed.

Well, is that all? Nay, if that were all we should owe you a humble apology. Our chief, "savage" though he be, is not insane. He *has* an object in view—which is more than can be said of everybody.

He has not been long gone, an hour or two, when the smooth surface of the river is broken in several places, and out burst two or three heads of hippopotami. Although, according to Disco Lillihammer, the personification of ugliness, these creatures do not the less enjoy their existence. They roll about in the stream like puncheons, dive under one another playfully, sending huge waves to the banks on either side. They gape hideously with their tremendous jaws, which look as though they had been split much too far back in the head by a rude hatchet—the tops of all the teeth having apparently been lopped off by the same clumsy blow. They laugh too, with a demoniacal "Ha! ha! ha!" as if they rejoiced in their excessive plainness, and knew that we—you and I, reader— are regarding them with disgust, not unmingled with awe.

Presently one of the herd betakes himself to the land. He is tired of play, and means to feed. Grass appears to be his only food, and to procure this he must needs go back from the river a short way, his enormous lips, like an animated mowing-machine, cutting a track of short cropped grass as he waddles along.

The form of that part of the bank is such that he is at least inclined, if not constrained, to pass directly under the suspended beam. Ha! we understand the matter now. Most people do understand, when a thing becomes obviously plain. The hippopotamus wants grass for supper; the "savage" chief wants hippopotamus. Both set about arranging their plans for their respective ends. The hippopotamus passes close to the forked stick, and touches the cord which sustains it in air like the sword of Damocles. Down comes the beam, driving the spike deep into his back. A cry follows, something between a grunt, a squeak, and a yell, and the wounded animal falls, rolls over, jumps up, with unexpected agility for such a sluggish, unwieldy creature, and rumbles, rushes, rolls, and stumbles back into the river, where his relatives take to flight in mortal terror. The unfortunate beast might perhaps recover from the wound, were it not that the spike has been tipped with poison. The result is that he dies in about an hour. Not long afterwards the chief returns with a band of his followers, who, being experts in the use of the knife and hatchet, soon make mincemeat of their game—laden with which they return in triumph to their homes.

Let us follow them thither.

CHAPTER TEN

DESCRIBES AFRICAN DOMESTICITY, AND MANY OTHER THINGS RELATIVE THERETO, BESIDES SHOWING THAT ALARMS AND FLIGHTS, SURPRISES AND FEASTS, ARE NOT CONFINED TO PARTICULAR PLACES

When our negro chief—whose name, by the way, was Kambira—left the banks of the river, followed by his men bearing the hippopotamus-flesh, he set off at a swinging pace, like to a man who has a considerable walk before him.

The country through which they passed was not only well wooded, but well watered by numerous rivulets. Their path for some distance tended upwards towards the hills, now crossing over mounds, anon skirting the base of precipitous rocks, and elsewhere dipping down into hollows; but although thus serpentine in its course, its upward tendency never varied until it led them to the highest parts of a ridge from which a magnificent prospect was had of hill and dale, lake, rivulet and river, extending so far that the distant scenery at the horizon appeared of a thin pearly-grey colour, and of the same consistency as the clouds with which it mingled.

Passing over this ridge, and descending into a wide valley which was fertilised and beautified by a moderately-sized rivulet, Kambira led his followers towards a hamlet which lay close to the stream, nestled in a woody hollow, and, like all other Manganja villages, was surrounded by an impenetrable hedge of poisonous euphorbia—a tree which casts a deep shade, and renders it difficult for bowmen to aim at the people inside.

In the immediate vicinity of the village the land was laid out in little gardens and fields, and in these the people—men, women, and children,—were busily engaged in hoeing the ground, weeding, planting, or gathering the fruits of their labour.

These same fruits were plentiful, and the people sang with joy as they worked. There were large crops of maize, millet beans, and ground-nuts; also patches of yams, rice, pumpkins, cucumbers, cassava, sweet potatoes, tobacco, cotton, and hemp, which last is also called "bang," and is smoked by the natives as a species of tobacco.

It was a pleasant sight for Kambira and his men to look upon, as they rested for a few minutes on the brow of a knoll near a thicket of bramble bushes, and gazed down upon their home. Doubtless they thought so, for their eyes glistened, so also did their teeth when they smilingly commented on the scene before them. They did not, indeed, become enthusiastic about scenery, nor did they refer to the picturesque grouping of huts and trees, or make any allusion whatever to light and shade; no, their thoughts were centred on far higher objects than these. They talked of wives and children, and hippopotamus-flesh; and their countenances glowed— although they were not white—and their strong hearts beat hard against their ribs—although they were not clothed, and their souls (for we repudiate Yoosoof's opinion that they had none), their souls appeared to take quiet but powerful interest in their belongings.

R. M. Ballantyne

It was pleasant also, for Kambira and his men to listen to the sounds that floated up from the valley,—sweeter far than the sweetest strains of Mozart or Mendelssohn,—the singing of the workers in the fields and gardens, mellowed by distance into a soft humming tone; and the hearty laughter that burst occasionally from men seated at work on bows, arrows, fishing-nets, and such-like gear, on a flat green spot under the shade of a huge banyan-tree, which, besides being the village workshop, was the village reception-hall, where strangers were entertained on arriving,—also the village green, where the people assembled to dance, and sing, and smoke "bang," to which last they were much addicted, and to drink beer made by themselves, of which they were remarkably fond, and by means of which they sometimes got drunk;—in all which matters the intelligent reader will not fail to observe that they bore a marked resemblance to many of the civilised European nations, except, perhaps, in their greater freedom of action, lightness of costume, and colour of skin.

The merry voices of children, too, were heard, and their active little black bodies were seen, while they engaged in the play of savages—though not necessarily in savage play. Some romped, ran after each other, caught each other, tickled each other, occasionally whacked each other—just as our own little ones do. Others played at games, of which the skipping-rope was a decided favourite among the girls, but the play of most of the older children consisted in imitating the serious work of their parents. The girls built little huts, hoed little gardens, made small pots of clay, pounded imaginary corn in miniature mortars, cooked it over ideal fires, and crammed it down the throats of imitation babies; while the boys performed deeds of chivalric daring with reed spears, small shields, and tiny bows and arrows, or amused themselves in making cattle-pens, and in sculpturing cows and crocodiles. Human nature, in short, was powerfully developed, without anything particular to suggest the idea of "savage" life, or to justify the opinion of Arabs and half-caste Portuguese that black men are all "cattle."

The scene wanted only the spire of a village church and the tinkle of a Sabbath bell to make it perfect.

But there *was* a tinkle among the other sounds, not unlike a bell which would have sounded marvellously familiar to English ears had they been listening. This was the ringing of the anvil of the village blacksmith. Yes, savage though they were, these natives had a blacksmith who wrought in iron, almost as deftly, and to the full as vigorously, as any British son of Vulcan. The Manganja people are an industrious race. Besides cultivating the soil extensively, they dig iron-ore out of the hills, and each village has its smelting-house, its charcoal-burners, its forge with a pair of goatskin bellows, and its blacksmith—we might appropriately say, its *very* blacksmith! Whether the latter would of necessity, and as a matter of course, sing bass in church if the land were civilised enough to possess a church, remains to be seen! At the time we write of he merely hummed to the sound of the hammer, and forged hoes, axes, spears, needles, arrow-heads, bracelets, armlets, necklets, and anklets, with surprising dexterity.

Pity that he could not forge a chain which would for ever restrain the murderous hands of the Arabs and half-caste Portuguese, who, for ages, have blighted his land with their pestilential presence!

After contemplating the picture for a time, Kambira descended the winding path that led to the village. He had not proceeded far when one of the smallest of the children—a creature so rotund that his body and limbs were a series of circles and ovals, and so black that it seemed an absurdity

R. M. Ballantyne

even to think of casting a shadow on him—espied the advancing party, uttered a shrill cry of delight, and ran towards them.

His example was followed by a dozen others, who, being larger, outran him, and, performing a war-dance round the men, possessed themselves, by amicable theft, of pieces of raw meat with which they hastened back to the village. The original discoverer of the party, however, had other ends in view. He toddled straight up to Kambira with the outstretched arms of a child who knows he will be welcomed.

Kambira was not demonstrative, but he was hearty. Taking the little ball of black butter by the arms, he whirled him over his head, and placed him on his broad shoulders, with a fat leg on each side of his neck, and left him there to look after himself. This the youngster did by locking his feet together under the man's chin, and fastening his fat fingers in his woolly hair, in which position he bore some resemblance to an enormous chignon.

Thus was he borne crowing to the chief's hut, from the door of which a very stout elderly woman came out to receive them.

There was no one else in the hut to welcome them, but Yohama, as the chief styled her, was sufficient; she was what some people call "good company." She bustled about making preparations for a feast, with a degree of activity that was quite surprising in one so fat—so very fat—asking questions the while with much volubility, making remarks to the child, criticising the hippopotamus-meat, or commenting on things in general.

Meanwhile Kambira seated himself in a corner and prepared to refresh himself with a pipe of bang in the most natural and civilised fashion imaginable; and young Obo—for so Yohama called him—entered upon a series of gymnastic exercises with his father—for such Kambira was—which partook of the playfulness of the kitten, mingled with the eccentricity and mischief of the monkey.

It would have done you good, reader, if you possess a spark of sympathy, to have watched these two as they played together. The way in which Obo assaulted his father, on whose visage mild benignity was enthroned, would have surprised you. Kambira was a remarkably grave, quiet and reserved man, but that was a matter of no moment to Obo, who threatened him in front, skirmished in his rear, charged him on the right flank with a reed spear, shelled him on the left with sweet potatoes, and otherwise harassed him with amazing perseverance and ingenuity.

To this the enemy paid no further attention than lay in thrusting out an elbow and raising a knee, to check an unusually fierce attack, or in giving Obo a pat on the back when he came within reach, or sending a puff of smoke in his face, as if to taunt and encourage him to attempt further deeds of daring.

While this was going on in the chief's hut, active culinary preparations were progressing all over the village—the women forsook their hoes and grinding-mortars, and the looms on which they had been weaving cotton cloth, the men laid down various implements of industry, and, long ere the sun began to descend in the west, the entire tribe was feasting with all the gusto, and twenty times the appetite, of aldermen.

During the progress of the feast a remarkably small, wiry old negro, entertained the chief and his party with a song, accompanying himself the while on a violin—not a

R. M. Ballantyne

European fiddle, by any means, but a native production—with something like a small keg, covered with goatskin, for a body, a longish handle, and one string which was played with a bow by the "Spider." Never having heard his name, we give him one in accordance with his aspect.

Talk of European fiddlers! No Paganini, or any other *nini* that ever astonished the Goths and Vandals of the north, could hold a candle—we had almost said a fiddle—to this sable descendant of Ham, who, squatted on his hams in the midst of an admiring circle, drew forth sounds from his solitary string that were more than exquisite,—they were excruciating.

The song appeared to be improvised, for it referred to objects around, as well as to things past, present, and to come; among others, to the fact that slave parties attacked villages and carried off the inhabitants.

At such points the minstrel's voice became low and thrilling, while his audience grew suddenly earnest, opened their eyes, frowned, and showed their teeth; but as soon as the subject was changed the feeling seemed to die away. It was only old memories that had been awakened, for no slavers had passed through their country for some time past, though rumours of an attack on a not very distant tribe had recently reached and greatly alarmed them.

Thus they passed the afternoon, and when the cool of the evening drew on a dance was proposed, seconded, and carried unanimously.

They were about to begin when a man was seen running down the path leading to the village at a speed which proved him to be the bearer of tidings. In a few minutes he burst into the midst of them with glaring eyeballs and labouring chest—for he had run fast, though not far, and told his news in rapid short sentences—to the effect that a band of slavers, led by Portuguese, were on their way to the valley, within a mile or so of it, even while he spoke; that he thought the leader was Marizano; and that they were *armed with the loud-sounding guns*!

The consternation consequent on this news was universal, and there was good ground for it, because Marizano was a well-known monster of cruelty, and his guns had rendered him invincible hitherto, wherever he went, the native spear and bow being utterly useless in the hands of men who, however courageous, were shot down before they could come within arrow-range of their enemies.

It is the custom of the slave-dealers, on going into the interior for the purpose of procuring slaves, to offer to buy them from such tribes as are disposed to sell. This most of the tribes are willing to do. Fathers do not indeed, sell their own children, or husbands their wives, from preference, but chiefs and head-men are by no means loath to get rid of their criminals in this way—their bad stock, as it were, of black ivory. They also sell orphans and other defenceless ones of their tribes, the usual rate of charge being about two or three yards of calico for a man, woman, or child.

But the Arab slave-dealer sometimes finds it difficult to procure enough of "cattle" in this way to make up a band sufficiently large to start with for the coast because he is certain to lose four out of every five, at the *lowest estimate*, on his journey down. The drove, therefore, must be large. In order to provide it he sends out parties to buy where they can, and to steal when they have the chance. Meanwhile he takes up his quarters near some tribe, and sets about deliberately to produce war. He rubs up old sores, foments existing quarrels, lends guns and ammunition, suggests

R. M. Ballantyne

causes of dispute, and finally gets two tribes to fight. Of course many are slaughtered, fearful barbarities and excesses are committed, fields are laid waste and villages are burnt, but this is a matter of no consequence to our Arab. Prisoners are sure to be taken, and he buys the prisoners; for the rest,—there are plenty of natives in Africa!

When all else fails, not being very particular, he sends off a party under some thorough-going scoundrel, well-armed, and with instructions to attack and capture wherever they go.

No wonder, then, that the rumoured approach of Marizano and his men caused the utmost alarm in Kambira's village, and that the women and children were ordered to fly to the bush without delay. This they required no second bidding to do, but, oh! it was a sad sight to see them do it. The younger women ran actively, carrying the infants and leading the smaller children by the hands, and soon disappeared; but it was otherwise with the old people. These, men and women, bowed with age, and tottering as much from terror as decrepitude, hobbled along, panting as they went, and stumbling over every trifling obstruction in their path, being sometimes obliged to stop and rest, though death might be the consequence; and among these there were a few stray little creatures barely able to toddle, who had probably been forgotten or forsaken by their mothers in the panic, yet were of sufficient age to be aware, in their own feeble way, that danger of some sort was behind them, and that safety lay before. By degrees all—young and old, strong and feeble—gained the shelter of the bush, and Kambira was left with a handful of resolute warriors to check the invaders and defend his home.

Well was it at that time for Kambira and his men that the approaching band was *not* Marizano and his robbers.

When the head of the supposed enemy's column appeared on the brow of the adjacent hill, the Manganja chief fitted an arrow to his bow, and, retiring behind a hut, as also did his followers, resolved that Marizano should forfeit his life even though his own should be the penalty. Very bitter were his thoughts, for his tribe had suffered from that villain at a former period, and he longed to rid the land of him.

As he thought thus he looked at his followers with an expression of doubt for he knew too well that the Manganja were not a warlike tribe, and feared that the few who remained with him might forsake him in the hour of need. Indeed, much of his own well-known courage was to be attributed to the fact, that his mother had belonged to a family more or less nearly connected with the Ajawa, who are very warlike—too much so, in truth, for it is they who, to a large extent are made use of by the slave-dealers to carry on war with the neighbouring tribes. Kambira's men, however, looked resolute, though very grave.

While he was thus meditating vengeance, he observed that one of the approaching band advanced alone without arms, and making signs of peace. This surprised him a little, but dreading treachery, he kept under the shelter of a hut until the stranger was close to the village; then, observing that the party on the hill had laid down their arms and seated themselves on the grass, he advanced, still, however, retaining his weapons.

The stranger was a little man, and appeared timid, but seeing that the chief evidently meant no mischief, and knowing that the guns of his friends had him within range, he drew near.

"Where come you from?" demanded Kambira.

To this Antonio—for it was he—replied that his party came

R. M. Ballantyne

from the coast; that they wanted to pass through the land to see it, and to find out what it produced and what its people had to sell; that it was led by two Englishmen, who belonged to a nation that detested slavery—the same nation that sent out Dr Livingstone, who, as everybody knew, had passed through that land some years before. They were also, he said, countrymen of the men of God who had come out to teach the Manganja the Truth, who had helped them in their troubles, delivered them from the slave-traders, and some of whom had died in their land. He added that there were Manganja men and women in their company.

The "men of God" to whom Antonio referred, and to whom he had been expressly told by Harold Seadrift to refer, were those devoted missionaries mentioned in a previous chapter, who, under the leadership of the amiable and true-hearted Bishop Mackenzie, established a mission among these very Manganja hills in the year 1861. By a rare combination of Christian love and manly courage under very peculiar circumstances, they acquired extraordinary power and influence over the natives in the space of a few months, and laid the foundation of what might have been—perhaps may yet be—true Christianity in Central Africa. But the country was unhappily involved at the time in one of the wars created by the Portuguese and Arab slave-traders. The region was almost depopulated by man-stealers, and by the famine that resulted from the culture of the land having been neglected during the panic. The good bishop and several of his devoted band sank under the combined effects of climate and anxiety, and died there, while the enfeebled remnant were compelled, sorrowfully, to quit the field, to the deep regret of the surviving Manganja. [*The Story of the Universities' Mission to Central Africa*, by the Reverend Henry Rowley.—We can heartily recommend this to the young—ay, and to the old— as being, next to the Adventures of Williams in the South Seas, one of the most interesting records of missionary enterprise that we ever read.]

When, therefore, Antonio mentioned Bishop Mackenzie and Dr Livingstone, a gleam of intelligent interest lit up Kambira's swarthy countenance, and he was about to speak, but suddenly checked himself, and a stern frown chased the gleam away.

"The Manganja," he said, after a few moments' silence, during which poor Antonio eyed him with some distrust, "know well that these men of God were not of the same country as the Arab and the Portuguese; that they hated slavery and loved the Manganja, and that the graves of some of them are with us now; but we know also that some white men are great liars. How am I to make sure that your leaders are English? Why did you not bring down the Manganja men and women you say are with you?"

"The women were footsore, and fell behind with their men," answered Antonio, "and we thought it best not to wait for them."

"Go," rejoined Kambira, waving his hand; "if you be true men let the Englishmen come to me, and also the Manganja, *without guns*, then I will believe you.—Go."

The peremptory manner in which this was said left no room for reply. Antonio therefore returned to his friends, and the chief to his cover.

On consultation and consideration it was agreed that Kambira's advice should be acted on, "For," said Disco, removing the pipe with which he had been solacing himself during Antonio's absence, "we can plant our fellers on the knoll here with a blunderbuss each, and arrange a signal so that, if there should be anything like foul play, we'd have nothin' to do but hold aloft a kercher or suthin o' that sort, an' they'd pour a broadside into 'em afore they could wink—d'ee see?"

"Not quite clearly," replied Harold, smiling, "because some of our fellows can't take an aim at all, much less a good one, so they'd be as likely to shoot us as them."

Disco pondered this a little, and shook his head, then shook the ashes out of his pipe, and said that on the whole he was willing to risk it—that they "could not expect to travel through Afriky without risking summat."

As Chimbolo with his wife and the rest of the party came up at that moment the case was put before him. He at once advised compliance with Kambira's request saying that the presence of himself and his friends would be quite sufficient to put the chief's mind at rest.

In a few minutes the plan was carried out and Kambira satisfied of the good faith of his visitors. Nevertheless he did not at once throw open his arms to them. He stood upon his dignity; asked them a good many questions, and answered a good many more, addressing himself always to Antonio as the spokesman, it being a point of etiquette not to address the principal of the party. Then, presents were exchanged, in the management of which a considerable time was spent. One of the warriors having in the meantime been despatched to recall the fugitives, these began to pour out of the woods, the frail old people and forsaken toddlers being the last to return, as they had been the last to fly.

After this, fires were kindled, fowls were chased, caught, slain, plucked, roasted, and boiled; hippopotamus-flesh was produced, the strangers were invited to make themselves at home, which they very soon did. Beer and bang were introduced; the celebrated fiddler was reinstated, the dance, which had been so long delayed, was at last fairly begun, and, as if to make the picture perfect and felicity complete, the moon came out from behind a thick cloud, and clothed the valley with a flood of silver light.

R. M. Ballantyne

CHAPTER ELEVEN

REVEALS DISCO'S OPINIONS ABOUT SAVAGES, AND THE SAVAGES' OPINIONS OF DISCO, AND OTHER WEIGHTY MATTERS

As two or three of Harold's people were not very well just at that time, he resolved to remain at Kambira's village for a few days to give them rest, and afterwards to push on to the country of his friend Chimbolo.

This arrangement he came to the more readily that he was short of provisions, and Kambira told him that a particular part of the country near the shores of a lake not far distant abounded with game of all sorts.

To Disco Lillihammer he explained his plans next day, while that worthy, seated under the shade of a banyan-tree, was busily engaged with what he styled his "mornin' dooties"— namely, the filling and smoking of his cutty-pipe.

"You see, Disco," he said, "it won't do to knock up the men with continuous travel, therefore I shall give them a spell of rest here. Kambira tells me that there is plenty of game, large and small, to be had not far off, so that we shall be able to replenish our stock of meat and perchance give the niggers a feast such as they have not been accustomed to of late, for it is not too much to expect that our rifles will do more execution, at all events among lions and elephants, than native spears. Besides, I wish to see something of the people, who, being what we may call pure out-and-out savages—"

"Savages!" interrupted Disco, removing his pipe, and pointing with the stem of it to the village on an eminence at the outskirts of which they were seated; "d'ee call them folk savages?"

Harold looked at the scene before him, and paused for a few moments; and well he might, for not fifty yards off the blacksmith was plying his work energetically, while a lad sat literally *between* a pair of native bellows, one of which he blew with his left hand, the other with his right and, beyond these, groups of men and women wrought at their primitive looms or tilled their vegetable gardens and patches of land.

"Savages!" repeated Disco, still pointing to the village with the stem of his pipe, and gazing earnestly at his companion, "humph!"

It is probable that Disco might have said more, but he was an accurate judge of the precise moment when a pipe is about to go out, and delay will prove fatal. He therefore applied himself diligently to suck and cherish the dying spark. Having revived its powers to such an extent that clouds enveloped his visage, and his nose, being red, loomed luridly through them, he removed the pipe, and again said, "Humph! They ain't a bit more savages, sir, than you or me is."

"Perhaps not," replied Harold. "To say truth, it would be difficult to point out any peculiarity that justifies the name, except the fact that they wear very little clothing, and neither go to school nor church."

R. M. Ballantyne

"They wears no clothin'," rejoined Disco, "'cause they don't need for to do so; an' they don't go to church or school, 'cause they hain't got none to go to—that same bein' not the fault o' the niggers, but o' them as knows better."

"There's truth in what you say, Disco," returned Harold, with a smile, "but come, you must admit that there is something savage in the custom they have of wearing these hideous lip-rings."

The custom to which he referred is one which prevails among several of the tribes of Africa, and is indeed so utterly hideous and outrageous that we should be justified in refusing to believe it, were we not assured of the fact by Dr Livingstone and other missionaries and travellers of unquestionable integrity. The ring is worn in the upper lip, not hanging from it but fitted into a hole in it in such a manner as to thrust the lip straight and far out from the face. As the ring is about the size of an ordinary napkin-ring, it may be easily believed, that time is required for the formation of the deformity. At an early age the middle of the upper lip of a girl is pierced close to the nose, and a small pin introduced to prevent the hole closing up. After it is healed the pin is taken out and a larger one forced into its place, and so for weeks, months, and years the process of increasing the size of the lip goes on, until a ring of two inches in diameter can be introduced. Nearly all the women in these parts use this ring, or, as it is called, pelele. Some make them of bamboo, others of ivory or tin. When a wearer of the pelele smiles, the action of the cheek muscles draws the lip tight which has the effect of raising the ring towards the eyebrows, so that the nose is seen in the middle of it, and the teeth are exposed, a revelation which shows that the latter have been chipped to sharp points so as to resemble the teeth of a cat or crocodile.

"No doubt," said Disco, in reply to Harold's remark, "the lip-rings are uncommon ugly, but the principle o' the thing, sir, that's w'ere it is, the principle ain't no wuss than ear-rings. The savages, as we calls 'em, bores holes in their lips an' sticks rings into 'em. The civilised folk, as we calls ourselves, bores holes in their ears an' sticks rings into 'em. W'ere's the difference? that's wot *I* want to know."

"There's not much difference in principle," said Harold, laughing, "but there is a great difference in appearance. Ear-rings hang gracefully; lip-rings stick out horribly."

"H'm! it appears to me that that's a matter o' taste, now. Howsoever, I do admit that lip-rings is wuss than ear-rings; moreover it must make kissin' somewhat difficult, not to say onpleasant, but, as I said before, so I says again, It's all in the principle w'ere it lies. W'y, look here, sir,—savages, as we call 'em, wear brass rings round their necks, our women wear gold and brass chains. The savages wear anklets, we wear bracelets. They have no end o' rings on their toes, we have 'em on our fingers. Some savages shave their heads, some of us shaves our faces. Their women are raither given to clothin' which is too short and too narrer, ours come out in toggery far too wide, and so long sometimes, that a feller daren't come within a fathom of 'em astarn without runnin' the risk o' trampin' on, an' carrying away some o' the canvas. The savage women frizzes out their hair into most fantastical shapes, till the very monkeys has to hold their sides sittin' in the trees larfin' at 'em—and wot do *we* do in regard to that? W'y, some of *our* women puts on a mixture o' hairy pads, an' combs, an' pins, an' ribbons, an' flowers, in a bundle about twice the size o' their heads, all jumbled together in such a way as to defy description; an' if the monkeys was to see *them*, they'd go off into such fits that they'd bu'st altogether an' the race would become extinct in Afriky. No, sir; it's my opinion that there ain't no such thing as savages—or, if you

R. M. Ballantyne

choose to put it the tother way, we're all savages together."

Disco uttered the last part of his speech with intense energy, winding it up with the usual slap on the thigh, delivered with unusual fervour, and then, becoming aware that the vital spark of the cutty had all but fled, he applied himself to its resuscitation, in which occupation he found relief to his feelings, and himself formed a brilliant illustration of his remarks on savage customs.

Harold admitted that there was much truth in what he said, but rather inclined to the opinion that of the two sets of savages the uncivilised were, if anything, the wildest. Disco however, contrary to his usual habits, had nailed his colours to the mast on that point and could not haul them down. Meanwhile Harold's opinion was to some extent justified by the appearance of a young man, who, issuing from the jungle close at hand, advanced towards them.

Most of the men at the village displayed a good deal of pride, if not taste, in the arrangement of their hair. Some wore it long and twisted into a coil which hung down their backs; others trained and stiffened it in such a way that it took the form of buffalo horns, while some allowed it to hang over the shoulders in large masses, and many shaved it either entirely, or partially in definite patterns. But the young dandy who now approached outdid all others, for he had twisted his hair into innumerable little tails, which, being stiffened by fillets of the inner bark of a tree, stuck straight out and radiated from the head in all directions. His costume otherwise was simple enough, consisting merely of a small kilt of white calico. He was accompanied by Antonio.

"We've be come from Kambira," said the interpreter, "to tell you for come to feast."

"All right," said Disco, rising; "always ready for wittles if you only gives us an hour or two between times.—I say, Tony," (he had by that time reduced the interpreter's name to this extent), "ask this feller what he means by makin' sitch a guy of hisself."

"Hims say it look well," said Antonio, with a broad grin.

"Looks well—eh? and ask him why the women wear that abominable pelele."

When this question was put to the black dandy, he looked at Disco evidently in surprise at his stupidity. "Because it is the fashion," he said.

"They wear it for beauty, to be sure! Men have beards and whiskers; women have none, and what kind of creature would woman be without whiskers, and without a pelele? She would have a mouth like a man, and no beard!"

The bare idea of such a state of things tickled the dandy so much that he went into roars of laughter, insomuch that all the radiating tails of his head quivered again. The effect of laughter and tails together was irresistible. Harold, Disco, and Antonio laughed in sympathy, till the tears ran down their cheeks, and then returned to the village where Kambira and his chief men awaited them.

While enjoying the feast prepared for them, Harold communicated his intentions and desires to the chief, who was delighted at the prospect of having such powerful allies on a hunting expedition.

The playful Obo meanwhile was clambering over his father's person like a black monkey. He appeared to be particularly fond of his father, and as love begets love, it is not surprising

R. M. Ballantyne

that Kambira was excessively fond of Obo. But Obo, becoming obstreperous, received an amicable punch from his father, which sent him headlong into a basket of boiled hippopotamus. He gave a wild howl of alarm as Disco snatched him out of the dish, dripping with fat, and set him on his knee.

"There, there, don't blubber," said the seaman, tenderly wiping off the fat while the natives, including Kambira, exploded with laughter. "You ain't burnt, are you?"

As Obo could not reply, Disco put his finger into the gravy from which the urchin had been rescued, and satisfied himself that it was not hot enough to have done the child injury. This was also rendered apparent by his suddenly ceasing to cry, struggling off Disco's knee, and renewing his assaults on his easy-going father.

Accepting an egg which was offered him by Yohama, Harold broke it, and entered into conversation with Kambira through the medium of Antonio.

"Is your boy's mother a—Hollo! there's a chick in this egg," he exclaimed, throwing the offensive morsel into the fire.

Jumbo, who sat near the place where it fell, snatched it up, grinned, and putting it into his cavernous mouth, swallowed it.

"Dem's betterer wid chickies," he said, resuming his gravity and his knife and fingers,—forks being held by him in light esteem.

"Ask him, Antonio, if Obo's mother is alive," said Harold, trying another egg, which proved to be in better condition.

The interpreter, instead of putting the question without

comment, as was his wont, shook his head, looked mysterious, and whispered—"No better ask dat. Hims lost him's wife. The slave-hunters cotch her some time ago, and carry her off when hims away hunting. Hims awful mad, worser dan mad elerphint when hims speak to 'bout her."

Harold of course dropped the subject at once, after remarking that he supposed Yohama was the child's grandmother.

"Yis," said Antonio; "she be Kambira's moder, an' Obo's gran'moder—bof at once."

This fact was, we may almost say, self-evident for Obo's attentions and favours were distributed exclusively between Yohama and Kambira, though the latter had unquestionably the larger share.

During the course of the feast, beer was served round by the little man who had performed so deftly on the violin the previous evening.

"Drink," said Kambira hospitably; "I am glad to see my white brothers here; drink, it will warm your hearts."

"Ay, an' it won't make us drunk," said Disco, destroying Jumbo's peace of mind by winking and making a face at him as he raised the calabash to his lips. "Here's long life to you, Kambira, an' death to slavery."

There can be no doubt that the chief and his retainers would have heartily applauded that sentiment if they had understood it, but at the moment Antonio was too deeply engaged with another calabash to take the trouble to translate it.

The beer, which was pink, and as thick as gruel, was indeed too weak to produce intoxication unless taken in very large quantities; nevertheless many of the men were so fond of it that they sometimes succeeded in taking enough to bring them to the condition which we style "fuddled." But at that time the particular brew was nearly exhausted, so that temperance was happily the order of the day.

Having no hops in those regions, they are unable to prevent fermentation, and are therefore obliged to drink up a whole brewing as quickly as possible after it is made.

"Man, why don't ye wash yer face?" said Disco to the little fiddler as he replenished his calabash; "it's awful dirty."

Jumbo laughed, of course, and the small musician, not understanding what was said, followed suit out of sympathy.

"Wash him's face!" cried Antonio, laughing, "him would as soon cut off him's head. Manganja nevair wash. Ah me! You laugh if you hear de womans ask me yesterday—'Why you wash?' dey say, 'our men nevair do.' Ho! ho! dey looks like it too."

"I'm sure that cannot be said of Kambira or any of his chief men," said Harold.

"Perhaps not," retorted Antonio, "but some of 'um nevair wash. Once 'pon a time one man of dis tribe foller a party me was with. Not go way for all we tell 'um. We said we shoot 'um. No matter, hims foller still. At last we say, 'You scoun'rel, we *wash* you!' Ho! how hims run! Jist like zebra wid lion at 'um's tail. Nevair see 'um after dat—nevair more!"

"Wot a most monstrous ugly feller that is sittin' opposite Kambira, on the other side o' the fire—the feller with the half-shaved head," said Disco in an undertone to Harold during a temporary pause in eating.

"A well-made man, however," replied Harold.—"I say, Disco," he added, with a peculiar smile, "you think yourself rather a good-looking fellow, don't you, now?"

The worthy seaman, who was indeed an exceptionally good-looking tar, modestly replied—"Well now, as you have put it so plump I don't mind if I do confess that I've had some wild suspicions o' that sort now and then."

"Then you may dismiss your suspicions now, for I can assure you that you are regarded in this land as a very monster of ugliness," said Harold, laughing.

"In the estimation of niggers your garments are hideous; your legs they think elephantine, your red beard frightful, and your blue eyes savage—*savage*! think of that."

"Well, well," retorted Disco, "your own eyes are as blue as mine, an' I don't suppose the niggers think more of a yaller beard than a red one."

"Too true, Disco; we are both ill-favoured fellows here, whatever we may be elsewhere; however, as we don't intend to take Manganja wives it won't matter much. But what think you of our plan, now that Kambira is ready to fall in with it?"

"It seems a good one. When do we start?"

"To-morrow," said Harold.

"Wery good," replied Disco, "I'm agreeable."

The morrow came, and with the early light all the people turned out to witness the departure of the hunters. Scouts had been previously sent out in all directions to make sure that no enemies or slave-traders were at that time in their immediate neighbourhood, and a strong force of the best warriors was left to guard the village.

Of Harold's band, two half-castes, Jose and Oliveira, volunteered to stay in camp with the guard, and two, Songolo and Mabruki, the freemen of Quillimane, remained in the village to recruit their health, which had failed. Chimbolo likewise remained, the wounds on his back not having healed sufficiently to admit of the hard labour of hunting. All the rest accompanied the hunters, and of these the three Makololo men, Jumbo, Zombo, and Masiko, were incomparably the best and bravest. Of course the volatile Antonio also went, being indispensable.

On setting out—each man with his sleeping-mat on his back and his little wooden pillow hung at his neck,—there was a great deal of shouting and ho-ho-ing and well-wishing on the part of those who remained behind, but above all the noise there arose a shrill cry of intense and agonising despair. This proceeded from the small windpipe of little Obo, who had not until the last moment made the appalling discovery that Kambira was going away without him!

There was something very touching in the cry of the urchin, and something which brought vividly to the minds of the Englishmen the infantine community of their own land. There was the same sudden gaze of horror on realising the true position of affairs,—the same sharp shriek and frantic struggle to escape from the grasp of those who held him back from following his father,—the same loud cry of agony on finding that his efforts were vain, and then, the wide-open mouth, the close-shut eyes, and the awful, prolonged silence—suggestive of fits—that betokens the concentration of mind, heart, and lungs into that tremendous roar of unutterable significance which appears to be the safety-valve of the human family, black and white, at that tender period of life.

Poor Obo! his sobs continued to burst out with steam-engine power, and his eyes to pour cataracts of tears into Yohama's sympathetic bosom, long after the hunting party had left the hills behind them, and advanced into the almost impenetrable jungles of the low grounds.

R. M. Ballantyne

CHAPTER TWELVE

DESCRIBES A HUNTING EXPEDITION WHICH WAS BOTH EXCITING AND SUCCESSFUL

Down by the reedy margin of a pretty large lake—where wild-fowl innumerable made the air vocal with their cries by day, and frogs, in numbers inconceivable, chirped and croaked a lullaby to men who slept, and a symphony to beasts that howled and growled and prowled at night in bush and brake—Kambira pitched his camp.

He did not indeed, select the moist level of the fever-breeding marshes, but he chose for his temporary habitation the dry summit of a wooded hill which overlooked the lake.

Here the natives of the neighbourhood said that elephants had been lately seen, and buffaloes, zebras, etcetera, were at all times numerous.

After two long days' march they had reached the spot, and encamped late in the evening. Next morning early the business of the expedition began. Various parties of natives, armed with bows and arrows and spears, were sent out in different directions, but the principal band was composed of Kambira and his chief men, with Harold and his party.

They did not go far before game was found. Guinea-fowl were numerous, and those who were aimed with bows soon procured a goodly supply of these, but our travellers did not waste their energies or powder on such small game. Besides these, monkeys peeped inquisitively at the hunters from among the trees, and myriads of turtle-doves were seen in the covers. As they advanced, wild pigs, elands, waterbucks, koodoos, and other creatures, were seen in herds, and the natives dropped off, or turned aside in pursuit of these, so that ere long the band remaining with Kambira was reduced to about forty men.

Coming to a small river in which were a number of deep pools and shallows, they saw several hippopotami lying asleep, their bodies nearly all out of the water, appearing like masses of black rock in the stream. But at the same place they discovered fresh traces of elephants and buffaloes, therefore the hippopotami were left unmolested, save that Harold sent a bullet amongst them, partly to let the natives hear the report of his gun, and partly to see how the animals would take it.

They all started to their feet at once, and stared around them with looks of stolid surprise that were almost equal to the looks of the natives, to whom fire-arms were little known, except by report. Another shot sent the whole herd with a heavy plunge into deep water.

"It's a queer country," observed Disco when they had resumed their march. "Just look at them there lizards with red and blue tails running about among the rocks an' eatin' up the white ants like one o'clock."

Disco might have said like twelve o'clock, if numbers would have added to the force of his remark, for the little creatures referred to were miraculously active in pursuit of their food.

"But I s'pose," continued Disco, "the niggers would think our country a queerer place than this."

"Undoubtedly they would," replied Harold; "just fancy what would be the feelings of Kambira if he were suddenly transported into the heart of London."

"Hallo!" exclaimed Disco, stopping suddenly and pointing to one of the men in advance, who had crouched and made signals to his friends to halt, "breakers ahead—eh?"

"More likely buffaloes," whispered Harold, as he cocked his rifle and advanced quickly with Kambira, who carried a short spear or javelin.

On reaching an opening in the bushes, a small herd of zebras was observed not much more than a hundred yards in advance.

"Will the white man's gun kill so far?" asked the chief, turning to Antonio.

The interpreter made no reply, but pointed to Harold, who was in the act of taking aim. The loud report was followed by the fall of the nearest zebra. Disco also fired and wounded another, which bounded away in wild alarm with its fellows.

The natives yelled with delight, and Disco cheered in sympathy.

"You've hit him," said Harold, as he reloaded.

"Ay, but I han't disabled him. Better luck next time. I think I took him somewhere on the port bow."

"If by that you mean the left shoulder," returned Harold, with a laugh, "it's likely he won't run far. What does Kambira think of the white man's gun?" he added, turning round.

The tall chief nodded approvingly, and said, with a grave countenance—"Good, good; it is good—better than this," shaking his short spear.

At that moment a small antelope, which had been startled and put to flight by some of the other bands of hunters, came crashing wildly towards them, ignorant of the enemy in its front until within about thirty yards. It turned at a sharp angle and plunged into the jungle, but the spear which Kambira had shaken whizzed though the air and pierced its heart before it had time to disappear.

"A splendid heave!" cried Disco, with enthusiasm; "why, man alive, you'd make yer fortin' as a harpooner if ye was to go to the whale-fishin'.—Hallo! there's somethin' else; w'y, the place is swarmin'. It's for all the world like a zoological ga'rdings let loose."

As he spoke, the hoofs of a herd of ponderous animals were heard, but the rank grass and underwood concealed them entirely from view. The whole party rushed to the nearest opening, and were just in time to see the tail of an irate buffalo make a magnificent flourish in the air as its owner plunged into cover.

There was no further attempt at conversation after this. The near presence of large game was too exciting, so that merely a word of advice, direction, or inquiry, passed as the party advanced rapidly—one or two of the most active going before as pioneers.

While Disco was striding along with flashing eyes, rifle ready, and head turning from side to side in momentary

R. M. Ballantyne

expectation of something bounding suddenly out of some-where, he chanced to cast his eyes upwards, and, to his horror, beheld two huge serpents coiled together among the branches of a tree close to his head.

Uttering a yell of alarm—for he entertained an almost superstitious dread of serpents—he fired blindly upwards, and dashed to one side so violently that he tumbled himself and Harold into a bush of wait-a-bit thorns, out of which the laughing natives found it difficult to extract them.

"What *is* the matter, man?" said Harold somewhat testily.

"Have a care! look! Avast! A bite'll be death, an' no mistake!" cried Disco, pointing to the reptiles.

Harold fired at once and brought them both down, and the natives, attacking them with sticks, soon killed them.

"No fear," said Antonio, with a chuckle. "Dem not harm nobody, though ums ugly an' big enough."

This was true. They were a couple of pythons, and the larger of the two, a female, was ten feet long; but the python is a harmless creature.

While they were talking, smoke was observed to rise from an isolated clump of long grass and bushes not far from the banks of the river, much to the annoyance of Kambira, who feared that the fire might spread and scare away the game. It was confined, however, to the place where it began, but it had the effect of driving out a solitary buffalo that had taken refuge in the cover. Jumbo chanced to be most directly in front of the infuriated animal when it burst out, and to him exclusively it directed its attentions.

Never since Jumbo was the size of Obo had that laughter-loving savage used his lithe legs with greater energy than on this occasion. An ostrich might have envied him as he rushed towards the river, into which he sprang headlong when the buffalo was barely six feet behind him.

Of course Harold fired, as well as Disco, and both shots told, as also a spear from Kambira, nevertheless the animal turned abruptly on seeing Jumbo disappear, and charged furiously up the bank, scattering its enemies right and left. Harold fired again at little more than fifty yards off, and heard the bullet thud as it went in just behind the shoulder, yet strange to say, it seemed to have no other effect than to rouse the brute to greater wrath, and two more bullets failed to bring him down.

This toughness of the buffalo is by no means uncommon, but different animals vary much in their tenacity of life. Some fall at once to the first well-directed shot; others die hard. The animal the hunters were now in pursuit of, or rather which was in pursuit of the hunters, seemed to be of the latter class. Harold fired another shot from behind a tree, having loaded with a shell-bullet, which exploded on hitting the creature's ribs. It fell, much to the satisfaction of Disco, of whom it happened to be in pursuit at the time. The seaman at once stopped and began to reload, and the natives came running forward, when Antonio, who had climbed a tree to be out of harm's way, slipped down and ran with great bravery up to the prostrate animal.

Just as he reached it the buffalo sprang up with the activity of a cat, and charged him. Antonio turned and ran with such rapidity that his little legs became almost invisible, like those of a sparrow in a hurry. He gained a tree, and had just time to climb into it when the buffalo struck it like a battering-ram, hard enough almost to have split both head and tree. It

R. M. Ballantyne

paused a few seconds, drew back several paces, glared savagely at Antonio, and then charged again and again, as if resolved either to shake him out of the tree, or give itself a splitting headache, but another shell from Harold, who could hardly take aim for laughing, stretched the huge animal dead upon the ground. Altogether, it took two shells and five large solid rifle-balls to finish him.

"That wos a pretty good spurt," said Disco, panting, as he joined Harold beside the fallen beast. "It's well-known that a starn chase is a long 'un, but this would have been an exception to the rule if you hadn't shot him, sir. He pretty nigh made short work o' *me*. He was a'most aboard of me w'en you fired."

"True," said Harold; "and had that tree not grown where it stands, and grown tough, too, I suspect he would have made short work of Antonio too."

"Bah!" said the interpreter, with affected carelessness, "him was but a slow brute, after all."

Disco looked at Jumbo, who was none the worse of his ducking, and shut his right eye smartly. Jumbo opened his cavernous mouth, and exploded so violently that his double row of brilliant teeth must have been blown out and scattered on the ground, had they not been miraculously strong.

"Come, now," said Kambira, who had just given orders to some of his followers to remain behind and look after the carcase, "we go to find elephants."

"Have we much chance of findin' them?" inquired Disco.

Kambira thought they had, because fresh traces had been recently seen in the neighbourhood, whereupon Disco said that he would prefer to go after lions, but Kambira assured him that these animals were not so easy to find, and much more dangerous when attacked. Admitting the force of this, though still asserting his preference of lions to elephants, the bloodthirsty son of Neptune shouldered his rifle and followed his leader.

While the main party of hunters were thus successfully pushing along, the other bands were not idle, though, possessing no fire-arms, they were less noisy. In fact their proceedings were altogether of the cat-catty. One fellow, as black as a coal, as lithe as an eel, and as long—according to Disco's standard—as a fathom of pump-water, having come upon a herd of buffalo unseen by them, and being armed with a small bow and quiver of arrows, suddenly dropped on all-fours and began to glide through the long grass.

Now there is a particular little bird in those regions which calls for special notice here. It is a very singular bird, inasmuch as it has constituted itself the guardian of the buffalo. It frequently sits upon that animal's back, and, whenever it sees the approach of man, or any other danger, it flaps its wings and screams to such an extent, that the buffalo rushes off without waiting to inquire or see what is the matter; and the small guardian seems to think itself sufficiently rewarded with the pickings it finds on the back of its fat friend. So vigilant is this little creature, that it actually renders the approach of the hunter a matter of great difficulty in circumstances when, but for it, he might approach with ease. [See Livingstone's *Zambesi and its Tributaries*, page 200.]

Our wary native was, however, aware of this little fellow's propensities, and took precautions to outwit the bird rather than the beast. It may perhaps cause some surprise to be told that a small bow and arrows were a sufficiently powerful

R. M. Ballantyne

species of artillery to bring to bear against such noble game, but the surprise will vanish when we state that the arrows were poisoned.

Having crawled to within range, the fathom of black pump-water suddenly arose and let fly an arrow. The missile went deep into the side of a majestic bull. The little bird fluttered and screamed too late. The bull at once dashed away at full speed, starting off the whole herd in alarm. The black fathom followed at the top of his speed, and was joined by a number of other black fathoms, who were quite aware of what had been done. The buffaloes were soon out of sight, but the fathoms followed the trail with the unerring pertinacity of fate. After a long run they came up with the stricken bull, which had fallen behind its fellows, and waited patiently until the poison took full effect. In a short time the animal fell, and the successful hunters fell to work upon his carcase with their knives.

Leaving them thus employed, we will return to Kambira and his friends.

They had not gone far when a fine water-buck was observed feeding beside a creek.

Kambira laid his hand on Harold's shoulder and pointed to it with a smile, which might have been interpreted, "Now, then, there's a chance for you!"

Harold fired, and the water-buck dropped.

"Good," said Kambira.

"Hallo!" exclaimed Disco.

And well he might, for at that moment an enormous

crocodile, which had evidently been watching the water-buck, seized and dragged it into the water. It was not deep, however, and the wounded animal made a desperate plunge, hauled the crocodile several yards, and tore itself out of its hideous jaws. It then jumped into the stream and was swimming across when another crocodile made a dash at it, but Harold sent a ball into its ugly head, which appeared to make it change its mind. It disappeared, and the water-buck turning, made for the bank from which it had started. Just as it reached it the vital spark fled—the fine head dropped and the body turned over.

It will be seen from what has been told, that on this occasion the rifles did most of the work. The natives who followed Harold had nothing to do but look on exultingly, glare, dance, show their teeth and gums, and secure the game. We cannot perhaps, expect the good-natured reader to follow us through all the details of that day's work; but it would be unpardonable were we to close the chapter without referring to the principal event of the day, which occurred a couple of hours after the shooting of the water-buck.

It happened thus:—When the hunters began to grow tired, and the prospect of falling in with large game became less hopeful, the chief determined to return to camp; but Disco felt so disappointed at not having seen an elephant or a lion, that he expressed a wish to continue the chase with a small select party. Harold laughed at the idea of the seaman leading such a party, but offered no objection, although he did not care to accompany his friend, having, as he said, had enough of it, and being desirous of having a long chat with the chief in camp.

"You see, sir," said Disco, patting the stock of his rifle with his right hand, "we chance to have got, so to speak, into the heart of a shoal o' big fish, an' there's no sayin' how soon

R. M. Ballantyne

they may take it into their heads to up anchor, and make sail for other grounds. Therefore, says I, blaze away at 'em while you've got the chance."

"But you may have as good a chance to-morrow, or next day," suggested Harold.

"We ain't sure o' that sir. To-morrow, they say, never comes," returned Disco. "It's my ambition to let fly a broadside at a lion or a elephant so I means for to go on; an' wot I says is, Who wolunteers to sail in company?"

When the party were given to understand what "wolunteers" meant, the three Makololo joined the tar with alacrity, also the Somali negroes Nakoda and Conda, and about a dozen of the natives, armed with spears. Disco's own men were armed with their guns. Antonio, being necessary to Harold, returned to camp; but this was a matter of little importance, as Jumbo and his fellow-countrymen knew enough of English to act as interpreters.

Every one who has had a few years' experience of life knows the truth of the proverb which asserts that "fortune favours the brave." Its truth was exemplified on the present occasion not more than an hour after the little band of heroes had set out.

Disco led the way, as a matter of course, holding, as he said, that no nigger could possibly be equal to a white sailor in the matter of steering, whether ashore or afloat. He steered by the sun, and directed his course to nowhere in particular, being influenced chiefly by the form of the ground and the appearance of the jungle.

Jumbo grinned a good deal at the sententious gravity with which the leader delivered his orders, and the self-important strides with which he passed over the land. He would have grinned still more, perhaps have laughed outright if he had understood that the occasional off-hand kicks which Disco bestowed on a thick bush here and there, were given in the hope that a lion might thereby be set up, as one dislodges a rabbit or a hare!

At last on reaching the crest of a mound which was comparatively free of underwood, Disco beheld a sight which caused him to drop on his hands and knees as though he had been shot.

Not more than fifty yards off a herd of cow elephants and their calves were seen feeding quietly on tall heavy-seeded grass in the plain below.

"Avast!" said Disco, in a hoarse whisper, at the same time crouching behind a bush, and making frantic signals to the rest of the party to advance with extreme caution.

"Wat 'um see?" inquired Jumbo in a low whisper, creeping up to his excited leader.

There was no need for a reply. A glance over the top of the bush sufficed.

"Be quiet as mice now, lads," said Disco, when all the members of his party had crept around him, and become aware of the presence of elephants. "Get your guns laid, and if any one of you dares to pull a trigger till I give the word, I'll keel-haul him."

This, or something distantly resembling it, having been explained to the men who carried guns, they lay down and took aim.

R. M. Ballantyne

The noise made by the hunters attracted the attention of the nearest elephant, and, with true motherly instinct she placed her young one between her fore-legs for protection.

"We fire right in de middel ob de lot?" inquired Zombo hastily.

"Not at all," whispered Disco; "let every man point at the nearest one—the one that lays broadside on to us, wi' the little un under her bows. Now—ready—present—fire!"

Bang went the seven guns with a degree of precision that might have put to shame any corps of volunteer riflemen in England; up went the trunks and tails of the elephants, little and big, and away rushed the whole herd in dire alarm. But the wounded animal suddenly stumbled and fell on its knees, then leaped up and ran on heavily.

Meanwhile Disco, who had discharged only one barrel of his heavy gun, leaped over the bushes, and rushed forward at a pace which for a few seconds enabled him to keep ahead even of the fleet natives. The elephants, however, easily left them all behind, and it appeared as if the affair were about to end in disappointment, when the wounded beast again stumbled.

"Hold on! halt!" cried Disco in a voice of thunder.

He kneeled at the same time, took aim, and fired.

Whether it was this last shot or the effects of previous loss of blood, we cannot tell; but after receiving it, the ponderous animal rolled over on its side, and died.

To say that the natives became temporarily insane would give but a feeble idea of what now took place, because few readers are likely to be aware of the amazing power of the negro to give expression to the vagaries of insanity. We shall therefore content ourselves by saying that they cheered, laughed, howled, shouted, danced, and yelled—and leave the rest to imagination.

"Now, then, boys, avast howlin'. Clap a stopper on your bellows, will 'ee?" said Disco, in a boatswain's roar, that effectually quelled the tumult. "Cut off to camp, every mother's son of you, an bring up Kambira an' all the boys, with as many knives and dishes as ye can muster, for this mountain of flesh ain't to be cut up in a hurry, an' the sun won't be long o' goin' to bed. Away with 'ee! Let's see how you can wag yer black legs, an' I'll keep watch over the carcase. If anything comes to have a look at it—a lion, for instance,—so much the worse for the lion!"

It was in vain that Jumbo explained there was no necessity for sending more than one of the party to the camp. Disco was a strict disciplinarian, and, having given the order, enforced it in a manner which admitted of no disobedience. They therefore departed, leaving the seaman seated on the elephant, smoking his pipe with his gun beside him.

But Jumbo did not go far. He soon turned aside from his companions, and returned to the scene of the hunt, resolved if possible to give his leader a fright. Gaining the skirts of the jungle which surrounded the open space where Disco kept watch, he crept cautiously as near to him as possible.

Disco still sat smoking and eyeing the elephant with a smile of satisfaction. Presently he rose,—retreated a few yards from the carcase, and stood admiring it with his head on one side, as if it were a picture and he a connoisseur. He had in this act approached somewhat nearer to Jumbo, who saluted him with a most awful growl.

No monkey in Africa could have dropped its pipe, had it been a smoker, or sprung to seize its gun, had it been a sportsman, with greater agility than did Disco Lillihammer on that trying occasion! Getting on the other side of the dead elephant he faced round, cocked both barrels, and prepared to receive whatever might come.

Jumbo, lying very low behind a bank of earth for safety, gave another low growl. Disco started and half raised his piece. Jumbo then threw a large stone towards a neighbouring bush, which it struck and caused to rustle.

This was enough for Disco, who took a quick aim, and let fly the contents of both barrels into the bush.

Jumbo noiselessly but swiftly crept back into the woods, chuckling as he went, leaving Disco to reload in wild haste. But his haste was uncalled for. There was no more growling; no more rustling in the bushes.

"I've done for him," muttered Disco, after waiting patiently at the "ready" for some time. "But it won't do for me to ventur' up to it all by myself. Pr'aps it's a lion, an' they do say that it's chancy work to go near a wounded lion. To be sure the growl wasn't so loud as I'd have expected o' the king o' the forest, but then they don't always growl loud. Anyhow I'll keep a bright look-out an' wait till the niggers return."

Philosophising thus, the bold seaman mounted guard over the elephant.

Meanwhile Jumbo, having got out of earshot of his friend, indulged in a loud laugh and made after his friends, but, observing the visage of a small yellow-coloured monkey among the leaves overhead, a thought flashed into his mind and induced him to change his plans.

Throwing his spear dexterously he transfixed the monkey and brought it down. Returning with great caution to the bush into which Disco had fired, and gliding with the noiseless motion of a snake the latter part of the way, he placed the dead monkey on the ground and left it there.

It was by that time too late to overtake his comrades. He therefore waited until they returned, and then joined the party in rear, as though he had followed them from the camp.

The same wild exhibition of delight was about to be enacted when the party came trooping up, but Disco quickly checked it by the astounding announcement that he thought he had shot a lion, or somethin' o' that sort!

"You don't mean it!" said Harold, rather excited.

"All I know is," said Disco, "that I heerd somethin' uncommon like a lion growl twice in yonder bush, an' saw the bush move too, so I fired a broadside that seemed to finish him at once, for there was no more rustlin' after that."

"An' no more growlin'?" asked Jumbo, with much simplicity of countenance.

"Not a growl, nor nothin' else," answered Disco.

"Well, get your guns ready, lads," said Harold, "and stand by to fire while we go and search the bush."

So saying, Harold and Disco advanced together with their rifles ready, while the natives, who were more or less alarmed, according to their respective degrees of courage, scattered in a semicircle well in rear. Kambira, armed with a spear, kept close to Harold, and Jumbo, with unwonted bravery, walked alongside of Disco. Antonio, quietly retiring, took refuge in a tree.

"Yoo's *sure* you hit um?" inquired Jumbo in a whisper.

"Can't say I'm *sure*," replied Disco, "but we'll soon see."

"Was um's growl very bad?" asked Jumbo.

"Hold yer long tongue!" said Disco testily, for he was becoming excited.

"Look! see dere!" exclaimed Jumbo in an energetic whisper.

"What? where?"

"Look! right troo de bush. Dis way. Dar, don' you zee um's skin,—t'other side? Fire!"

"Why, eh!" exclaimed Disco, peering keenly through the leaves, "yellow hair! yes—its—"

Stopping abruptly he pointed his gun at the bush and poured the contents of both barrels into it. Then, clubbing his weapon and brandishing it in the air, he uttered a wild cry— went crashing through the bush, and next moment stood aghast before the yellow monkey, whose little carcase he had almost blown to atoms.

We won't chronicle the roars of laughter, the yells of delight that followed,—the immense amount of chaffing, the innumerable witticisms and criticisms that ensued—no, no! regard for the gallant seaman constrains us to draw a veil over the scene and leave it, as we have left many things before, and shall leave many things yet to come, to the reader's vivid imagination.

Fortunately for Disco, the superior attractions of the dead elephant soon drew off attention from this exploit. The natives proceeded to cut up the huge mass of meat, and this was indeed an amazing spectacle. At first the men stood round the carcase in dead silence, while Kambira delivered a species of oration, in which he pointed out minutely the particular parts of the animal which were to be apportioned to the head-men of the different fires of which the camp was composed,—the left hind-leg and the parts around the eyes being allotted to his English visitors. These points settled, the order was given to "cut up," and immediately the excitement which had been restrained burst forth again with tenfold violence. The natives seemed to be quite unable to restrain their feelings of delight, as they cut away at the carcase with spears and knives. They screamed as well as danced with glee. Some attacked the head, others the flanks, jumping over the animal or standing on it the better to expedite their operations; some ever and anon ran off screaming with masses of bloody meat, threw it on the grass and went back for more, while others, after cutting the carcase open, jumped inside and wallowed about in their eagerness to reach and cut out the precious fat—all talking and shouting at the utmost pitch of their voices.

"Well, now," said Disco to Harold, with a grin of amusement, "the likes o' that I never did see nowheres. Cuttin' up a Greenland whale is nothin' to it."

"Come, come," said Harold, checking his laughter and seizing an excited negro by the shoulder, "no fighting allowed."

This had reference to two who chanced to have taken a fancy for the same mass of meat, and were quarrelling so violently over it that blows seemed on the point of following, but having let off part of their superabundant energy in words, they rushed back to expend the remainder on their dead friend.

Suddenly a sharp agonised yell was heard inside the carcase. Next moment Zombo jumped out all bloody and furious, holding up his right hand. While groping about inside, one of his too eager comrades outside had laid about rather incautiously with his knife, drove it through the meat and sliced Zombo's left hand. He was easily soothed, however; Harold bound up the cut with a piece of rag, and Zombo went to work as recklessly as ever.

In a marvellously short time tons of meat were cut up and divided amongst the band, and, before daylight had quite disappeared, the hunters were on their way back to camp, while a troop of hyenas and other carnivora were gorging themselves with the elephant's remains.

CHAPTER THIRTEEN

THE ENCAMPMENT AND THE SUPPER—
DISCUSSIONS, POLITICAL AND OTHERWISE—
KAMBIRA RECEIVES A SHOCK, AND OUR
WANDERERS ARE THROWN INTO PERPLEXITY

Turn we now to a more peaceful scene. The camp is almost quiet, the stars are twinkling brightly overhead, the fires are glimmering fitfully below. The natives, having taken the edge off their appetites, have stretched their dusky forms on their sleeping-mats, and laid their woolly heads on their little wooden pillows. The only persons moving are Harold Seadrift and Disco Lillihammer—the first being busy making notes in a small book, the second being equally busy in manufacturing cloudlets from his unfailing pipe, gazing the while with much interest at his note-making companion.

"They was pretty vigorous w'en they wos at it, sir," said Disco, in reference to supper, observing that his companion looked up from his book, "but they wos sooner done than I had expected."

"Yes, they weren't long about it," replied Harold, with an abstracted air, as he resumed his writing.

Lest the reader should erroneously imagine that supper is

over, it is necessary here to explain what taking the edge off a free African's appetite means.

On reaching camp after the cutting up of the elephant, as detailed in the last chapter, the negroes had set to work to roast and boil with a degree of vigour that would have surprised even the *chefs de cuisine* of the world's first-class hotels. Having gorged themselves to an extent that civilised people might perhaps have thought dangerous, they had then commenced an uproarious dance, accompanied by stentorian songs, which soon reduced them to the condition of beings who needed repose. Proceeding upon the principle of overcoming temptation by giving way to it, they at once lay down and went to sleep.

It was during this stage of the night's proceedings that Disco foolishly imagined that supper had come to a close. Not many minutes after the observation was made, and before the black cutty-pipe was smoked out, first one and then another of the sleepers awoke, and, after a yawn or two, got up to rouse the fires and put on the cooking-pots. In less than a quarter of an hour the whole camp was astir, conversation was rife, and the bubbling of pots that had not got time to cool, and the hissing of roasts whose fat had not yet hardened, mingled with songs whose echoes were still floating in the brains of the wild inhabitants of the surrounding jungle. Roasting, boiling, and eating were recommenced with as much energy as if the feast had only just begun.

Kambira, having roused himself, gave orders to one of his men, who brought one of the elephant's feet and set about the cooking of it at Harold's fire. Kambira and Disco, with Antonio and Jumbo, sat round the same fire.

There was a hole in the ground close beside them which contained a small fire; the embers of this were stirred up and replenished with fuel. When the inside was thoroughly heated, the elephant's foot was placed in it, and covered over with hot ashes and soil, and another fire kindled above the whole.

Harold, who regarded this proceeding with some surprise, said to Kambira—through Antonio—"Who are you cooking that for?"

"For my white guests," replied the chief.

"But we have supped already," said Harold; "we have already eaten as much as we can hold of the elephant's trunk and tongue, both of which were excellent—why prepare more?"

"This is not for to-night, but for to-morrow," returned Kambira, with a smile. "The foot takes all night to cook."

This was a sufficient explanation, and in truth the nature of the dish required that it should be well done. When, on the morrow, they were called to partake of it they found that it was, according to Disco's estimation, "fust-rate!" It was a whitish mass, slightly gelatinous and sweet, like marrow, and very palatable. Nevertheless, they learned from experience that if the effect of bile were to be avoided, a long march was necessary after a meal of elephant's foot!

Meanwhile the proceedings of the natives were food enough for our travellers for the time being. Like human creatures elsewhere, they displayed great variety of taste. Some preferred boiled meat, others roast; a few indulged in porridge made of mapira meal. The meal was very good, but the porridge *was* doubtful, owing to the cookery. It would appear that in Africa, as in England, woman excels in the culinary art. At all events, the mapira meal was better

R. M. Ballantyne

managed by them, than by the men. On the present occasion the hunters tumbled in the meal by handfuls in rapid succession as soon as the water was hot, until it became too thick to be stirred about, then it was lifted off the fire, and one man held the pot while another plied the porridge-stick with all his might to prevent the solid mass from being burnt. Thus it was prepared, and thus eaten, in enormous quantities. No wonder that dancing and profuse perspiration were esteemed a necessary adjunct to feeding!

At the close of the second edition of supper, which went into four or five editions before morning, some of the men at the fire next to that of Kambira engaged in a debate so furious, that the curiosity of Disco and Harold was excited, and they caused Antonio to translate much of what was said. It is not possible to give a connected account of this debate as translated by Antonio. To overcome the difficulty we shall give the substance of it in what Disco styled Antonio's "lingo."

There were about a dozen natives round the fire, but two of them sustained the chief part in the debate. One of these was a large man with a flat nose; the other was a small man with a large frizzy head.

"Hold 'oos tongue," said Flatnose (so Antonio named him); "tongue too long—far!"

"Boh! 'oos brains too short," retorted Frizzyhead contemptuously.

An immense amount of chattering by the others followed these pithy remarks of the principals.

The question in debate was, Whether the two toes of the ostrich represented the thumb and forefinger in man, or the little and ring fingers? But in a few minutes the subject changed gradually, and somehow unaccountably, to questions of a political nature,—for, strange to say, in savage Africa, as in civilised England, politics are keenly discussed, doubtless at times with equal wisdom in the one land as in the other.

"What dat 'oo say?" inquired Flatnose, on hearing some muttered remarks of Frizzyhead in reference to the misgovernment of chiefs. Of course there, as here, present company was understood to be excepted.

"Chiefs ob no use—no use at all!" said Frizzyhead so vehemently that the men at several of the nearest fires ceased to talk, and began to listen.

"Ob no use?" cried Flatnose, with vehemence so superior that the attention of the whole camp was arrested.

"No!" replied Frizzyhead, still more energetically, "ob no use at all. We could govern ourselves betterer, so what de use of 'um? The chief 'ums fat an' hab plenty wife, but we, who do all de hard work, hab hunger, an' only one wife, prehaps none at all. Dis is bad, unjust, wrong."

There was a general shout of "eehee!" from all quarters, which was equivalent to our "hear, hear."

"'Oo know noting at all," retorted Flatnose, who was a loyal subject. "Is not de chief de fader of de peepil? Can dere be peepil widout a fader—eh? God made de chief—who says dat chief is not wise? He *is* wise, but um's child'n am big fools!"

Kambira nodded his head and smiled at this, and there was a general inclination on the part of most of the audience to applaud, for there, as elsewhere, men have a tendency to be blown about by every wind of doctrine.

It was amusing to observe the earnestness and freedom with which men of the lowest grade assaulted the opinions of their betters on this occasion. Unable at other times, or in any other way, to bring themselves into importance, they were glad of the opportunity to do so with their tongues, and, like their civilised types, they assumed an air of mock modesty.

"Oh!" cried one of these, in reply to Flatnose, "we is littil infants; we is still holdin' on to de boosums ob our moders; we not able to walk alone; we knows notin' at all; but on *dis* point, we knows that you old men speak like de ignorint peepil. We nebber hear such nonsense—nebber!"

No notice was taken of this, but Frizzyhead, whose passion was rising to white heat in consequence of the glibness of his opponent's tongue, cried out—"'Oo cannot prove wat 'ou says?"

"Oh yes, can prove it well 'nuff," replied Flatnose, "but 'oos no' got brain for onerstand."

This last was too much for poor Frizzyhead, who leaped up, stuttered, and cried—"Can 'oo outrun me, then?"

"Ye—ye—yes!" gasped Flatnose, springing up.

Away they went like two hunted springboks, and ran for a mile, then turned and came back into camp streaming with perspiration, little Frizzyhead far ahead of the big man, and rejoicing in the fact that he could beat his opponent in a race, if not in an argument. Thus was peace restored. Pity that civilised arguments cannot be terminated in the same way!

While these discussions were going on, Disco observed that hyenas were occasionally to be seen prowling near the verge of the bushes around them, as if anxious to join in the feast, which no doubt was the case.

"Don't they do mischief sometimes?" he inquired of Antonio.

"No; him a cowardly beast. Him come at mans when sleepin' or dyin', but not at oder time. 'Oo like see me catch um?"

"Why, yes, if 'ee can do it," answered Disco, with a slight look of contempt at his friend, who bore too much resemblance in some points to the hyena.

"Come here, den."

They went together into the jungle a little distance, and halted under the branch of a large tree. To this Antonio suspended a lump of raw flesh, at such a height from the ground that a hyena could only reach it by leaping. Directly underneath it he planted a short spear in the earth with its point upward.

"Now, come back to fire," he said to Disco; "'ou soon hear sometin'."

Antonio was right. In a short time afterwards a sharp yell was heard, and, on running to the trap, they found a hyena in its death-agonies. It had leaped at the meat, missed it, and had come down on the spear and impaled itself.

"Well, of all the fellers I ever know'd for dodges," said Disco, on reseating himself at the fire, "the men in these latitudes are the cleverest."

By this time dancing was going on furiously; therefore, as it would have been impossible to sleep, Disco refilled his pipe and amused himself by contemplating the intelligent countenance of Kambira, who sat smoking bang out of a huge native meerschaum on the other side of the fire.

"I wonder," said Harold, who lay stretched on a sleeping-mat, leaning on his right arm and gazing contemplatively at the glowing heart of the fire; "I wonder what has become of Yoosoof?"

"Was 'ee thinkin' that he deserved to be shoved in there?" asked Disco, pointing to the fire.

"Not exactly," replied Harold, laughing; "but I have frequently thought of the scoundrel, and wondered where he is and what doing now. I have sometimes thought too, about that girl Azinte, poor thing. She—"

He paused abruptly and gazed at Kambira with great surprise, not unmixed with alarm, for the chief had suddenly dropped his pipe and glared at him in a manner that cannot be described. Disco observed the change also, and was about to speak, when Kambira sprang over the fire and seized Harold by the arm.

There was something in the movement, however, which forbade the idea of an attack, therefore he lay still.

"What now, Kambira?" he said.

"Antonio," cried the chief, in a voice that brought the interpreter to his side in a twinkling; "what name did the white man speak just now?"

"Azinte," said Harold, rising to a sitting posture.

Kambira sat down, drew up his knees to his chin, and clasped his hands round them.

"Tell me all you know about Azinte," he said in a low, firm voice.

It was evident that the chief was endeavouring to restrain some powerful feeling, for his face, black though it was, indicated a distinct degree of pallor, and his lips were firmly compressed together. Harold therefore, much surprised as well as interested, related the little he knew about the poor girl,—his meeting with her in Yoosoof's hut; Disco's kindness to her, and her subsequent departure with the Arab.

Kambira sat motionless until he had finished.

"Do you know where she is gone?" he inquired.

"No. I know not; but she was not in the boat with the other slaves when we sailed, from which I think it likely that she remained upon the coast.—But why do you ask, Kambira, why are you so anxious about her?"

"She is my wife," muttered the chief between his teeth; and, as he said so, a frown that was absolutely diabolical settled down on his features.

For some minutes there was a dead silence, for both Harold and Disco felt intuitively that to offer consolation or hope were out of the question.

Presently Kambira raised his head, and a smile chased the frown away as he said—"You have been kind to Azinte, will you be kind to her husband?"

"We should be indeed unworthy the name of Englishmen if

we said no to that," replied Harold, glancing at Disco, who nodded approval.

"Good. Will you take me with you to the shores of the great salt lake?" said Kambira, in a low, pathetic tone, "will you make me your servant, your slave?"

"Most gladly will I take you with me as *a friend*," returned Harold. "I need not ask why you wish to go," he added,— "you go to seek Azinte?"

"Yes," cried the chief, springing up wildly and drawing himself up to his full height, "I go to seek Azinte. Ho! up men! up! Ye have feasted enough and slept enough for one night. Who knows but the slavers may be at our huts while we lie idly here? Up! Let us go!"

The ringing tones acted like a magic spell. Savage camps are soon pitched and sooner raised. In a few minutes the obedient hunters had bundled up all their possessions, and in less than a quarter of an hour the whole band was tracking its way by moonlight through the pathless jungle.

The pace at which they travelled home was much more rapid than that at which they had set out on their expedition. Somehow, the vigorous tones in which Kambira had given command to break up the camp, coupled with his words, roused the idea that he must have received information of danger threatening the village, and some of the more anxious husbands and fathers, unable to restrain themselves, left the party altogether and ran back the whole way. To their great relief, however, they found on arriving that all was quiet. The women were singing and at work in the fields, the children shouting at play, and the men at their wonted occupation of weaving cotton cloth, or making nets and bows, under the banyan-trees.

Perplexity is not a pleasant condition of existence, neverthe-less, to perplexity mankind is more or less doomed in every period of life and in every mundane scene—particularly in the jungles of central Africa, as Harold and his friends found out many a time to their cost.

On arriving at the native village, the chief point that perplexed our hero there was as to whether he should return to the coast at once, or push on further into the interior. On the one hand he wished very much to see more of the land and its inhabitants; on the other hand, Kambira was painfully anxious to proceed at once to the coast in search, of his lost wife, and pressed him to set off without delay.

The chief was rather an exception in regard to his feelings on this point. Most other African potentates had several wives, and in the event of losing one of them might have found consolation in the others. But Kambira had never apparently thought of taking another wife after the loss of Azinte, and the only comfort he had was in his little boy, who bore a strong resemblance, in some points, to the mother.

But although Harold felt strong sympathy with the man, and would have gone a long way out of his course to aid him, he could not avoid perceiving that the case was almost, if not altogether, a hopeless one. He had no idea to what part of the coast Azinte had been taken. For all he knew to the contrary, she might have been long ago shipped off to the northern markets, and probably was, even while he talked of her, the inmate of an Arab harem, or at all events a piece of goods—a "chattel"—in the absolute possession of an irresponsible master. Besides the improbability of Kambira ever hearing what had become of his wife, or to what part of the earth she had been transported, there was also the difficulty of devising any definite course of action for the chief himself, because the instant he should venture to leave the protection

R. M. Ballantyne

of the Englishmen he would be certain to fall into the hands of Arabs or Portuguese, and become enslaved.

Much of this Harold had not the heart to explain to him. He dwelt, however, pretty strongly on the latter contingency, though without producing much effect. Death, the chief replied, he did not fear, and slavery could easily be exchanged for death.

"Alas! not so easily as you think," said Harold, pointing to Chimbolo, whose sad story he had heard; "they will try *every* kind of torture before they kill you."

Chimbolo nodded his head, assenting, and ground his teeth together fiercely when this was said.

Still Kambira was unmoved; he did not care what they did to him. Azinte was as life to him, and to search for her he would go in spite of every consideration.

Harold prevailed on him, however, to agree to wait until he should have spent another month in visiting Chimbolo's tribe, after which he promised faithfully to return and take him along with his party to the coast.

Neither Harold nor Disco was quite at ease in his mind after making this arrangement, but they both agreed that no other course could be pursued, the former saying with a sigh that there was no help for it, and the latter asserting with a grunt that the thing "wos unawoidable."

On the following day the journey of exploration was resumed. Kambira accompanied his friends a few miles on the road, and then bade them farewell. On the summit of an elevated ridge the party halted and looked back. Kambira's manly form could be seen leaning on his spear. Behind him the little village lay embosomed in luxuriant verdure, and glowing in the bright sunshine, while songs and sounds of industry floated towards them like a sweet melody. It was with a feeling of keen regret that the travellers turned away, after waving their hands in reply to a parting salute from the stalwart chief, and, descending to the plain, pushed forward into the unknown wilderness beyond.

R. M. Ballantyne

CHAPTER FOURTEEN

CAMPING, TRAVELLING, SHOOTING, DREAMING, POETISING, PHILOSOPHISING, AND SURPRISING, IN EQUATORIAL AFRICA

At sunset the travellers halted in a peculiarly wild spot and encamped under the shelter of a gigantic baobab tree.

Two rousing fires were quickly kindled, round which the natives busied themselves in preparing supper, while their leaders sat down, the one to write up his journal, the other to smoke his pipe.

"Well, sir," said Disco, after a few puffs delivered with extreme satisfaction, "you do seem for to enjoy writin'. You go at that log of yours every night, as if it wos yer last will and testament that ye couldn't die happy without exikootin' an' signin' it with yer blood."

"A better occupation, isn't it," replied Harold, with a sly glance, "than to make a chimney-pot of my mouth?"

"Come, sir," returned Disco, with a deprecatory smile, "don't be too hard on a poor feller's pipe. If you can't enjoy it, that's no argiment against it."

"How d'you know I can't enjoy it?"

"Why? cos I s'pose you'd take to it if you did."

"Did *you* enjoy it when you first began?" asked Harold.

"Well, I can't 'zactly say as I did."

"Well, then, if you didn't, that proves that it is not *natural* to smoke, and why should I acquire an unnatural and useless habit?"

"Useless! why, sir, on'y think of wot you loses by not smokin'—wot a deal of enjoyment!"

"Well, I *am* thinking," replied Harold, affecting a look of profound thoughtfulness, "but I can't quite make it out— enjoyment? let me see. Do I not enjoy as good health as you do?"

"O, cer'nly, sir, cer'nly. You're quite up to the mark in that respect."

"Well then, I enjoy my food as well, and can eat as much, can't I?"

"No doubt of it," replied Disco, with a grin; "I was used to be considered raither a dab at wittles, but I must say I knocks under to *you*, sir."

"Very good," rejoined Harold, laughing; "then as to sleep, I enjoy sleep quite as soundly as yourself; don't I?"

"I can't say as to that," replied Disco. "You see, sir, as I never opens my eyes arter shuttin' of 'em till the bo's'n pipes all hands ahoy, I've no means of knowin' wot you accomplish in that way."

"On the whole, then, it seems that I enjoy everything as much as you do, and—"

"No, not everything; you don't enjoy baccy, you know.—But please, sir, don't go for to moralise; I can't stand it. You'll spile my pipe if ye do!"

"Well, I shall spare you," said Harold, "all the more that I perceive supper is about—"

At that moment Antonio, who had gone down to a streamlet which trickled close at hand, gave utterance to a hideous yell, and came rushing into camp with a face that was pea-green from terror.

"Ach!" he gasped, "a lion! queek! your guns!" Every one leaped up and seized his weapon with marvellous alacrity on receiving an alarm so violent and unlooked-for.

"Where away?" inquired Disco, blazing with excitement, and ready at a moment's notice to rush into the jungle and fire both barrels at whatever should present itself.

"No, no, don' go," cried Antonio in alarm; "be cautionous."

The interpreter's caution was enforced by Chimbolo, who laid his hand on Disco's arm, and looked at him with such solemnity that he felt it necessary to restrain his ardour.

Meanwhile Antonio with trembling steps led Harold to a point in the thicket whence he beheld two bright phosphoric-looking objects which his companion said were the lion's eyes, adding that lion's eyes always shone in that way.

Harold threw forward his rifle with the intention of taking aim, but lowered it quickly, for he felt convinced that no lion could possibly have eyes so wide apart unless its head were as large as that of an elephant.

"Nonsense, Antonio!" he said, laughing; "that cannot be a lion."

"Ho, yis, him's a lion, for sure," Antonio returned, positively.

"We shall see."

Harold raised his rifle and fired, while Antonio turned and fled, fully expecting the wounded beast to spring. Harold himself half looked for some such act, and shrank behind a bush by way of precaution, but when the smoke cleared away, he saw that the two glowing eyes were gazing at him as fixedly as ever.

"Pooh!" exclaimed Disco, brushing past; "I knows wot it is. Many a time I've seed 'em in the West Injies."

Saying which, he went straight up to the supposed lion, picked up a couple of glow-worms, and brought them to the camp-fires, much to the amusement of the men, especially of Jumbo, and greatly to the confusion of the valorous interpreter, who, according to his invariable custom when danger threatened, was found to have sought refuge in a tree.

This incident furnished ground for much discussion and merriment during supper, in which Antonio, being in no wise ashamed of himself, joined noisily; and Chimbolo took occasion to reprove Disco for his rashness, telling him that it was impossible to kill lions in the jungle during the darkness of night, and that, if they did pay them a visit, it would be wise to let them be, and trust to the camp-fires keeping them at a respectful distance. To which Disco retorted that he didn't believe there was any lions in Afriky, for he'd heard a deal about 'em an' travelled far, but had not yet heard the sound of their woices, an', wot was more, didn't expect to.

Before that night was far advanced, Disco was constrained to acknowledge himself in error, for a veritable lion did actually prowl down to the camp, and salute them with a roar which had a wonderfully awe-inspiring effect on every member of the party, especially on those who heard it for the first time in their lives.

Just before the arrival of this nocturnal visitor, one of the men had been engaged in some poetic effusions, which claim preliminary notice here, because they were rudely terminated by the lion.

This man was one of Kambira's people, and had joined the party by permission. He was one of those beings who, gifted with something like genius, or with superior powers of some sort, have sprung up in Africa, as elsewhere, no doubt from time immemorial, to dazzle their fellows for a little, and then pass away, leaving a trail of tradition behind them. The existence there, in time past, of men of mind far in advance of their fellows, as well as of heroes whose physical powers were marvellous, may be assumed from the fact that some such exist at the present time, as well as from tradition. Some of these heroes have excited the admiration of large districts by their wisdom, others by their courage or their superior dexterity with the spear and bow, like William Tell and Robin Hood, but the memory of these must soon have been obliterated for want of literature. The man who had joined Harold was a poet and a musician. He was an *improvvisatore*, composed verses on the incidents that occurred as they travelled along, and sang them with an accompaniment on an instrument called the *sansa*, which had nine iron keys and a calabash for a sounding-board.

The poet's name was Mokompa. With the free and easy disposition of his race, he allowed his fancy to play round the facts of which he sang, and was never at a loss, for, if the right word did not come readily, he spun out the measure with musical sounds which meant nothing at all.

After supper was over, or rather when the first interval of repose occurred, Mokompa, who was an obliging and hearty little fellow, was called on for a song. Nothing loath, he seized his sansa and began a ditty, of which the following, given by Antonio, may be regarded as a remarkably free, not to say easy, translation:—

MOKOMPA'S SONG.

Kambira goes to hunt,
Yo ho!
Him's spear am nebber blunt,
Yo ho!
Him kill de buff'lo quick,
An' lub de porridge thick;
Him chase de lion too,
An' stick um troo an' troo.
De 'potimus as well,
An' more dan me can tell,
Hab down before um fell,
Yo ho!
De English come to see,
Yo ho!
Dat werry good for we,
Yo ho!
No' take us 'way for slaves,
Nor put us in our graves,
But set de black mans free,

R. M. Ballantyne

W'en cotch um on de sea.
Dem splendid shooters, too,
We knows what dey can do
Wid boil an' roast an' stew,
Yo ho!
One makes um's gun go crack,
Yo ho!
An elephant on um's back,
Yo ho!
De drefful lion roar,
De gun goes crack once more,
De bullet fly an' splits
One monkey into bits,
Yo ho!
De glow-worm next arise,
De Englishman likewise
Wid werry much surprise,
An' hit um 'tween de eyes,
"Hooray! hooray!" um cries,
An' run to fetch um's prize—
Yo ho!

The last "Yo ho!" was given with tremendous energy, and followed by peals of laughter.

It was at this point that the veritable lion thought proper to join in, which he did, as we have said, with a roar so tremendous that it not only put a sudden stop to the music, but filled the party with so much alarm that they sprang to their arms with surprising agility.

Mindful of Chimbolo's previous warning, neither Harold nor Disco sought to advance, but both looked at their savage friend for advice.

Now, in some parts of Africa there exists a popular belief

that the souls of departed chiefs enter into lions and render them sacred, and several members of Harold Seadrift's party entertained this notion. Chimbolo was one of these. From the sounds of growling and rending which issued from the thicket, he knew that the lion in question was devouring part of their buffalo-meat which had been hung on the branch of a neighbouring tree, not, however, near enough to the fires to be visible. Believing that the beast was a chief in disguise, Chimbolo advanced a little towards the place where he was, and, much to our traveller's amusement, gave him a good scolding.

"*You* call yourself a chief, do you—eh?" he said sternly. "What kind of a chief can *you* be, to come sneaking about in the dark like this, trying to steal our buffalo-meat! Are you not ashamed of yourself? A pretty chief, truly; you are like the scavenger-beetle, and think of yourself only; you have not the heart of a chief. Why don't you kill your own beef? You must have a stone in your chest, and no heart at all."

"That's werry flowery lingo, but it don't seem to convince him," said Disco, with a quiet smile, as the lion, which had been growling continuously over its meal all the time, wound up Chimbolo's speech with another terrific roar.

At this point another believer in transmigration of souls, a quiet man who seldom volunteered remarks on any subject, stepped forward and began seriously to expostulate with the lion.

"It is very wrong of you," he said, "to treat strangers in this fashion. You might have more respect for Englishmen who have come to see your land, and never did you any harm. We are travelling peaceably through the country; we never kill anybody, and never steal anything; the buffalo-meat is ours, not yours, and it ill becomes a great chief like you to be prowling about in the dark, like a hyena, trying to steal the meat of strangers. Surely you can hunt for yourself—there is plenty of meat in the forest." [See Livingstone's *Zambesi and its Tributaries*, page 160.]

As the lion was equally deaf to this man's reasoning, Harold thought it right to try a more persuasive plan. He drew up in a line all the men who had guns, and at a word of command they fired a volley of balls into the jungle, in the direction whence the sounds issued. A dead silence followed, but it was deemed advisable not to venture in to see the effect, as men had frequently lost their lives by so doing. A watch, however, was kept during the night, and the fires were well replenished, for they knew that the king of the forest usually shrinks from doing his evil deeds in the light of a strong camp-fire. We say usually—because they are not always thus shy. Authentic instances are on record of lions having leaped into the centre of a bivouac, and carried off one of the men in spite of being smitten in the face with flaming firebrands. Fortunately the lion of which we write thought "discretion the better part of valour." He retired peaceably, nevertheless Disco and his friend continued to dream of him all night so vividly that they started up several times, and seized their rifles, under the impression that he had roared his loudest into their very ears, and after each of these occasions they crept back into their sleeping bags to re-dream of the lion!

The "bag" which formed each man's couch was made simply of two mats sewed together, and left open, not at one of the ends but at one of the sides, so that a man could roll out of or into it more easily than he could have slid, feet first, into a sack. It was large enough also for two to sleep inside together, always supposing that the two were of accommodating dispositions!

That they had now reached a land which swarmed with wild

animals was intimated to some extent by the running past, within fifty yards of their bivouac, of a troop of elephants. It was daybreak at the time, so that, having been thus rudely aroused, they did not deem it necessary to return to rest but after taking a hasty mouthful of food, set forth on their journey.

The usual mode of proceeding on the march was as follows:—They rose about five o'clock, or soon after the appearance of dawn, and swallowed a cup of tea, with a bit of biscuit, then some of the men folded up the blankets and stowed them away in the bags, others tied up the cooking utensils, etcetera, in bundles, and hung them at the ends of carrying-sticks, which they bore upon their shoulders. The process did not take long. They were soon on the march, either in single file, if the path were narrow, or in groups, according to fancy, where the ground admitted of their spreading out. About nine, a convenient spot was chosen for a halt to breakfast, which meat, although not "*eaten* the night before in order to save time in the morning," was at all events *cooked* on the previous evening for the same end, so that it only needed warming up. Then the march was resumed; a short rest was allowed in the heat of the day, when, of course, Disco had a pipe and much sagacious intercourse with his fellows, and they finally encamped for the remainder of the day and night early in the afternoon. Thus they travelled five or six hours at a stretch, and averaged from twelve to fifteen miles a day, which is about as much as Europeans can stand in a hot climate without being oppressed. This Disco called "taking it easy," and so it was when compared with the custom of some travellers, whose chief end would appear to be the getting over as much ground as possible in a given time, in order that they may afterwards boast of the same, and for the accomplishment of which they are obliged to abuse and look ferocious at the blacks, cock their pistols, and flourish their whips, in a

R. M. Ballantyne

manner which is only worthy of being styled contemptible and cowardly. We need not say that our friends Harold and Disco had no such propensities. They had kindly consideration for the feelings of their "niggers," coupled with great firmness; became very sociable with them, and thus got hearty, willing work out of them. But to return from this digression.

During the day, the number of animals of all sorts that were seen was so great as to induce Disco to protest, with a slap of his thigh, that the whole land, from stem to stern, seemed to him to be one prodigious zoological garden—it did, an' no mistake about it.

Disco was not far wrong. He and Harold having started ahead of the party, with Chimbolo as their guide, came on a wonderful variety of creatures in rapid succession. First, they fell in with some large flocks of guinea-fowl, and shot a few for dinner. As they advanced, various birds ran across their path, and clouds of turtle-doves filled the air with the blatter of their wings as they rose above the trees. Ducks, geese, and francolins helped to swell the chorus of sounds.

When the sun rose and sent a flood of light over a wide and richly wooded vale, into which they were about to descend, a herd of pallahs stood gazing at the travellers in stupid surprise, and allowed them to approach within sixty yards before trotting leisurely away. These and all other animals were passed unmolested, as the party had sufficient meat at the time, and Harold made it a point not to permit his followers to shoot animals for the mere sake of sport, though several of them were uncommonly anxious to do so. Soon afterwards a herd of waterbucks were passed, and then a herd of koodoos, with two or three magnificently-horned bucks amongst them, which hurried off to the hillsides on seeing the travellers. Antelopes also were seen, and buffaloes, grazing beside their path.

Ere long they came upon a small pond with a couple of elephants standing on its brink, cooling their huge sides by drawing water into their trunks and throwing it all over themselves. Behind these were several herds of zebras and waterbucks, all of which took to flight on "getting the wind" of man. They seemed intuitively to know that he was an enemy. Wild pigs, also, were common, and troops of monkeys, large and small, barked, chattered, grinned, and made faces among the trees.

After pitching the camp each afternoon, and having had a mouthful of biscuit, the two Englishmen were in the habit of going off to hunt for the daily supply of fresh meat accompanied by Chimbolo as their guide and game-carrier, Antonio as their interpreter, and Mokompa as their poet and jester. They did not indeed, appoint Mokompa to that post of honour, but the little worthy took it upon himself, for the express purpose of noting the deeds of the white men, in order to throw his black comrades into convulsions over supper by a poetic recital of the same.

"It pleases them, an' it don't hurt us," was Disco's observation on this head.

On the afternoon, then, of which we write, the party of four went out to hunt, while the encampment was being prepared under the superintendence of Jumbo, who had already proved himself to be an able manager and cook, as also had his countrymen Masiko and Zombo.

"What a rich country!" exclaimed Harold, looking round in admiration from the top of a small hillock on as fine a scene as one could wish to behold, "and what a splendid cotton country it might be if properly cultivated!"

"So it is," said Disco, "an' I shouldn't wonder if there wos lots of gold too, if we only knew where to look for it."

"Gold!" exclaimed Antonio, who sat winking placidly on the stump of a fallen tree; "dere be lots ob gold near Zambesi—an' oder ting too."

"Let's hear wot are some of the other things," said Disco.

"What are dere?—oh, let me see: der be coal, lots ob coal on Zambesi, any amount ob it, an' it burn fuss-rate, too. Dere be iron-ore, very much, an' indigo, an' sugar-cane, an ivory; you hab hear an' see yooself about de elephants an' de cottin, an' tobacco. [See Livingstone's *Zambesi and its Tributaries*, page 52.] Oh! great plenty ob eberyting eberywhere in dis yere country, but," said Antonio, with a shrug of his shoulders, "no can make noting out ob it on account ob de slave-trade."

"Then I 'spose 'ee don't approve of the slave-trade?" said Disco.

"No, dat am true," replied Antonio; "de country very good for slave-trader, but no good for man like me what want to trade proper."

"H'm! I've more respect for 'ee than I had," said Disco. "I 'spose you've bin up in these parts before now, have 'ee?"

"No, nevah, but I hab sister what marry one nigger, one slave, what sold himself, an' him tell me much 'bout it. Hims bin up here many time."

"Sold himself!" repeated Harold in surprise. "What do you mean?"

"Mean dat," returned Antonio. "Him was a black free-man—call him Chibanti; him was all alone in de world, lose fader, moder, broder, sister, wife, eberyting by slave-trader, who steal dem all away or murder dem. So Chibanti him say, 'What de use of be free?' So him go to one master, who berry good to hims niggers—gib dem plenty to eat an' little to do—an' sole hisself to him."

"An' wot did he get for himself?" asked Disco.

"Got ninety yard ob cottin cloth."

"Did he consider himself cheap or dear at that?" inquired Disco.

"Oh, dear—awful dear!"

"What has come of him now?" asked Harold.

"Dunno," answered Antonio. "After him got de cloth, hims master send him to Quillimane wid cargo ob ivory, an' gib him leave to do leetil trade on hims own account; so him bought a man, a woman, an' a boy, for sixty yard ob cottin, an' wid de rest hired slaves for de voyage down, an' drove a mos' won'erful trade. But long time since me hear ob him. P'raps hims good master be dead, an' him go wid de rest of de goods an' chattels to a bad master, who berry soon make him sorry him sole hisself."

Pushing forward for several days in the manner which we have attempted to describe, our travellers passed through many varied scenes, which, however, all bore one mark in common, namely, teeming animal and vegetable life. Human beings were also found to be exceedingly numerous, but not so universally distributed as the others, for, although many villages and hamlets were passed, the inhabitants of which were all peacefully inclined and busy in their fields, or with their native cotton, iron, and pottery manufactures, vast expanses of rich ground were also traversed, which, as far as man was concerned, appeared to be absolute solitudes.

Entering upon one of these about noon of a remarkably fine day, Harold could not help remarking on the strange stillness which pervaded the air. No sound was heard from beast, bird, or insect; no village was near, no rippling stream murmured, or zephyr stirred the leaves; in short, it was a scene which, from its solitude and profound silence, became oppressive.

"W'y, sir," said Disco, whose face was bathed in perspiration, "it do seem to me as if we'd got to the fag-end of the world altogether. There ain't nothin' nowhere."

Harold laughed, and said it looked like it. But Disco was wrong. It was only the hour when animals seem to find a *siesta* indispensable, and vegetables as well as air had followed their example. A few minutes sufficed to prove their mistake, for, on entering a piece of woodland, a herd of pallahs, and another of water-bucks, appeared, standing as quiet and still as if they were part of a painted landscape. Then, in passing a thick clump of thorns, they could see, through openings in the bushes, the dim phantom-like forms of buffaloes, with heads lowered and eyes glaring at them, ready to charge, if need be, though too lazy from heat, apparently, to begin the 'fray, and willing to act on the principle of "let be for let be." Still farther on, a native was observed keeping at a respectful distance. He had seen the travellers from afar, and come with noiseless tread to get a nearer view.

Halting to rest the party for a few minutes in a shady hollow, Harold threw himself at full length on the grass, but Disco, who, strange to say, did not feel inclined to smoke at the moment—probably because he had only just finished his fifth pipe a few minutes previously—sauntered on alone to the top of the next ridge.

He had barely reached the summit when Harold, who chanced to be looking after him, observed that he crouched suddenly behind a bush, and, after gazing steadfastly for a few seconds over the hill, turned and ran back, making excessively wild demonstrations with head and arms, but uttering no sound.

Of course the whole party sprang up and ran towards the excited mariner, and soon were near enough to understand that his violent actions were meant to caution them to make no noise.

"Hush!" he said eagerly, on coming near enough to be heard; "keep quiet as mice. There's a slave-gang, or somethin' uncommon like it, goin' along on right athwart us."

Without a word of reply, the whole party hurried forward and gained a point of observation behind the low bushes which crowned the ridge.

R. M. Ballantyne

CHAPTER FIFTEEN

SHOWS SOME OF THE EFFECTS OF THE SLAVE-TRADE AT THE FOUNTAIN-HEAD

Down in a gorge, just below the spot where Harold Seadrift and his men lay concealed, a strange sight met the eyes of the two Englishmen, in regard to which, despite all that they had heard and seen, and were prepared to see, they were as much shocked as if it had never been presented even to their imaginations up to that moment.

It was a gang of slaves winding its way slowly but steadily through the gorge.

The head of the dusky procession was just emerging on the open ground beyond the gorge when the travellers first came upon it. The slaves advanced towards the spot where they lay, passing under it so closely that they could see the very expressions on the faces of the men, women, and children who composed the gang. These expressions were varied and very terrible. Our travellers had now reached the fountain-head whence the perennial stream of "Black Ivory" flows out of Africa. The process of manufacture, although considerably advanced, had not yet reached that perfection of callous subjection and settled despair which had struck our Englishmen so forcibly in the slave-market of Zanzibar.

There was anxiety not unmingled with faint hope in the faces of some of the women; and a few of the more stalwart and courageous among the men wore a fierce, determined aspect which told of manhood not yet absolutely prostrated in the dust of abject servility, while, in regard to some of the children, surprise at the peculiar circumstances of their surroundings had not yet been swallowed up in a condition of chronic terror.

They marched in a long line, fastened to each other by chains and ropes and heavy "gorees" or slave-sticks. The latter implements were poles from six to seven feet long, with a fork at the end of each, in which the necks of the men were fitted and secured by means of an iron bolt, passing across the throat and riveted at both ends. To render marching possible with such encumbrances, the men went in couples, one behind the other, so that the slave-stick of the leading man could be tied to the stick of his fellow behind, which was slewed round to the front for the purpose. Their wrists were also tied, some in front, others behind their backs. Secured thus, Hercules himself might have been reduced to obedience, especially if he had felt the frequent sting of the cruel lash that was laid on these captives, a lash whose power was made manifest by the numerous seams and scars which crossed and recrossed their backs and limbs. The women and children were deemed sufficiently secure by being fastened to each other with ropes and iron rings round their necks. All were naked, with the exception of a little piece of cloth round the loins, and some of the women had infants of a few weeks old strapped to their backs by means of this shred of cloth, while others carried baskets on their heads containing meal for the sustenance of the party during their journey.

In advance of the line marched a tall, powerfully-built half-caste, armed with a musket and small axe, and clad in a loose

R. M. Ballantyne

coat, short drawers reaching the knees, and straw hat. He was obviously the commander of the band. Behind him came several negroes, also armed with muskets, and with thick wands for the purpose of flagellation. These wore loin-cloths and turbans or red caps, but nothing more. They laughed, talked and strutted as they went along, forming a marked contrast to the silent and depressed slaves.

At intervals along the line, and in rear, there were stationed one or two of these drivers, who urged on their "cattle" with more or less cruelty, according to their individual impulses or natures.

We need scarcely say that this sight filled Harold and Disco not only with feelings of horror and pity, but with sensations of towering indignation that almost suffocated them. Those who only read of such things at home can form but a faint conception of what it is actually to behold them.

"We must fight!" muttered Harold between his teeth.

Disco could not speak, but he looked at his companion, and gave a nod that plainly indicated the state of his feelings.

"'Sh!" hissed Chimbolo, creeping up at that moment and laying his hand, which trembled violently, on Harold's shoulder, "Marizano!"

"What! the scoundrel in advance?"

Chimbolo pointed to the leader of the slave-gang, and almost foamed at the mouth with suppressed rage.

At that moment their attention was attracted to a woman who walked immediately behind the slavers. She was a young and, according to African ideas, a comely girl, but was apparently very weak—so weak that she panted and stumbled as she went along, a circumstance which was accounted for by the little infant tied to her back, which could not have been more than a couple of weeks old. Stumbling against the fallen branch of a tree, she fell at last with a low wail to the ground, and made no effort, as on previous occasions, to recover herself.

The whole gang stopped, and Marizano, turning back, pushed the woman with his foot.

A fine-looking young man, who was the leader in a couple secured by a slave-stick, seemed to regard this woman with a degree of interest that argued near relationship. He started forward half involuntarily when the Portuguese half-caste kicked her. He had forgotten for an instant his fellow in rear, as well as the bar of the goree across his throat, which checked him violently; at the same time one of the drivers, who had observed the movement, laid a supple wand across his bare back so sharply as to draw forth a terrific yell of agony.

This was too much for Disco Lillihammer. Unable to restrain himself, he leaped up, seized his rifle by the muzzle with both hands, and, swinging it round his head, rushed upon Marizano with a bursting shout of rage and defiance.

It is probable that the half-caste leader, who was by no means destitute of courage, would have stood his ground had his assailant been a man of colour, but this unexpected apparition of a white man with a fiery countenance and blue eyes that absolutely flashed as he rushed forward with irresistible fury, was too much for him. Firing hastily, and with bad aim, Marizano turned and fled into the woods, followed by all his men. There was however a large band of Ajawa savages in rear, armed with bows and poisoned

R. M. Ballantyne

arrows. When he encountered these the Portuguese chief halted, and, rallying his men, took shelter behind trees and began to fire at the advancing enemy.

Seeing this, Harold drew his men together and made them fire a united volley, which had the effect of utterly routing the slavers. Disco meanwhile, finding that he could not overtake Marizano, at last did what he ought to have done at first—kneeled down, took deliberate aim at him, and fired. His agitation prevented accuracy of aim; nevertheless he succeeded in sending a bullet through the fleshy part of the man's arm, above the elbow, which effectually put him to flight.

Returning to the slaves, who had been left standing where they were first stopped, in a state of great surprise and perplexity, he assisted his companions in freeing them. This was easy enough in regard to the women and children, but the gorees on the men were very difficult to remove. Being riveted, as we have said, it became necessary to split the forks with hatchets, an operation which endangered the heads of the poor captives and hurt their galled necks considerably. It was accomplished however in the midst of a deal of excitement and hurried conversation, while Jumbo and his comrades kindled fires, and Harold bade the women cook the meal—which they had hitherto carried—for themselves and their children. They seemed to consider this too good news to be true, but on being encouraged, began with alacrity.

"Don't be afeared, lass," cried Disco, patting a young woman on the head, "eat as much as 'ee like. You need it, poor thing, an' stuff the childer till they can't hold no more. Bu'st 'em if 'ee can. The slavers won't come back here in a hurry. Ha! I only wish they would, an' let us have a brush with 'em. But there's no such luck. Cowards never fight 'xcept w'en they're sure to win.—Now, piccaninny, here you are," he said, stuffing some raw mapira meal into the open mouth of a thin little girl of about six or seven, who was gazing at him in open-eyed surprise; "don't put off time, you're half-starved already!"

The little black skeleton began to chew the dry meal with evident satisfaction, but without taking her eyes off her deliverer.

"Who are *you*?" asked a somewhat older girl of Harold, whom she regarded with looks of reverence and wonder.

Of course Harold did not understand her, but he immediately called Antonio, who translated.

"Who are you?" she said; "the other people tied and starved us, but you cut the ropes and tell us to eat; what sort of people are you? Where did you come from?"

To this Harold replied briefly that he was an Englishman, who hated slavers and slavery, but he said nothing more at that time, as he intended to have a palaver and explanation with the freed captives after their meal was over.

There was a great clapping of hands among the slaves, expressive of gratitude, on hearing that they were free.

About a hundred sat down to that meal, most of whom were women and children, and the manner in which they devoured the food set before them, told eloquently of their previous sufferings. At first they timidly held back, scarce venturing to believe that their new captors, as they thought them, were in earnest. But when their doubts and fears were removed, they attacked the mapira porridge like ravening wolves. Gradually the human element began to reappear, in the shape of a comment or a smile, and before long the women were chatting together, and a few of the stronger among the young children were making feeble attempts to play.

When the oldest man of the party, who appeared to be between twenty and thirty, was brought forward and questioned, he gave some interesting and startling information.

"Tell him," said Harold to Antonio, "that we are Englishmen; that we belong to the same nation as the great white man Dr Livingstone, who travelled through this land some years ago—the nation which hates slavery because the Great God hates it, and would have all men to be free, to serve each other in love, and to do to other people as they would have other people do to them. Ask him, also, where he comes from, and who captured him and his companions."

To this the negro replied—"What the white man says may be true, but the white men seem to tell lies too much. The men who killed our warriors, burned our villages, and took our women and children away, came to us saying that they were friends; that they were the servants of the same people as the white man Livingstone, and wanted to trade with us. When we believed and trusted them, and were off our guard, they fired on us with their guns. We know not what to think or to believe."

Harold was much perplexed by this reply, for he knew not what evidence to cite in proof that he, at least was not a deceiver.

"Tell him," he said at length, "that there are false white men as well as true, and that the best proof I can give him that I am one of the true is, to set him and his friends at liberty. They are now as free to go where they please as we are."

On receiving this assurance the negro retired to consult with his friends. Meanwhile Antonio, who seemed to have been touched by the unvarying kindness with which he had been treated by his employers, opened his mind to them, and gave them a good deal of information, of which the substance is as follows:—

At that time the merchants of the Portuguese inland town of Tette, on the Zambesi, were carrying on the slave-trade with unusual vigour, for this reason, that they found it difficult to obtain ivory except in exchange for slaves. In former years they had carried on a trade in ivory with a tribe called the Banyai, these Banyai being great elephant-hunters, but it happened that they went to war with another tribe named the Matabele, who had managed to steal from them all their women and children. Consequently, the forlorn Banyai said to the Tette merchants, when they went to trade with them as they had been accustomed to do, "We do not want your merchandise. Bring us women and children, and you shall have as much ivory as you wish."

These good people of Tette—being chiefly half-caste Portuguese, and under Portuguese government, and claiming, as they do, to be the possessors of that region of Africa—are so utterly incapable of holding their own, that they are under the necessity of paying tribute to a tribe of savages who come down annually to Tette to receive it, and who, but for that tribute, would, as they easily could, expel them from the land. These merchants of Tette, moreover, in common with all the Portuguese in Africa, are by the laws of Portugal prohibited from engaging in the *export* slave-trade. They are not, however, forbidden to engage temporarily in the "domestic slave-trade," hence they had sent out slaving parties—in other words, robbers, kidnappers, murderers—who hired the warlike Ajawa tribe to aid them in killing the Manganja men, and robbing them of their wives and little ones, by which means they were enabled to supply the demand for such "cattle" among the Banyai, and thus obtained the desired supply of ivory! So vigorously had this slave traffic been carried on, at the time of which we write, that no fewer than two hundred people—mostly women and children—were carried out of the hill-country every week. [See *The Universities' Mission to Central Africa*, page 112.]

In a short time the negro returned to the place where Harold and Disco were seated, and said that he believed his white deliverers were true men, but added that he and his people had no home to go to; their village having been burnt, and all the old people and warriors killed or dispersed by Marizano, who was a terribly cruel man. In proof of this assertion he said that only the day before, Marizano had shot two of the women for attempting to untie their thongs; a man had been killed with an axe because he had broken-down with fatigue; and a woman had her infant's brains dashed out because she was unable to carry it, as well as the load assigned to her.

"It is difficult to decide what one should do in these circumstances," said Harold to Disco. "You know it would never do to leave these helpless people here to starve; but if we take them on with us our progress will be uncommonly slow."

"We'd better take 'em back," said Disco.

"Back! Where to?"

"W'y, to the last village wot we passed through. It ain't more than a day's march, an' I'm sure the old feller as is capting of it would take care o' the lot."

"There is good advice in that, yet I grudge to go back," said Harold; "if there were a village the same distance in advance,

I would rather take them on."

"But there ain't," returned Disco. "Hallo! I say, wot's wrong with Tony?"

The interpreter came forward with a look of much excitement as he spoke.

"What now, Antonio?"

"Oh! it's drefful," replied the interpreter. "Dey tells me have hear Marizano speak ob anoder slaving party what go straight to Kambira's village for attack it."

"Who told you that? Are they sure?" asked Harold hastily.

"Two, t'ree mans tole me," replied Antonio. "All say same ting. Too late to help him now, me's 'fraid."

"Never say too late," cried Disco, starting up; "never say die while there's a shot in the locker. It may be time enough yet if we only look sharp. I votes that we leave nearly all the provisions we have with these poor critters here; up anchor, 'bout ship, clap on all sail, and away this werry minit."

Harold agreed with this advice heartily, and at once acted on it. The arrangements were quickly made, the provisions distributed, an explanation made, and in less than an hour the travellers were retracing their steps in hot haste.

By taking a straight line and making forced marches, they arrived in sight of the ridge where they had last seen Kambira, on the evening of the third day. As they drew near Harold pushed impatiently forward, and, outrunning his companions, was first to reach the summit. Disco's heart sank within him, for he observed that his companion stood still, bowed his head, and covered his face with both hands. He soon joined him, and a groan burst from the seaman's breast when he saw dense volumes of smoke rising above the spot where the village had so recently lain a picture of peaceful beauty.

Even their followers, accustomed though they were, to scenes and deeds of violence and cruelty, could not witness the grief of the Englishmen unmoved.

"P'raps," said Disco, in a husky voice, "there's some of 'em left alive, hidin' in the bushes."

"It may be so," replied Harold, as he descended the slope with rapid strides. "God help them!"

A few minutes sufficed to bring them to the scene of ruin, but the devastation caused by the fire was so great that they had difficulty in recognising the different spots where the huts had stood. Kambira's hut was, however, easily found, as it stood on a rising ground. There the fight with the slavers had evidently been fiercest, for around it lay the charred and mutilated remains of many human bodies. Some of these were so far distinguishable that it could be told whether they belonged to man, woman, or child.

"Look here!" said Disco, in a deep, stern voice, as he pointed to an object on the ground not far from the hut.

It was the form of a woman who had been savagely mangled by her murderers. The upturned and distorted face proved it to be Yohama, the grandmother of little Obo. Near to her lay the body of a grey-haired negro, who might to judge from his position, have fallen in attempting to defend her.

"Oh! if the people of England only saw this sight!" said

Harold, in a low tone; "if they only believed in and *realised* this fact, there would be one universal and indignant shout of 'No toleration of slavery anywhere throughout the world!'"

"Look closely for Kambira or his son," he added, turning to his men.

A careful search among the sickening remains was accordingly made, but without any discovery worth noting being made, after which they searched the surrounding thickets. Here sad evidence of the poor fugitives having been closely pursued was found in the dead bodies of many of the old men and women, and of the very young children and infants; also the bodies of a few of the warriors. All these had been speared, chiefly through the back. Still they were unsuccessful in finding the bodies of the chief or his little boy.

"It's plain," said Disco, "that they have either escaped or been took prisoners."

"Here is some one not quite dead," said Harold,—"Ah! poor fellow!"

He raised the unfortunate man's head on his knee, and recognised the features of the little man who had entertained them with his tunes on the native violin.

It was in vain that Antonio tried to gain his attention while Disco moistened his lips with water. He had been pierced in the chest with an arrow. Once only he opened his eyes, and a faint smile played on his lips, as if he recognised friends, but it faded quickly and left the poor musician a corpse.

Leaving, with heavy hearts, the spot where they had spent such pleasant days and nights, enjoying the hospitality of Kambira and his tribe, our travellers began to retrace their steps to the place where they had left the rescued slaves, but that night the strong frame of Disco Lillihammer succumbed to the influence of climate. He was suddenly stricken with African fever, and in a few hours became as helpless as a little child.

In this extremity Harold found it necessary to encamp. He selected the highest and healthiest spot in the neighbourhood, caused his followers to build a rude, but comparatively comfortable, hut and set himself diligently to hunt for, and to tend, his sick friend.

CHAPTER SIXTEEN

TREATS OF LOVE, HATRED, AND SORROW, AND PROVES THAT SLAVERY AND ITS CONSEQUENCES ARE NOT CONFINED TO BLACK MEN AND WOMEN

We must now change the scene to the garden of that excellent Governor, Senhor Francisco Alfonso Toledo Bignoso Letotti, and the date to three months in advance of the period in which occurred the events related in the last chapter.

"Maraquita, I am sorry to find that you still persist in encouraging that morbid regret for the loss of one who cannot now be recovered."

Thus spoke the Governor in tones that were unusually petulant for one who idolised his child.

"Father, why did you sell her without saying a word to me about your intention? It was very, very, *very* unkind—indeed it was."

Poor Maraquita's eyes were already red and swollen with much weeping, nevertheless she proceeded to increase the redness and the swelling by a renewed burst of passionate distress.

The worthy Governor found it difficult to frame a reply or to administer suitable consolation, for in his heart he knew that he had sold Azinte, as it were surreptitiously, to Marizano for an unusually large sum of money, at a time when his daughter was absent on a visit to a friend. The noted Portuguese kidnapper, murderer, rebel and trader in black ivory, having recovered from his wound, had returned to the town, and, being well aware of Azinte's market value, as a rare and remarkably beautiful piece of ivory of extra-superfine quality, had threatened, as well as tempted, Governor Letotti beyond his powers of resistance. Marizano did not want the girl as his own slave. He wanted dollars, and, therefore, destined her for the markets of Arabia or Persia, where the smooth-tongued and yellow-skinned inhabitants hold that robbery, violence, and cruelty, such as would make the flesh of civilised people creep, although horrible vices in themselves, are nevertheless, quite justifiable when covered by the sanction of that miraculous talisman called a "domestic institution." The British Government had, by treaty, agreed to respect slavery in the dominions of the Sultan of Zanzibar, as a domestic institution with which it would not interfere!

Governor Letotti's heart had smitten him at first for he really was an amiable man, and felt kindly disposed to humanity at large, slaves included. Unfortunately the same kindliness was concentrated with tenfold power on himself, so that when self-interest came into play the amiable man became capable of deeds that Marizano himself might have been proud of. The only difference, in fact, between the two was that the Governor, like the drunkard, often felt ashamed of himself, and sometimes wished that he were a better man, while the man-stealer gloried in his deeds, and had neither wish nor intention to improve.

"Maraquita," said Senhor Letotti, still somewhat petulantly, though with more of remonstrance in his tone, "how can you speak so foolishly? It was out of my power you know, to speak to you when you were absent about what I intended to do. Besides, I was, at the time, very much in need of some ready money, for, although I am rich enough, there are times when most of my capital is what business men called 'locked up,' and therefore not immediately available. In these circumstances, Marizano came to me with a very tempting offer. But there are plenty of good-looking, amiable, affectionate girls in Africa. I can easily buy you another slave quite as good as Azinte."

"As good as Azinte!" echoed Maraquita wildly, starting up and gazing at her father with eyes that flashed through her tears, "Azinte, who has opened her heart to me—her bursting, bleeding heart—and told me all her former joys and all her present woes, and who loves me as she loves—ay, better than she loves—her own soul, merely because I dropped a few tears of sympathy on her little hand! Another as good as Azinte!" she cried with increasing vehemence; "would *you* listen with patience to any one who should talk to you of another as good as Maraquita?"

"Nay, but," remonstrated the Governor, "you are now raving; your feelings towards Azinte cannot be compared with my love for *you*."

"If you loved me as I thought you did, you would not—you could not—have thus taken from me my darling little maid. Oh! shame, shame on you, father—"

She could say no more, but rushed from the room to fling herself down and sob out her feelings in the privacy of her own chamber, where she was sought out by the black cook, who had overheard some of the conversation, and was a sympathetic soul. But that amiable domestic happened to be inopportunely officious; she instantly fled from the chamber, followed by the neatest pair of little slippers imaginable, which hit her on the back of her woolly head,—for Maraquita, like other spoilt children, had made up her mind *not* to be comforted.

Meanwhile the Governor paced the floor of his drawing-room with uneasy feelings, which, however, were suddenly put to flight by the report of a gun. Hastening to the window, he saw that the shot had been fired by a war-steamer which was entering the bay.

"Ha! the 'Firefly;' good!" exclaimed the Governor, with a gratified look; "this will put it all right."

He said nothing more, but left the room hastily. It may however be as well to explain that his remark had reference to the mutual affection which he was well aware existed between his daughter and the gallant Lieutenant Lindsay. He had not, indeed, the most remote intention of permitting Maraquita to wed the penniless officer, but he had no objection whatever to their flirting as much as they pleased; and he readily perceived that nothing would be more likely to take the Senhorina's thoughts off her lost maid than the presence of her lover.

There was a bower in a secluded corner of the Governor Letotti's garden, a very charming bower indeed, in which Lieutenant Lindsay had been wont at times when duty to the Queen of England permitted, to hold sweet converse with the "queen of his soul." What that converse was it neither becomes us to say nor the reader to inquire. Perhaps it had reference to astronomy, perchance to domestic economy. At all events it was always eminently satisfactory to both parties engaged, save when the Senhorina indulged in a little touch of waywardness, and sent the poor officer back to his ship with a heavy heart, for the express purpose of teaching him the extent of her power and the value of her favour. She overclouded him now and then, just to make him the more ardently long for sunshine, and to convince him that in the highest sense of the word he was a slave!

To this bower, then, the Senhorina returned with a sad heart and swollen eyes, to indulge in vain regrets. Her sorrows had overwhelmed her to such an extent that she failed to observe the 'Firefly's' salute. It was therefore with a look of genuine surprise and agitation that she suddenly beheld Lieutenant Lindsay, who had availed himself of the first free moment, striding up the little path that led to the bower.

"Maraquita!" he exclaimed, looking in amazement at the countenance of his lady-love, which was what Norsemen style "begrutten."

But Maraquita was in no mood to be driven out of her humour, even by her lover.

"I am miserable," she said with vehemence, clenching one of her little fists as though she meditated an assault on the lieutenant—"utterly, absolutely, inconsolably miserable."

If Lindsay had entertained any doubt regarding the truth of her assertion, it would have been dispelled by her subsequent conduct, for she buried her face in a handkerchief and burst into tears.

"Beloved, adorable, tender, delicious Maraquita," were words which leapt into the lieutenant's mind, but he dare not utter them with his lips. Neither did he venture to clasp Maraquita's waist with his left arm, lay her pretty little head on his breast and smooth her luxuriant hair with his right hand, though he felt almost irresistibly tempted so to do— entirely from feelings of pity, of course,—for the Senhorina had hitherto permitted no familiarities beyond a gentle pressure of the hand on meeting and at parting.

It is unnecessary to repeat all that the bashful, though ardent, man of war said to Maraquita, or all that Maraquita said to the man of war; how, ignoring the celestial orbs and domestic economy, she launched out into a rhapsodical panegyric of Azinte; told how the poor slave had unburdened her heart to her about her handsome young husband and her darling little boy in the far off interior, from whom she had been rudely torn, and whom she never expected to see again; and how she, Maraquita, had tried to console Azinte by telling her that there was a heaven where good people might hope to meet again, even though they never met on earth, and a great deal more besides, to all of which the earnest lieutenant sought to find words wherewith to express his pity and sympathy, but found them not, though he was at no loss to find words to tell the queen of his soul that, in the peculiar circumstances of the case, and all things considered, his love for her (Maraquita) was tenfold more intense than it had ever been before!

"Foolish boy," said the Senhorina, smiling through her tears, "what is the use of telling me that? Can it do any good to Azinte?"

"Not much, I'm afraid," replied the lieutenant. "Well, then, don't talk nonsense, but tell me what I am to do to recover my little maid."

"It is impossible for me to advise," said the lieutenant with a perplexed look.

"But you *must* advise," said Maraquita, with great decision.

"Well, I will try. How long is it since Azinte was taken away from you?"

"About two weeks."

"You say that Marizano was the purchaser. Do you know to what part of the coast he intended to convey her?"

"How should I know? I have only just heard of the matter from my father."

"Well then, you must try to find out from your father all that he knows about Marizano and his movements. That is the first step. After that I will consider what can be done."

"Yes, Senhor," said Maraquita, rising suddenly, "you must consider quickly, and you must act at once, for you must not come here again until you bring me news of Azinte."

Poor Lindsay, who knew enough of the girl's character to believe her to be thoroughly in earnest, protested solemnly that he would do his utmost.

All that Maraquita could ascertain from her father was, that Marizano meant to proceed to Kilwa, the great slave-depot of the coast, there to collect a large cargo of slaves and proceed with them to Arabia, whenever he had reason to believe that the British cruisers were out of the way. This was not much to go upon, but the Senhorina was as unreasonable as were the Egyptians of old, when they insisted on the Israelites making bricks without straw.

He was unexpectedly helped out of his dilemma by Captain Romer, who called him into his cabin that same evening, told him that he had obtained information of the movements of slavers, which induced him to think it might be worth while to watch the coast to the northward of Cape Dalgado, and bade him prepare for a cruise in charge of the cutter, adding that the steamer would soon follow and keep them in view.

With a lightened heart Lindsay went off to prepare, and late that night the cutter quietly pulled away from the 'Firefly's' side, with a well-armed crew, and provisioned for a short cruise.

Their object was to proceed as stealthily as possible along the coast, therefore they kept inside of islands as much as possible, and cruised about a good deal at nights, always sleeping on board the boat, as the low-lying coast was very unhealthy, but landing occasionally to obtain water and to take a survey of the sea from convenient heights.

Early one morning as they were sailing with a very light breeze, between two small islands, a vessel was seen looming through the haze, not far from shore.

Jackson, one of the men, who has been introduced to the reader at an earlier part of this narrative, was the first to observe the strangers.

"It's a brig," he said; "I can make out her royals."

"No, it's a barque," said the coxswain.

A little midshipman, named Midgley, differed from both, and said it was a large dhow, for he could make out the top of its lateen sail.

"Whatever it is, we'll give chase," said Lindsay, ordering the men to put out the oars and give way, the sail being of little use.

In a few minutes the haze cleared sufficiently to prove that

Midgley was right. At the same time it revealed to those on board the dhow that they were being chased by the boat of a man-of-war. The little wind that blew at the time was insufficient to enable the dhow to weather a point just ahead of her, and the cutter rowed down on her so fast that it was evidently impossible for her to escape.

Seeing this, the commander of the dhow at once ran straight for the shore. Before the boat could reach her she was among the breakers on the bar, which were so terrible at that part of the coast as to render landing in a small boat quite out of the question. In a few minutes the dhow was hurled on the beach and began to break up, while her crew and cargo of slaves swarmed into the sea and tried to gain the shore. It seemed to those in the boat that some hundreds of negroes were struggling at one time in the seething foam.

"We must risk it, and try to save some of the poor wretches," cried Lindsay; "give way, lads, give way!"

The boat shot in amongst the breakers, and was struck by several seas in succession, and nearly swamped ere it reached the shore. But they were too late to save many of the drowning. Most of the strongest of the slaves had gained the shore and taken to the hills in wild terror, under the impression so carefully instilled into them by the Arabs, that the only object the Englishmen had in view was to catch, cook, and eat them! The rest were drowned, with the exception of two men and seven little children, varying from five to eight years of age, who were found crawling on the beach, in such a state of emaciation that they could not follow their companions into the bush. They tried, however, in their own feeble, helpless way, to avoid capture and the terrible fate which they thought awaited them.

These were soon lifted tenderly into the boat.

R. M. Ballantyne

"Here, Jackson," cried Lindsay, lifting one of the children in his strong arms, and handing it to the sailor, "carry that one very carefully, she seems to be almost gone. God help her, poor, poor child!"

There was good cause for Lindsay's pity, for the little girl was so thin that every bone in her body was sticking out— her elbow and knee-joints being the largest parts of her shrunken limbs, and it was found that she could not rise or even stretch herself out, in consequence, as was afterwards ascertained, of her having been kept for many days in the dhow in a sitting posture, with her knees doubled up against her face. Indeed, most of the poor little things captured were found to be more or less stiffened from the same cause.

An Arab interpreter had been sent with Lindsay, but he turned out to be so incapable that it was scarcely possible to gain any information from him. He was either stupid in reality, or pretended to be so. The latter supposition is not improbable, for many of the interpreters furnished to the men-of-war on that coast were found to be favourable to the slavers, insomuch that they have been known to mislead those whom they were paid to serve.

With great difficulty the cutter was pulled through the surf. That afternoon the 'Firefly' hove in sight, and took the rescued slaves on board.

Next day two boats from the steamer chased another dhow on shore, but with even less result than before, for the whole of the slaves escaped to the hills. On the day following, however, a large dhow was captured, with about a hundred and fifty slaves on board, all of whom were rescued, and the dhow destroyed.

The dhows which were thus chased or captured were all

regular and undisguised slavers. Their owners were openly engaged in what they knew was held to be piracy alike by the Portuguese, the Sultan of Zanzibar, and the English. They were exporting slaves from Africa to Arabia and Persia, which is an illegal species of traffic. In dealing with these, no difficulty was experienced except the difficulty of catching them. When caught, the dhows were invariably destroyed and the slaves set free—that is to say, carried to those ports where they might be set free with safety.

But there were two other sorts of traffickers in the bodies and souls of human beings, who were much more difficult to deal with.

There were, first the legal slave-traders, namely, the men who convey slaves by sea from one part of the Sultan of Zanzibar's dominions to another. This kind of slavery was prosecuted under the shelter of what we have already referred to as a domestic institution! It involved, as we have said before, brutality, injustice, cruelty, theft, murder, and extermination, but, being a domestic institution of Zanzibar, it was held to be *legal*, and the British Government have recognised and tolerated it by treaty for a considerable portion of this century!

It is, however, but justice to ourselves to say, that our Government entered into the treaty with the view of checking, limiting, and mitigating the evils of the slave-trade. We have erred in recognising any form of slavery, no matter how humane our object was—one proof of which is that we have, by our interference, unintentionally increased the evils of slavery instead of abating them.

It is worth while remarking here, that slavery is also a domestic institution in Arabia and Persia. If it be right that we should not interfere with the Zanzibar institution, why should we interfere with that of Arabia or Persia? Our treaty appears to have been founded on the principle that we ought to respect domestic institutions. We maintain a squadron on the east coast of Africa to stop the flow of Africans to the latter countries, while we permit the flow by *treaty*, as well as by practice, to the former. Is this consistent? The only difference between the two cases is one of distance, not of principle.

But to return to our point—the legal traders. In consequence of the Sultan's dominions lying partly on an island and partly on the mainland, his domestic institution necessitates boats, and in order to distinguish between his boats and the pirates, there is a particular season fixed in which he may carry his slaves by sea from one part of his dominions to another; and each boat is furnished with papers which prove it to be a "legal trader." This is the point on which the grand fallacy of *our* interference hinges. The "domestic institution" would be amply supplied by about 4000 slaves a year. The so-called legal traders are simply legalised deceivers, who transport not fewer than 30,000 slaves a year! It must be borne in mind that these 30,000 represent only a portion—the Zanzibar portion—of the great African slave-trade. From the Portuguese settlements to the south, and from the north by way of Egypt, the export of negroes as slaves is larger. It is estimated that the total number of human beings enslaved on the east and north-east coast of Africa is about 70,000 a year. As all authorities agree in the statement that, at the *lowest* estimate, only *one* out of every five captured survives to go into slavery, this number represents a loss to Africa of 350,000 human beings a year. They leave Zanzibar with full cargoes continually, with far more than is required for what we may term home-consumption. Nevertheless, correct papers are furnished to them by the Sultan, which protects them from British cruisers within the prescribed limits, namely, between Cape Dalgado and Lamoo, a line of coast about 1500 miles in extent. But it is easy for them to evade the cruisers in these wide seas and extensive coasts, and the value of Black Ivory is so great that the loss of a few is but a small matter. On reaching the northern limits the legal traders become pirates. They run to the northward, and take their chance of being captured by cruisers.

The reason of all this is very obvious. The Sultan receives nearly half a sovereign a head for each slave imported into Zanzibar, and our Governments, in time past, have allowed themselves to entertain the belief, that, by treaty, the Sultan could be induced to destroy this the chief source of his revenue!

Surely it is not too much to say, that *Great Britain ought to enter into no treaty whatever in regard to slavery, excepting such as shall provide for the absolute, total, and immediate extirpation thereof by whatsoever name called.*

Besides these two classes of slavers,—the open, professional pirates, and the sneaking, deceiving "domestic" slavers,—there are the slave-smugglers. They are men who profess to be, and actually are, legal traders in ivory, gum, copal, and other produce of Africa. These fellows manage to smuggle two or three slaves each voyage to the Black Ivory markets, under pretence that they form part of the crew of their dhows. It is exceedingly difficult, almost impossible, for the officers of our cruisers to convict these smugglers—to distinguish between slaves and crews, consequently immense numbers of slaves are carried off to the northern ports in this manner. Sometimes these dhows carry Arab or other passengers, and when there are so many slaves on board that it would be obviously absurd to pretend that they formed part of the crew, the owner dresses the poor wretches up in the habiliments that come most readily to hand, and passes them off as the wives or servants of these passengers. Any one might see at a glance that the stupid, silent, timid-looking creatures, who have had almost every human element beaten out of them, are nothing of the sort, but there is no means of *proving* them other than they are represented to be. If an interpreter were to ask them they would be ready to swear anything that their owner had commanded; hence the cruisers are deceived in every way—in many ways besides those now mentioned—and our philanthropic intentions are utterly thwarted; for the rescuing and setting free of 1000 or 2000 negroes a year out of the 30,000 annually exported, is not an adequate result for our great expense in keeping a squadron on the coast, especially when we consider that hundreds, probably thousands, of slaves perish amid horrible sufferings caused by the efforts of the man-stealers to avoid our cruisers. These would probably not lose their lives, and the entire body of slaves would suffer less, if we did not interfere at all.

From this we do not argue that non-interference would be best, but that as our present system of repression does not effectively accomplish what is aimed at, it ought to be changed. What the change should be, many wise and able men have stated. Their opinion we cannot quote here, but one thing taught to us by past experience is clear, we cannot cure the slave-trade by merely limiting it. Our motto in regard to slavery ought to be—*Total and immediate extinction everywhere.*

CHAPTER SEVENTEEN

STRONG MEASURES LEAD TO
UNEXPECTED DISCOVERIES

"I'm terribly worried and perplexed," said Lieutenant Lindsay one afternoon to Midshipman Midgley, as they were creeping along the coast in the neighbourhood of Cape Dalgado.

"Why so?" inquired the middy.

"Because I can learn nothing whatever about the movements of Marizano," replied the Lieutenant. "I have not spoken to you about this man hitherto, because—because—that is to say—the fact is, it wasn't worth while, seeing that you know no more about him than I do, perhaps not so much. But I can't help thinking that we might have learned something about him by this time, only our interpreter is such an unmitigated ass, he seems to understand nothing—to pick up nothing."

"Indeed!" exclaimed the midshipman; "I'm surprised to hear you say so, because I heard Suliman whispering last night with that half-caste fellow whom we captured along with the other niggers, and I am confident that he mentioned the name of Marizano several times."

R. M. Ballantyne

"Did he? Well now, the rascal invariably looks quite blank when I mention Marizano's name, and shakes his head, as if he had never heard of it before."

"Couldn't you intimidate him into disgorging a little of his knowledge?" suggested Midgley, with an arch look.

"I have thought of that," replied Lindsay, with a frown. "Come, it's not a bad idea; I'll try! Hallo! Suliman, come aft, I want you."

Lieutenant Lindsay was one of those men who are apt to surprise people by the precipitancy of their actions. He was not, indeed, hasty; but when his mind was made up he was not slow in proceeding to action. It was so on the present occasion, to the consternation of Suliman, who had hitherto conceived him to be rather a soft easy-going man.

"Suliman," he said, in a low but remarkably firm tone of voice, "you know more about Marizano than you choose to tell me. Now," he continued, gazing into the Arab's cold grey eyes, while he pulled a revolver from his coat-pocket and cocked it, "I intend to make you tell me all you know about him, or to blow your brains out."

He moved the pistol gently as he spoke, and placed his forefinger on the trigger.

"I not know," began Suliman, who evidently did not believe him to be quite in earnest; but before the words had well left his lips the drum of his left ear was almost split by the report of the pistol, and a part of his turban was blown away.

"You don't know? very well," said Lindsay, recocking the pistol, and placing the cold muzzle of it against the Arab's yellow nose.

This was too much for Suliman. He grew pale, and suddenly fell on his knees.

"Oh! stop! no—no! not fire! me tell you 'bout 'im."

"Good, get up and do so," said the Lieutenant, uncocking the revolver, and returning it to his pocket; "and be sure that you tell me all, else your life won't be worth the value of the damaged turban on your head."

With a good deal of trepidation the alarmed interpreter thereupon gave Lindsay all the information he possessed in regard to the slaver, which amounted to this, that he had gone to Kilwa, where he had collected a band of slaves sufficient to fill a large dhow, with which he intended, in two days more, to sail, in company with a fleet of slavers, for the north.

"Does he intend to touch at Zanzibar?" inquired Lindsay.

"Me tink no," replied the interpreter; "got many pritty garls—go straight for Persia."

On hearing this the Lieutenant put the cutter about, and sailed out to sea in search of the 'Firefly,' which he knew could not at that time be at any great distance from the shore.

He found her sooner than he had expected; and, to his immense astonishment as well as joy, one of the first persons he beheld on stepping over the side of his ship was Azinte.

"You have captured Marizano, sir, I see," he said to Captain Romer.

"Not the scoundrel himself, but one of his dhows," replied the Captain. "He had started for the northern ports with two heavily-laden vessels. We discovered him five days ago, and, fortunately, just beyond the protected water, so that he was a fair and lawful prize. The first of his dhows, being farthest out from shore, we captured, but the other, commanded by himself, succeeded in running ashore, and he escaped; with nearly all his slaves—only a few of the women and children being drowned in the surf. And now, as our cargo of poor wretches is pretty large, I shall run for the Seychelles. After landing them I shall return as fast as possible, to intercept a few more of these pirates."

"To the Seychelles!" muttered the Lieutenant to himself as he went below, with an expression on his countenance something between surprise and despair.

Poor Lindsay! His mind was so taken up with, and confused by, the constant and obtrusive presence of the Senhorina Maraquita that the particular turn which affairs had taken had not occurred to him, although that turn was quite natural, and by no means improbable. Marizano, with Azinte on board of one of his piratical dhows, was proceeding to the north. Captain Romer, with his war-steamer, was on the look-out for piratical dhows. What more natural than that the Captain should fall in with the pirate? But Lieutenant Lindsay's mind had been so filled with Maraquita that it seemed to be, for the time, incapable of holding more than one other idea— that idea was the fulfilment of Maraquita's commands to obtain information as to her lost Azinte. To this he had of late devoted all his powers, happy in the thought that it fell in with and formed part of his duty, to his Queen and country, as well as to the "Queen of his soul." To rescue Azinte from Marizano seemed to the bold Lieutenant an easy enough matter; but to rescue her from his own Captain, and send her back into slavery! "Ass! that I am," he exclaimed, "not to have thought of this before. Of course she can *never* be returned to Maraquita, and small comfort it will be to the

Senhorina to be told that her favourite is free in the Seychelles Islands, and utterly beyond her reach, unless she chooses to go there and stay with her."

Overwhelmed with disgust at his own stupidity, and at the utter impossibility of doing anything to mend matters, the unfortunate Lieutenant sat down to think, and the result of his thinking was that he resolved at all events to look well after Azinte, and see that she should be cared for on her arrival at the Seychelles.

Among the poor creatures who had been rescued from Marizano's dhow were nearly a hundred children, in such a deplorable condition that small hopes were entertained of their reaching the island alive. Their young lives, however, proved to be tenacious. Experienced though their hardy rescuers were in rough and tumble work, they had no conception what these poor creatures had already gone through, and, therefore, formed a mistaken estimate of their powers of endurance. Eighty-three of them reached the Seychelles alive. They were placed under the care of a warm-hearted missionary, who spared no pains for their restoration to health; but despite his utmost efforts, forty of these eventually died—their little frames had been whipped, and starved, and tried to such an extent, that recovery was impossible.

To the care of this missionary Lieutenant Lindsay committed Azinte, telling him as much of her sad story as he was acquainted with. The missionary willingly took charge of her, and placed her as a nurse in the temporary hospital which he had instituted for the little ones above referred to. Here Azinte proved herself to be a most tender, affectionate, and intelligent nurse to the poor children, for whom she appeared to entertain particular regard, and here, on the departure of the 'Firefly' shortly afterwards, Lindsay left her in a state of comfort, usefulness, and comparative felicity.

R. M. Ballantyne

CHAPTER EIGHTEEN

DESCRIBES SOME OF THE DOINGS OF YOOSOOF AND HIS MEN IN PROCURING BLACK IVORY FROM THE INTERIOR OF AFRICA

A dirty shop, in a filthy street in the unhealthy town of Zanzibar, is the point to which we now beg leave to conduct our reader—whom we also request to leap, in a free and easy way, over a few months of time!

It is not for the sake of the shop that we make this leap, but for the purpose of introducing the two men who, at the time we write of, sat over their grog in a small back-room connected with that shop. Still the shop itself is not altogether unworthy of notice. It is what the Americans call a store—a place where you can purchase almost every article that the wants of man have called into being. The prevailing smells are of oil, sugar, tea, molasses, paint, and tar, a compound which confuses the discriminating powers of the nose, and, on the principle that extremes meet, removes the feeling of surprise that ought to be aroused by discovering that these odours are in close connexion with haberdashery and hardware. There are enormous casks, puncheons, and kegs on the floor; bales on the shelves; indescribable confusion in the corners; preserved meat tins piled to the ceiling; with dust and dirt encrusting everything. The walls, beams, and rafters, appear to be held together by means of innumerable cobwebs. Hosts of flies fatten on, without diminishing, the stock, and squadrons of cockroaches career over the earthen floor.

In the little back-room of this shop sat the slave-dealer Yoosoof, in company with the captain of an English ship which lay in the harbour.

Smoke from the captain's pipe filled the little den to such an extent that Yoosoof and his friend were not so clearly distinguishable as might have been desired.

"You're all a set of false-hearted, wrong-headed, low-minded, scoundrels," said the plain-spoken captain, accompanying each asseveration with a puff so violent as to suggest the idea that his remarks were round-shot and his mouth a cannon.

The Briton was evidently not in a complimentary mood. It was equally evident that Yoosoof was not in a touchy vein, for he smiled the slightest possible smile and shrugged his shoulders. He had business to transact with the captain which was likely to result very much to his advantage, and Yoosoof was not the man to let feelings stand in the way of business.

"Moreover," pursued the captain, in a gruff voice, "the trade in slaves is illegally conducted in one sense, namely, that it is largely carried on by British subjects."

"How you make that out?" asked Yoosoof.

"How? why, easy enough. Aren't the richest men in Zanzibar the Banyans, and don't these Banyans, who number about 17,000 of your population, supply you Arabs with money to carry on the accursed slave-trade? And ain't these Banyans

Indian merchants—subjects of Great Britain?"

Yoosoof shrugged his shoulders again and smiled.

"And don't these opulent rascals," continued the Briton, "love their ease as well as their money, and when they want to increase the latter without destroying the former, don't they make advances to the like of you and get 100 per cent out of you for every dollar advanced?"

Yoosoof nodded his head decidedly at this, and smiled again.

"Well, then, ain't the whole lot of you a set of mean scoundrels?" said the captain fiercely.

Yoosoof did not smile at this; he even looked for a moment as if he were going to resent it, but it was only for a moment. Self-interest came opportunely to his aid, and made him submissive.

"What can we do?" he asked after a short silence. "You knows what the Sultan say, other day, to one British officer, 'If you stop slave-trade you will ruin Zanzibar.' We mus' not do that. Zanzibar mus' not be ruin."

"Why not?" demanded the captain, with a look of supreme contempt, "what if Zanzibar *was* ruined? Look here, now, Yoosoof, your dirty little island—the whole island observe— is not quite the size of my own Scotch county of Lanark. Its population is short of 250,000 all told—scarce equal to the half of the population of Lanark—composed of semi-barbarians and savages. That's one side of the question. Here's the other side: Africa is one of the four quarters of the earth, with millions of vigorous niggers and millions of acres of splendid land, and no end of undeveloped resources, and you have the impudence to tell me that an enormous lump of this land must be converted into a desert, and something like 150,000 of its best natives be drawn off *annually*—for what?—for what?" repeated the sailor, bringing his fist down on the table before him with such force that the glasses danced on it and the dust flew up; "for what? I say; for a paltry, pitiful island, ruled by a sham sultan, without army or navy, and with little money, save what he gets by slave-dealing; an island which has no influence for good on the world, morally, religiously, or socially, and with little commercially, though it has much influence for evil; an island which has helped the Portuguese to lock up the east coast of Africa for centuries; an island which would not be missed—save as a removed curse—if it were sunk this night to the bottom of the sea, and all its selfish, sensual, slave-dealing population swept entirely off the face of the earth."

The captain had risen and dashed his pipe to atoms on the floor in his indignation as he made these observations. He now made an effort to control himself, and then, sitting down, he continued—"Just think, Yoosoof; you're a sharp man of business, as I know to my cost. You can understand a thing in a commercial point of view. Just try to look at it thus: On the one side of the world's account you have Zanzibar sunk with all its Banyan and Arab population; we won't sink the niggers, poor wretches. We'll suppose them saved, along with the consuls, missionaries, and such-like. Well, that's a loss of somewhere about 83,000 scoundrels,—a gain we might call it, but for the sake of argument we'll call it a loss. On the other side of the account you have 30,000 niggers—fair average specimens of humanity—saved from slavery, besides something like 150,000 more saved from death by war and starvation, the results of the slave-trade; 83,000 from 150,000 leaves 67,000! The loss, you see, would be more than wiped off, and a handsome balance left at the world's credit the very first year! To say nothing of the opening up of legitimate commerce to one of the richest countries on earth, and the consequent introduction of Christianity."

The captain paused to take breath. Yoosoof shrugged his shoulders, and a brief silence ensued, which was happily broken, not by a recurrence to the question of slavery, but by the entrance of a slave. He came in search of Yoosoof for the purpose of telling him that his master wished to speak with him. As the slave's master was one of the wealthy Banyans just referred to, Yoosoof rose at once, and, apologising to the captain for quitting him so hurriedly, left that worthy son of Neptune to cool his indignation in solitude.

Passing through several dirty streets the slave led the slaver to a better sort of house in a more salubrious or, rather, less pestilential, part of the town. He was ushered into the presence of an elderly man of quiet, unobtrusive aspect.

"Yoosoof," said the Banyan in Arabic, "I have been considering the matter about which we had some conversation yesterday, and I find that it will be convenient for me to make a small venture. I can let you have three thousand dollars."

"On the old terms?" asked Yoosoof.

"On the old terms," replied the merchant. "Will you be ready to start soon?"

Yoosoof said that he would, that he had already completed the greater part of his preparations, and that he hoped to start for the interior in a week or two.

"That is well; I hope you may succeed in doing a good deal of business," said the merchant with an amiable nod and smile, which might have led an ignorant onlooker to imagine that Yoosoof's business in the interior was work of a purely philanthropic nature!

"There is another affair, which, it has struck me, may lie in your way," continued the merchant. "The British consul is, I am told, anxious to find some one who will undertake to make inquiries in the interior about some Englishmen, who are said to have been captured by the black fellows and made slaves of."

"Does the consul know what tribe has captured them?" asked Yoosoof.

"I think not; but as he offers five hundred dollars for every lost white man who shall be recovered and brought to the coast alive, I thought that you might wish to aid him!"

"True," said Yoosoof, musing, "true, I will go and see him."

Accordingly, the slave-dealer had an interview with the consul, during which he learned that there was no absolute certainty of any Englishmen having been captured. It was only a vague rumour; nevertheless it was sufficiently probable to warrant the offer of five hundred dollars to any one who should effect a rescue; therefore Yoosoof, having occasion to travel into the interior at any rate, undertook to make inquiries.

He was also told that two Englishmen had, not long before, purchased an outfit, and started off with the intention of proceeding to the interior by way of the Zambesi river, and they, the consul said, might possibly be heard of by him near the regions to which he was bound; but these, he suggested, could not be the men who were reported as missing.

Of course Yoosoof had not the most remote idea that these were the very Englishmen whom he himself had captured on the coast, for, after parting from them abruptly, as described in a former chapter, he had ceased to care or think about them, and besides, was ignorant of the fact that they had been to Zanzibar.

Yoosoof's own particular business required a rather imposing outfit. First of all, he purchased and packed about 600 pounds worth of beads of many colours, cloth of different kinds, thick brass wire, and a variety of cheap trinkets, such as black men and women are fond of, for Yoosoof was an "honest" trader, and paid his way when he found it suitable to do so. He likewise hired a hundred men, whom he armed with guns, powder, and ball, for Yoosoof was also a dishonest trader, and fought his way when that course seemed most desirable.

With this imposing caravan he embarked in a large dhow, sailed for the coast landed at Kilwa, and proceeded into the interior of Africa.

It was a long and toilsome journey over several hundred miles of exceedingly fertile and beautiful country, eminently suited for the happy abode of natives. But Yoosoof and his class who traded in black ivory had depopulated it to such an extent that scarce a human being was to be seen all the way. There were plenty of villages, but they were in ruins, and acres of cultivated ground with the weeds growing rank where the grain had once flourished. Further on in the journey, near the end of it, there was a change; the weeds and grain grew together and did battle, but in most places the weeds gained the victory. It was quite evident that the whole land had once been a rich garden teeming with human life— savage life, no doubt still, not so savage but that it could manage to exist in comparative enjoyment and multiply. Yoosoof—passed through a hundred and fifty miles of this land; it was a huge grave, which, appropriately enough, was profusely garnished with human bones. [See Livingstone's *Tributaries of the Zambesi*, page 391.]

At last the slave-trader reached lands which were not utterly forsaken.

Entering a village one afternoon he sent a present of cloth and beads to the chief, and, after a few preliminary ceremonies, announced that he wished to purchase slaves.

The chief, who was a fine-looking young warrior, said that he had no men, women or children to sell, except a few criminals to whom he was welcome at a very low price,—about two or three yards of calico each. There were also one or two orphan children whose parents had died suddenly, and to whom no one in the village could lay claim. It was true that these poor orphans had been adopted by various families who might not wish to part with them; but no matter, the chief's command was law. Yoosoof might have the orphans also for a very small sum,—a yard of calico perhaps. But nothing would induce the chief to compel any of his people to part with their children, and none of the people seemed desirous of doing so.

The slave-trader therefore adopted another plan. He soon managed to ascertain that the chief had an old grudge against a neighbouring chief. In the course of conversation he artfully stirred up the slumbering ill-will, and carefully fanned it into a flame without appearing to have any such end in view. When the iron was sufficiently hot he struck it—supplied the chief with guns and ammunition, and even, as a great favour, offered to lend him a few of his own men in order that he might make a vigorous attack on his old enemy.

The device succeeded to perfection. War was begun without any previous declaration; prisoners were soon brought in—

R. M. Ballantyne

not only men, but women and children. The first were coupled together with heavy slave-sticks, which were riveted to their necks; the latter were attached to each other with ropes; and thus Yoosoof, in a few days, was enabled to proceed on his journey with a goodly drove of "black cattle" behind him.

This occurred not far from Lake Nyassa, which he intended should be his headquarters for a time, while his men, under a new leader whom he expected to meet there, should push their victorious arms farther into the interior.

On reaching the shores of the noble lake, he found several birds of the same feather with himself—Arabs engaged in the same trade. He also found his old friend and trusty ally, Marizano. This gratified him much, for he was at once enabled to hand over the charge of the expedition to his lieutenant, and send him forth on his mission.

That same evening—a lovely and comparatively cool one— Yoosoof and the half-caste sauntered on the margin of the lake, listening to the sweet melody of the free and happy birds, and watching the debarkation, from a large boat, of a band of miserable slaves who had been captured or purchased on the other side.

"Now, Marizano," said Yoosoof, addressing the half-caste in his native tongue, "I do not intend to cumber you with cloth or beads on this expedition. I have already spent a good deal in the purchase of slaves, who are now in my barracoon, and I think it will be both cheaper and easier to make up the rest of the gang by means of powder and lead."

"It is lighter to carry, and more effectual," remarked Marizano, with a nod of approval.

"True," returned Yoosoof, "and quicker. Will a hundred men and guns suffice?"

"Eighty are enough to conquer any of the bow and spear tribes of this region," replied the half-caste carelessly.

"Good!" continued Yoosoof. "Then you shall start to-morrow. The tribes beyond this lake are not yet afraid of us—thanks to the mad Englishman, Livingstone, who has opened up the country and spread the information that white men are the friends of the black, and hate slavery." [Livingstone tells us that he found, on ascending the Shire river, that the Portuguese slave-traders had followed closely in the footsteps of his previous discoveries, and passed themselves off as his friends, by which means they were successful in gaining the confidence of the natives whom they afterwards treacherously murdered or enslaved.]

"You may try to pass yourself off as a white man, though your face is not so white as might be desired; however, you can comfort yourself with the knowledge that it is whiter than your heart!"

The Arab smiled and glanced at his lieutenant. Marizano smiled, bowed in acknowledgment of the compliment, and replied that he believed himself to be second to no one except his employer in that respect.

"Well, then," continued Yoosoof, "you must follow up the discoveries of this Englishman; give out that you are his friend, and have come there for the same purposes; and, when you have put them quite at their ease, commence a brisk trade with them—for which purpose you may take with you just enough of cloth and beads to enable you to carry out the deception. For the rest I need not instruct; you know what to do as well as I."

Marizano approved heartily of this plan, and assured his chief that his views should be carried out to his entire satisfaction.

"But there is still another point," said Yoosoof, "on which I have to talk. It appears that there are some white men who have been taken prisoners by one of the interior tribes—I know not which—for the finding of whom the British consul at Zanzibar has offered me five hundred dollars. If you can obtain information about these men it will be well. If you can find and rescue them it will be still better, and you shall have a liberal share of the reward."

While the Arab was speaking, the half-caste's visage betrayed a slight degree of surprise.

"White men!" he said, pulling up his sleeve and showing a gun-shot wound in his arm which appeared to be not very old. "A white man inflicted that not long ago, and not very far from the spot on which we stand. I had vowed to take the life of that white man if we should ever chance to meet, but if it is worth five hundred dollars I may be tempted to spare it!"

He laughed lightly as he spoke, and then added, with a thoughtful look,—"But I don't see how these men—there were two of them, if not more—can be prisoners, because, when I came across them, they were well-armed, well supplied, and well attended, else, you may be sure, they had not given me this wound and freed my slaves. But the scoundrels who were with me at the time were cowards."

"You are right," said Yoosoof. "The white men you met I heard of at Zanzibar. They cannot be the prisoners we are asked to search for. They have not yet been long enough away, I should think, to have come by any mischance, and the white men who are said to be lost have been talked about in Zanzibar for a long time. However, make diligent inquiries, because the promise is, that the five hundred dollars shall be ours if we rescue *any* white man, no matter who he may chance to be. And now I shall show you the cattle I have obtained on the way up."

The barracoon, to which the Arab led his lieutenant, was a space enclosed by a strong and high stockade, in which slaves were kept under guard until a sufficient number should be secured to form a gang, wherewith to start for the coast. At the entrance stood a savage-looking Portuguese half-caste armed with a gun. Inside there was an assortment of Yoosoof's Black Ivory. It was in comparatively good condition at that time, not having travelled far, and, as it was necessary to keep it up to a point of strength sufficient to enable it to reach the coast, it was pretty well fed except in the case of a few rebellious articles. There were, however, specimens of damaged goods even there. Several of the orphans, who had become Yoosoof's property, although sprightly enough when first purchased, had not stood even the short journey to the lake so well as might have been expected. They had fallen off in flesh to such an extent that Yoosoof was induced to remark to Marizano, as they stood surveying them, that he feared they would never reach the coast alive.

"That one, now," he said, pointing to a little boy who was tightly wedged in the midst of the group of slaves, and sat on the ground with his face resting on his knees, "is the most troublesome piece of goods I have had to do with since I began business; and it seems to me that I am going to lose him after all."

"What's the matter with him?" asked the half-caste.

"Nothing particular, only he is a delicate boy. At first I

refused him, but he is so well-made, though delicate, and such a good-looking child, and so spirited, that I decided to take him; but he turns out to be *too* spirited. Nothing that I can do will tame him,—oh, *that* won't do it," said Yoosoof, observing that Marizano raised the switch he carried in his hand with a significant action; "I have beaten him till there is scarcely a sound inch of skin on his whole body, but it's of no use. Ho! stand up," called Yoosoof, letting the lash of his whip fall lightly on the boy's shoulders.

There was, however, no response; the Arab therefore repeated the order, and laid the lash across the child's bare back with a degree of force that would have caused the stoutest man to wince; still the boy did not move. Somewhat surprised, Yoosoof pushed his way towards him, seized him by the hair and threw back his head.

The Arab left him immediately and remarked in a quiet tone that he should have no more trouble with him—he was dead!

"What's the matter with that fellow?" asked Marizano, pointing to a man who was employed in constantly rolling up a bit of wet clay and applying it to his left eye.

"Ah, he's another of these unmanageable fellows," replied Yoosoof. "I have been trying to tame *him* by starvation. The other morning he fell on his knees before the man who guards the barracoon and entreated him to give him food. The guard is a rough fellow, and had been put out of temper lately by a good many of the slaves. Instead of giving him food he gave him a blow in the eye which burst the ball of it, and of course has rendered him worthless; but *he* won't trouble us long."

In another place a woman crouched on the ground, having something wrapped in leaves which she pressed to her dried breast. It was the body of a child to which she had recently given birth in that place of woe.

Leaving his cringing and terrified goods to the guardian of the barracoon, the Arab returned to his tent beside the beautiful lake, and there, while enjoying the aroma of flowers and the cool breeze, and the genial sunshine, and the pleasant influences which God has scattered with bountiful hand over that luxuriant portion of the earth, calmly concerted with Marizano the best method by which he could bring inconceivable misery on thousands of its wretched inhabitants.

CHAPTER NINETEEN

TELLS OF MISFORTUNES THAT BEFELL OUR WANDERERS; OF FAMILIAR TOYS UNDER NEW ASPECTS, ETCETERA

When Harold Seadrift and Disco Lillihammer were stopped in their journey, as related in a former chapter, by the sudden illness of the bold seaman, an event was impending over them which effectually overturned their plans. This was the sudden descent of a band of armed natives who had been recently driven from their homes by a slaving party. The slavers had taken them by surprise during the night, set their huts on fire, captured their women and children, and slaughtered all the men, excepting those who sought and found safety in flight. It was those who had thus escaped that chanced to come upon the camp of our travellers one evening about sunset.

Disco was recovering from his attack of fever at the time, though still weak. Harold was sitting by his couch of leaves in the hut which had been erected for him on the first day of the illness. Jumbo was cutting up a piece of flesh for supper, and Antonio was putting the kettle on the fire. The rest of the party were away in the woods hunting.

No guard was kept; consequently the savages came down on

them like a thunderbolt, and found them quite unprepared to resist even if resistance had been of any use.

At first their captors, bitterly infuriated by their recent losses, proposed to kill their prisoners, without delay, by means of the most excruciating tortures that they could invent, but from some unknown cause, changed their minds; coupled Harold and Disco together by means of two slave-sticks; tied Antonio and Jumbo with ropes, and drove them away.

So suddenly was the thing done, and so effectually, that Disco was far from the camp before he could realise that what had occurred was a fact, and not one of the wild feverish dreams that had beset him during his illness.

The natives would not listen to the earnest explanation of Antonio that Harold and Disco were Englishmen, and haters of slavery. They scowled as they replied that the same had been said by the slavers who had attacked their village; from which remark it would seem that Yoosoof was not quite the originator of that device to throw the natives off their guard. The Portuguese of Tette on the Zambesi had also thought of and acted on it!

Fortunately it was, as we have said, near sunset when the capture was made, and before it became quite dark the band encamped, else must poor Disco have succumbed to weakness and fatigue. The very desperation of his circumstances, however, seemed to revive his strength, for next morning he resumed his journey with some hope of being able to hold out. The continued protestations and assurances of Antonio, also, had the effect of inducing their captors to remove the heavy slave-sticks from the necks of Harold and Disco, though they did not unbind their wrists. Thus were they led further into the country, they knew not whither, for several days and nights, and at last reached a large village where they were all thrust into a hut, and left to their meditations, while their captors went to palaver with the chief man of the place.

This chief proved to be a further-sighted man than the men of the tribe who had captured the Englishmen. His name was Yambo. He had heard of Dr Livingstone, and had met with men of other tribes who had seen and conversed with the great traveller. Thus, being of a thoughtful and inquiring disposition, he had come to understand enough of the good white man's sentiments to guard him from being imposed on by pretended Christians.

Yambo's name signified "how are you?" and was probably bestowed on him because of a strongly benevolent tendency to greet friend and stranger alike with a hearty "how d'ee do?" sort of expression of face and tone of voice.

He was a tall grave man, with a commanding firm look, and, withal, a dash of child-like humour and simplicity. On hearing his visitors' remarks about their captives, he at once paid them a visit and a few leading questions put to Harold through Antonio convinced him that the prisoners were true men. He therefore returned to his black visitors, told them that he had perfect confidence in the good faith of the white men, and said that he meant to take charge of them. He then entertained his black brothers hospitably, gave them a few presents, and sent them on their way. This done he returned to his guests and told them that they were free, that their captors were gone, and that they might go where they pleased, but that it would gratify him much if they would consent to spend some time hunting with him in the neighbourhood of his village.

"Now," said Disco, after Yambo left them, "this is wot I call the most uncommon fix that ever wos got into by man since

Adam an' Eve began housekeepin' in the garden of Eden."

"I'm not quite sure," replied Harold, with a rueful look, "that it is absolutely the *worst* fix, but it is bad enough. The worst of it is that this Yambo has let these rascals off with all our fire-arms and camp-equipage, so that we are absolutely helpless—might as well be prisoners, for we can't quit this village in such circumstances."

"Wot's wuss than that to my mind, sir, is, that here we are at sea, in the heart of Afriky, without chart, quadrant, compass, or rudder, an' no more idea of our whereabouts than one o' them spider monkeys that grins among the trees. Hows'ever, we're in luck to fall into the hands of a friendly chief, so, like these same monkeys, we must grin an' bear it; only I can't help feelin' a bit cast down at the loss of our messmates. I fear there's no chance of their findin' us."

"Not the least chance in the world, I should say," returned Harold. "They could not guess in which direction we had gone, and unless they had hit on the right road at first, every step they took afterwards would only widen the distance between us."

"It's lucky I was beginnin' to mend before we was catched," said Disco, feeling the muscles of his legs; "true, I ain't much to boast of yet but I'm improvin'."

"That is more than I can say for myself," returned Harold, with a sigh, as he passed his hand across his forehead; "I feel as if this last push through the woods in the hot sun, and the weight of that terrible slave-stick had been almost too much for me."

Disco looked earnestly and anxiously into the face of his friend.

R. M. Ballantyne

"Wot," asked he, "does you feel?"

"I can scarcely tell," replied Harold, with a faint smile. "Oh, I suppose I'm a little knocked up, that's all. A night's rest will put me all right."

"So I thought myself, but I wos wrong," said Disco. "Let's hear wot your feelin's is, sir; I'm as good as any doctor now, I am, in regard to symptoms."

"Well, I feel a sort of all-overishness, a kind of lassitude and sleepiness, with a slight headache, and a dull pain which appears to be creeping up my spine."

"You're in for it sir," said Disco. "It's lucky you have always carried the physic in your pockets, 'cause you'll need it, an' it's lucky, too, that I am here and well enough to return tit for tat and nurse you, 'cause you'll have that 'ere pain in your spine creep up your back and round your ribs till it lays hold of yer shoulders, where it'll stick as if it had made up its mind to stay there for ever an' a day. Arter that you'll get cold an' shivering like ice—oh! doesn't I know it well—an' then hot as fire, with heavy head, an' swimming eyes, an' twisted sight, an' confusion of—"

"Hold! hold!" cried Harold, laughing, "if you go on in that way I shall have more than my fair share of it! Pray stop, and leave me a little to find out for myself."

"Well, sir, take a purge, and turn in at once, that's my advice. I'll dose you with quinine to-morrow mornin', first thing," said Disco, rising and proceeding forthwith to arrange a couch in a corner of the hut, which Yambo had assigned them.

Harold knew well enough that his follower was right. He

took his advice without delay, and next morning found himself little better than a child, both physically and mentally, for the disease not only prostrated his great strength—as it had that of his equally robust companion—but, at a certain stage, induced delirium, during which he talked the most ineffable nonsense that his tongue could pronounce, or his brain conceive.

Poor Disco, who, of course, had been unable to appreciate the extent of his own delirious condition, began to fear that his leader's mind was gone for ever, and Jumbo was so depressed by the unutterably solemn expression of the mariner's once jovial countenance, that he did not once show his teeth for a whole week, save when engaged with meals.

As for Antonio, his nature not being very sympathetic, and his health being good, he rather enjoyed the quiet life and good living which characterised the native village, and secretly hoped that Harold might remain on the sick-list for a considerable time to come.

How long this state of affairs lasted we cannot tell, for both Harold and Disco lost the correct record of time during their respective illnesses.

Up to that period they had remembered the days of the week, in consequence of their habit of refraining from going out to hunt on Sundays, except when a dearth of meat in the larder rendered hunting a necessity. Upon these Sundays Harold's conscience sometimes reproached him for having set out on his journey into Africa without a Bible. He whispered, to himself at first, and afterwards suggested to Disco, the excuse that his Bible had been lost in the wreck of his father's vessel, and that, perhaps, there were no Bibles to be purchased in Zanzibar, but his conscience was a troublesome one, and refused to tolerate such bad reasoning, reminding

R. M. Ballantyne

him, reproachfully, that he had made no effort whatever to obtain a Bible at Zanzibar.

As time had passed, and some of the horrors of the slave-trade had been brought under his notice, many of the words of Scripture leaped to his remembrance, and the regret that he had not carried a copy with him increased. That touch of thoughtlessness, so natural to the young and healthy—to whom life has so far been only a garden of roses—was utterly routed by the stern and dreadful realities which had been recently enacted around him, and just in proportion as he was impressed with the lies, tyranny, cruelty, and false-hood of man, so did his thoughtful regard for the truth and the love of God increase, especially those truths that were most directly opposed to the traffic in human flesh, such as—"love your enemies," "seek peace with all men," "be kindly affectioned one to another," "whatsoever ye would that men should do unto you, do ye even so to them." An absolute infidel, he thought, could not fail to perceive that a most blessed change would come over the face of Africa if such principles prevailed among its inhabitants, even in an extremely moderate degree.

But to return, the unfortunate travellers were now "at sea" altogether in regard to the Sabbath as well as the day of the month. Indeed their minds were not very clear as to the month itself!

"Hows'ever," said Disco, when this subject afterwards came to be discussed, "it don't matter much. Wot is it that the Scriptur' says,—'Six days shalt thou labour an' do all that thou hast to do, but the seventh day is the Sabbath of the Lord thy God. In it thou shalt do no work.' I wos used always to stick at that pint w'en my poor mother was a-teachin' of me. Never got past it. But it's enough for present use anyhow, for the orders is, work six days an' don't work the seventh. Werry good, we'll begin to-day an' call it Monday; we'll work for six days, an' w'en the seventh day comes we'll call it Sunday. If it ain't the right day, *we* can't help it; moreover, wot's the odds? It's the *seventh* day, so that to us it'll be the Sabbath."

But we anticipate. Harold was still—at the beginning of this digression—in the delirium of fever, though there were symptoms of improvement about him.

One afternoon one of these symptoms was strongly manifested in a long, profound slumber. While he slept Disco sat on a low stool beside him, busily engaged with a clasp-knife on some species of manufacture, the nature of which was not apparent at a glance.

His admirer, Jumbo, was seated on a stool opposite, gazing at him open-mouthed, with a countenance that reflected every passing feeling of his dusky bosom.

Both men were so deeply absorbed in their occupation—Disco in his manufacture, and Jumbo in staring at Disco—that they failed for a considerable time to observe that Harold had wakened suddenly, though quietly, and was gazing at them with a look of lazy, easy-going surprise.

The mariner kept up a running commentary on his work, addressed to Jumbo indeed, but in a quiet interjectional manner that seemed to imply that he was merely soliloquising, and did not want or expect a reply.

"It's the most 'stror'nary notion, Jumbo, between you and me and the post, that I ever did see. Now, then, this here bullet-head wants a pair o' eyes an' a nose on it; the mouth'll do, but it's the mouth as is most troublesome, for you niggers have got such wappin' muzzles—it's quite a caution, as the

Yankees say,"—(a pause)—"on the whole, however, the nose is very difficult to manage on a flat surface, 'cause w'y?—if I leaves it quite flat, it don't look like a nose, an' if I carves it out ever so little, it's too prominent for a nigger nose. There, ain't that a good head, Jumbo?"

Thus directly appealed to, Jumbo nodded his own head violently, and showed his magnificent teeth from ear to ear, gums included.

Disco laid down the flat piece of board which he had carved into the form of a human head, and took up another piece, which was rudely blocked out into the form of a human leg—both leg and head being as large as life.

"Now this limb, Jumbo," continued Disco, slowly, as he whittled away with the clasp-knife vigorously, "is much more troublesome than I would have expected; for you niggers have got such abominably ill-shaped legs below the knee. There's such an unnat'ral bend for'ard o' the shin-bone, an' such a rediklous sticking out o' the heel astarn, d'ee see, that a feller with white man notions has to make a study of it, if he sets up for a artist; in course, if he *don't* set up for a artist any sort o' shape'll do, for it don't affect the jumpin'. Ha! there they go," he exclaimed, with a humorous smile at a hearty shout of laughter which was heard just outside the hut, "enjoyin' the old 'un; but it's nothin' to wot the noo 'un'll be w'en it's finished."

At this exhibition of amusement on the countenance of his friend, Jumbo threw back his head and again showed not only his teeth and gums but the entire inside of his mouth, and chuckled softly from the region of his breast-bone.

"I'm dreaming, of course," thought Harold, and shut his eyes.

Poor fellow! he was very weak, and the mere act of shutting his eyes induced a half-slumber. He awoke again in a few minutes, and re-opening his eyes, beheld the two men still sitting, and occupied as before.

"It is a wonderfully pertinacious dream," thought Harold. "I'll try to dissipate it."

Thinking thus, he called out aloud,—"I say, Disco!"

"Hallo! that's uncommon like the old tones," exclaimed the seaman, dropping his knife and the leg of wood as he looked anxiously at his friend.

"What old tones?" asked Harold.

"The tones of your voice," said Disco.

"Have they changed so much of late?" inquired Harold in surprise.

"Have they? I should think they have, just. W'y, you haven't spoke like that, sir, for—but, surely—are you better, or is this on'y another dodge o' yer madness?" asked Disco with a troubled look.

"Ah! I suppose I've been delirious, have I?" said Harold with a faint smile.

To this Disco replied that he had not only been delirious, but stark staring mad, and expressed a very earnest hope that, now he had got his senses hauled taut again, he'd belay them an' make all fast for, if he didn't, it was his, Disco's opinion, that another breeze o' the same kind would blow 'em all to ribbons.

"Moreover," continued Disco, firmly, "you're not to talk. I once nursed a messmate through a fever, an' I remember that the doctor wos werry partikler w'en he began to come round, in orderin' him to hold his tongue an' keep quiet."

"You are right Disco. I will keep quiet, but you must first tell me what you are about, for it has roused my curiosity, and I can't rest till I know."

"Well, sir, I'll tell you, but don't go for to make no obsarvations on it. Just keep your mouth shut an' yer ears open, an' I'll do all the jawin'. Well, you must know, soon after you wos took bad, I felt as if I'd like some sort o' okipation w'en sittin' here watchin' of you—Jumbo an' me's bin takin' the watch time about, for Antony isn't able to hold a boy, much less *you* w'en you gits obstropolous—Well, sir, I had took a sort o' fancy for Yambo's youngest boy, for he's a fine, brave little shaver, he is, an' I thought I'd make him some sort o' toy, an' it struck me that the thing as 'ud please him most 'ud be a jumpin'-jack, so I set to an' made him one about a futt high.

"You never see such a face o' joy as that youngster put on, sir, w'en I took it to him an' pulled the string. He give a little squeak of delight he did, tuk it in his hands, an' ran home to show it to his mother. Well, sir, wot d'ee think, the poor boy come back soon after, blubberin' an' sobbin', as nat'ral as if he'd bin an English boy, an' says he to Tony, says he, 'Father's bin an' took it away from me!' I wos surprised at this, an' went right off to see about it, an' w'en I come to Yambo's hut wot does I see but the chief pullin' the string o' the jumpin'-jack, an' grinnin' an' sniggerin' like a blue-faced baboon in a passion—his wife likewise standin' by holdin' her sides wi' laughin'. Well, sir, the moment I goes in, up gits the chief an' shouts for Tony, an' tells him to tell me that I must make him a jumpin'-jack! In course I says I'd do it with all the pleasure in life; and he says that I must make it full size, as big as hisself! I opened my eyes at this, but he said he must have a thing that was fit for a man—a chief—so there was nothin' for it but to set to work. An' it worn't difficult to manage neither, for they supplied me with slabs o' timber an inch thick an' I soon blocked out the body an' limbs with a hatchet an' polished 'em off with my knife, and then put 'em together. W'en the big jack wos all right Yambo took it away, for he'd watched me all the time I wos at it, an' fixed it up to the branch of a tree an' set to work.

"I never, no I never, did," continued Disco, slapping his right thigh, while Jumbo grinned in sympathy, "see sitch a big baby as Yambo became w'en he got that monstrous jumpin'-jack into action—with his courtiers all round him, their faces blazin' with surprise, or conwulsed wi' laughter. The chief hisself was too hard at work to laugh much. He could only glare an' grin, for, big an' strong though he is, the jack wos so awful heavy that it took all his weight an' muscle haulin' on the rope which okipied the place o' the string that we're used to.

"'Haul away, my hearty,' thought I, w'en I seed him heavin', blowin', an' swettin' at the jack's halyards, 'you'll not break that rope in a hurry.'"

"But I was wrong, sir, for, although the halyards held on all right, I had not calkilated on such wiolent action at the joints. All of a sudden off comes a leg at the knee. It was goin' the up'ard kick at the time, an' went up like a rocket, slap through a troop o' monkeys that was lookin' on aloft, which it scattered like foam in a gale. Yambo didn't seem to care a pinch o' snuff. His blood was up. The sweat was runnin' off him like rain. 'Hi!' cries he, givin' another most awful tug. But it wasn't high that time, for the other leg came off at the hip-jint on the down kick, an' went straight into the buzzum of a black warrior an' floored him wuss than he ever wos

R. M. Ballantyne

floored since he took to fightin'. Yambo didn't care for that either. He gave another haul with all his might, which proved too much for jack without his legs, for it threw his arms out with such force that they jammed hard an' fast, as if the poor critter was howlin' for mercy!

"Yambo looked awful blank at this. Then he turned sharp round and looked at me for all the world as if he meant to say 'wot d'ee mean by that? eh!'

"'He shouldn't ought to lick into him like that,' says I to Tony, 'the figure ain't made to be druv by a six-horse power steam-engine! But tell him I'll fix it up with jints that'll stand pullin' by an elephant, and I'll make him another jack to the full as big as that one an' twice as strong.'"

"This," added Disco in conclusion, taking up the head on which he had been engaged, "is the noo jack. The old un's outside working away at this moment like a win'-mill. Listen; don't 'ee hear 'em?"

Harold listened and found no difficulty in hearing them, for peals of laughter and shrieks of delight burst forth every few minutes, apparently from a vast crowd outside the hut.

"I do believe," said Disco, rising and going towards the door of the hut "that you can see 'em from where you lay."

He drew aside the skin doorway as he spoke, and there, sure enough, was the gigantic jumping-jack hanging from the limb of a tree, clearly defined against the sky, and galvanically kicking about its vast limbs, with Yambo pulling fiercely at the tail, and the entire tribe looking on steeped in ecstasy and admiration.

It may easily be believed that the sight of this, coupled with

Disco's narrative, was almost too much for Harold's nerves, and for some time he exhibited, to Disco's horror, a tendency to repeat some antics which would have been much more appropriate to the jumping-jack, but, after a warm drink administered by his faithful though rough nurse, he became composed, and finally dropped into a pleasant sleep, which was not broken till late the following morning.

Refreshed in body, happy in mind, and thankful in spirit he rose to feel that the illness against which he had fought for many days was conquered, and that, although still very weak, he had fairly turned the corner, and had begun to regain some of his wonted health and vigour.

R. M. Ballantyne

CHAPTER TWENTY

HAROLD APPEARS IN A NEW CHARACTER, AND TWO OLD CHARACTERS REAPPEAR TO HAROLD

The mind of Yambo was a strange compound—a curious mixture of gravity and rollicking joviality; at one time displaying a phase of intense solemnity; at another exhibiting quiet pleasantry and humour, but earnestness was the prevailing trait of his character. Whether indulging his passionate fondness for the jumping-jack, or engaged in guiding the deliberations of his counsellors, the earnest chief was equally devoted to the work in hand. Being a savage—and, consequently, led entirely by feeling, which is perhaps the chief characteristic of savage, as distinguished from civilised, man,—he hated his enemies with exceeding bitterness, and loved his friends with all his heart.

Yambo was very tender to Harold during his illness, and the latter felt corresponding gratitude, so that there sprang up between the two a closer friendship than one could have supposed to be possible, considering that they were so different from each other, mentally, physically, and socially, and that their only mode of exchanging ideas was through the medium of a very incompetent interpreter.

Among other things Harold discovered that his friend the chief was extremely fond of anecdotes and stories. He, therefore, while in a convalescent state and unable for much physical exercise, amused himself, and spent much of his time, in narrating to him the adventures of Robinson Crusoe. Yambo's appetite for mental food increased, and when Crusoe's tale was finished he eagerly demanded more. Some of his warriors also came to hear, and at last the hut was unable to contain the audiences that wished to enter. Harold, therefore, removed to an open space under a banyan-tree, and there daily, for several hours, related all the tales and narratives with which he was acquainted, to the hundreds of open-eyed and open-mouthed negroes who squatted around him.

At first he selected such tales as he thought would be likely to amuse, but these being soon exhausted, he told them about anything that chanced to recur to his memory. Then, finding that their power to swallow the marvellous was somewhat crocodilish, he gave them Jack the Giant-killer, and Jack of Beanstalk notoriety, and Tom Thumb, Cinderella, etcetera, until his entire nursery stock was exhausted, after which he fell back on his inventive powers; but the labour of this last effort proving very considerable, and the results not being adequately great, he took to history, and told them stories about William Tell, and Wallace, and Bruce, and the Puritans of England, and the Scottish Covenanters, and the discoveries of Columbus, until the eyes and mouths of his black auditors were held so constantly and widely on the stretch, that Disco began to fear they would become gradually incapable of being shut, and he entertained a fear that poor Antonio's tongue would, ere long, be dried up at the roots.

At last a thought occurred to our hero, which he promulgated to Disco one morning as they were seated at breakfast on the floor of their hut.

　　　　　R. M. Ballantyne

"It seems to me, Disco," he said, after a prolonged silence, during which they had been busily engaged with their knives and wooden spoons, "that illness must be sent sometimes, to teach men that they give too little of their thoughts to the future world."

"Werry true, sir," replied Disco, in that quiet matter-of-course tone with which men generally receive axiomatic verities; "we *is* raither given to be swallered up with this world, which ain't surprisin' neither, seein' that we've bin putt into it, and are surrounded by it, mixed up with it, steeped in it, so to speak, an' can't werry well help ourselves."

"That last is just the point I'm not quite so sure about," rejoined Harold. "Since I've been lying ill here, I have thought a good deal about forgetting to bring a Bible with me, and about the meaning of the term Christian, which name I bear; and yet I can't, when I look honestly at it, see that I do much to deserve the name."

"Well, I don't quite see that, sir," said Disco, with an argumentative curl of his right eyebrow; "you doesn't swear, or drink, or steal, or commit murder, an' a many other things o' that sort. Ain't that the result o' your being a Christian."

"It may be so, Disco, but that is only what may be styled the *don't* side of the question. What troubles me is, that I don't see much on the *do* side of it."

"You says your prayers, sir, don't you?" asked Disco, with the air of a man who had put a telling question.

"Well, yes," replied Harold; "but what troubles me is that, while in my creed I profess to think the salvation of souls is of such vital importance, in my practice I seem to say that it is of no importance at all, for here have I been, for many weeks, amongst these black fellows, and have never so much as mentioned the name of our Saviour to them, although I have been telling them no end of stories of all kinds, both true and fanciful."

"There's something in that sir," admitted Disco. Harold also thought there was so much in it that he gave the subject a great deal of earnest consideration, and finally resolved to begin to tell the negroes Bible stories. He was thus gradually led to tell them that "old, old story" of God the Saviour's life and death, and love for man, which he found interested, affected, and influenced the savages far more powerfully than any of the tales, whether true or fanciful, with which he had previously entertained them. While doing this a new spirit seemed to actuate himself, and to influence his whole being.

While Harold was thus led, almost unconsciously, to become a sower of the blessed seed of God's Word, Marizano was working his way through the country, setting forth, in the most extreme manner, the ultimate results of man's sinful nature, and the devil's lies.

One of his first deeds was to visit a village which was beautifully situated on the banks of a small but deep river. In order to avoid alarming the inhabitants, he approached it with only about thirty of his men, twenty of whom were armed. Arrived at the outskirts, he halted his armed men, and advanced with the other ten, calling out cheerfully, "We have things for sale! have you anything to sell?" The chief and his warriors, armed with their bows and arrows and shields, met him, and forbade him to pass within the hedge that encircled the village, but told him to sit down under a tree outside. A mat of split reeds was placed for Marizano to sit on; and when he had explained to the chief that the object of his visit was to trade with him for ivory—in proof of which he pointed to the bales which his men carried,—he was well received, and a great clapping of hands ensued. Presents were then exchanged, and more clapping of hands took place, for this was considered the appropriate ceremony. The chief and his warriors, on sitting down before Marizano and his men, clapped their hands together, and continued slapping on their thighs while handing their presents, or when receiving those of their visitors. It was the African "thank you." To have omitted it would have been considered very bad manners.

Soon a brisk trade was commenced, in which the entire community became ere long deeply and eagerly absorbed.

Meanwhile Marizano's armed men were allowed to come forward. The women prepared food for the strangers; and after they had eaten and drunk of the native beer heartily, Marizano asked the chief if he had ever seen fire-arms used.

"Yes," replied the chief, "but only once at a great distance off. It is told to me that your guns kill very far off—much further than our bows. Is that so?"

"It is true," replied Marizano, who was very merry by this time under the influence of the beer, as, indeed, were also his men and their entertainers. "Would you like to see what our guns can do?" asked the half-caste. "If you will permit me, I shall let you hear and see them in use."

The unsuspecting chief at once gave his consent. His visitors rose; Marizano gave the word; a volley was poured forth which instantly killed the chief and twenty of his men. The survivors fled in horror. The young women and children were seized; the village was sacked—which means that the old and useless members of the community were murdered in cold blood, and the place was set on fire—and Marizano marched away with his band of captives considerably augmented, leaving a scene of death and horrible desolation behind him. [See Livingstone's *Zambesi and its Tributaries*, pages 201, 202.]

Thus did that villain walk through the land with fire and sword procuring slaves for the supply of the "domestic institution" of the Sultan of Zanzibar.

By degrees the murderer's drove of black "cattle" increased to such an extent that when he approached the neighbour-hood of the village in which Harold and Disco sojourned, he began to think that he had obtained about as many as he could conveniently manage, and meditated turning his face eastward, little dreaming how near he was to a thousand dollars' worth of property, in the shape of ransom for two white men!

He was on the point of turning back and missing this when he chanced to fall in with a villager who was out hunting, and who, after a hot chase, was captured. This man was made much of, and presented with some yards of cloth as well as a few beads, at the same time being assured that he had nothing to fear; that the party was merely a slave-trading one; that the number of slaves required had been made up, but that a few more would be purchased if the chief of his village had any to dispose of.

On learning from the man that his village was a large one, fully two days' march from the spot where he stood, and filled with armed men, Marizano came to the conclusion that it would not be worth his while to proceed thither, and was about to order his informant to be added to his gang with a slave-stick round his neck, when he suddenly bethought him of inquiring as to whether any white men had been seen in these parts. As he had often made the same inquiry before without obtaining any satisfactory answer, it was with great surprise that he now heard from his captive of two white men being in the very village about which he had been conversing.

At once he changed his plan, resumed his march, and, a couple of days afterwards, presented himself before the astonished eyes of Harold Seadrift and Disco Lillihammer, while they were taking a walk about a mile from the village.

Disco recognised the slave-trader at once, and, from the troubled as well as surprised look of Marizano, it was pretty evident that he remembered the countenance of Disco.

When the recollection of Marizano's cruelty at the time of their first meeting flashed upon him, Disco felt an almost irresistible desire to rush upon and strangle the Portuguese, but the calm deportment of that wily man, and the peaceful manner in which he had approached, partly disarmed his wrath. He could not however, quite restrain his tongue.

"Ha!" said he, "you are the blackguard that we met and pretty nigh shot when we first came to these parts, eh? Pity we missed you, you black-hearted villain!"

As Marizano did not understand English, these complimentary remarks were lost on him. He seemed, however, to comprehend the drift of them, for he returned Disco's frown with a stare of defiance.

"Whatever he was, or whatever he is," interposed Harold, "we must restrain ourselves just now, Disco, because we cannot punish him as he deserves, however much we may wish to, and he seems to have armed men enough to put us and our entertainers completely in his power. Keep quiet while I speak to him."

Jumbo and Antonio, armed with bows and arrows,—for they were in search of small game wherewith to supply the pot—came up, looking very much surprised, and the latter a good deal frightened.

"Ask him, Antonio," said Harold, "what is his object in visiting this part of the country."

"To procure slaves," said Marizano, curtly.

"I thought so," returned Harold; "but he will find that the men of this tribe are not easily overcome."

"I do not wish to overcome them," said the half-caste. "I have procured enough of slaves, as you see," (pointing to the gang which was halted some hundred yards or so in rear of his armed men), "but I heard that you were prisoners here, and I have come to prove to you that even a slave-trader can return good for evil. *You* did this," he said, looking at Disco, and pointing to his old wound in the arm; "I now come to deliver you from slavery."

Having suppressed part of the truth, and supplemented the rest of it with this magnificent lie, Marizano endeavoured to look magnanimous.

"I don't believe a word of it," said Disco, decidedly.

"I incline to doubt it too," said Harold; "but he may have some good reason of his own for his friendly professions towards us. In any case we have no resource left but to assume that he speaks the truth."

Turning to Marizano, he said:—

"We are not prisoners here. We are guests of the chief of

R. M. Ballantyne

this village."

"In that case," replied the half-caste, "I can return to the coast without you."

As he said this a large band of the villagers, having discovered that strangers had arrived, drew near. Marizano at once advanced, making peaceful demonstrations, and, after the requisite amount of clapping of hands on both sides, stated the object for which he had come. He made no attempt to conceal the fact that he was a slave-trader, but said that, having purchased enough of slaves, he had visited their village because of certain rumours to the effect that some white men had been lost in these regions, and could not find their way back to the coast. He was anxious, he said, to help these white men to do so, but, finding that the white men then at the village were *not* the men he was in search of, and did not want to go to the coast, he would just stay long enough with the chief to exchange compliments, and then depart.

All this was translated to the white men in question by their faithful ally Antonio, and when they retired to consult as to what should be done, they looked at each other with half amused and half perplexed expressions of countenance.

"Werry odd," said Disco, "how contrairy things turns up at times!"

"Very odd indeed," assented Harold, laughing. "It is quite true that we are, in one sense, lost and utterly unable to undertake a journey through this country without men, means, or arms; and nothing could be more fortunate than that we should have the chance, thus suddenly thrown in our way, of travelling under the escort of a band of armed men; nevertheless, I cannot bear the idea of travelling with or being indebted to a slave-trader and a scoundrel like Marizano."

"That's w'ere it is, sir," said Disco with emphasis, "I could stand anything a'most but that."

"And yet," pursued Harold, "it is our only chance. I see quite well that we may remain for years here without again having such an opportunity or such an escort thrown in our way."

"There's no help for it, I fear," said Disco. "We must take it like a dose o' nasty physic—hold our nobs, shut our daylights, an' down with it. The only thing I ain't sure of is your ability to travel. You ain't strong yet."

"Oh, I'm strong enough now, or very nearly so, and getting stronger every day. Well, then, I suppose it's settled that we go?"

"Humph! I'm agreeable, an' the whole business werry disagreeable," said Disco, making a wry face.

Marizano was much pleased when the decision of the white men was made known to him, and the native chief was naturally much distressed, for, not only was he about to lose two men of whom he had become very fond, but he was on the point of being bereft of his story-teller, the opener up of his mind, the man who, above all others, had taught him to think about his Maker and a future state.

He had sense enough, however, to perceive that his guests could not choose but avail themselves of so good an opportunity, and, after the first feeling of regret was over, made up his mind to the separation.

Next day Harold and Disco, with feelings of strong revulsion, almost of shame, fell into the ranks of the slave-gang, and for many days thereafter marched through the land in company with Marizano and his band of lawless villains.

Marizano usually walked some distance ahead of the main body with a few trusty comrades. Our adventurers, with their two followers, came next in order of march, the gang of slaves in single file followed, and the armed men brought up the rear. It was necessarily a very long line, and at a distance resembled some hideous reptile crawling slowly and tortuously through the fair fields and plains of Africa.

At first there were no stragglers, for the slaves were as yet, with few exceptions, strong and vigorous. These exceptions, and the lazy, were easily kept in the line by means of rope and chain, as well as the rod and lash.

Harold and Disco studiously avoided their leader during the march. Marizano fell in with their humour and left them to themselves. At nights they made their own fire and cooked their own supper, as far removed from the slave camp as was consistent with safety, for they could not bear to witness the sufferings of the slaves, or to look upon their captors. Even the food that they were constrained to eat appeared to have a tendency to choke them, and altogether their situation became so terrible that they several times almost formed the desperate resolution of leaving the party and trying to reach the coast by themselves as they best might, but the utter madness and hopelessness of such a project soon forced itself on their minds, and insured its being finally abandoned.

One morning Marizano threw off his usual reserve, and, approaching the white men, told them that in two hours they would reach the lake where his employer was encamped.

"And who is your master?" asked Harold.

"A black-faced or yellow-faced blackguard like himself, I doubt not," growled Disco.

Antonio put Harold's question without Disco's comment, and Marizano replied that his master was an Arab trader, and added that he would push on in advance of the party and inform him of their approach.

Soon afterwards the lake was reached. A large dhow was in readiness, the gang was embarked and ferried across to a place where several rude buildings and barracoons, with a few tents, indicated that it was one of the inland headquarters of the trade in Black Ivory.

The moment our travellers landed Marizano led them to one of the nearest buildings, and introduced them to his master.

"Yoosoof!" exclaimed Disco in a shout of astonishment.

It would have been a difficult question to have decided which of the three faces displayed the most extreme surprise. Perhaps Disco's would have been awarded the palm, but Yoosoof was undoubtedly the first to regain his self-possession.

"You be surprised," he said, in his *very* broken English, while his pale-yellow visage resumed its placid gravity of expression.

"Undoubtedly we are," said Harold.

"Bu'stin'!" exclaimed Disco.

"You would be not so mush surprised,—did you know dat I comes to here every year, an' dat Engleesh consul ask me for 'quire about you."

"If that be so, how comes it that *you* were surprised to see us?" asked Harold.

R. M. Ballantyne

"'Cause why, I only knows dat some white mans be loss theirselfs—not knows *what* mans—not knows it was *you*."

"Well now," cried Disco, unable to restrain himself as he turned to Harold, "did ever two unfortnits meet wi' sitch luck? Here have we bin' obliged for days to keep company with the greatest Portugee villian in the country, an' now we're needcessitated to be under a obligation to the greatest Arab scoundrel in Afriky."

The scoundrel in question smiled and shrugged his shoulders.

"Yoosoof," cried Disco, clenching his fist and looking full in the trader's eyes, "when I last saw yer ugly face, I vowed that if ever I seed it again I'd leave my mark on it pretty deep, I did; and now I does see it again, but I haven't the moral courage to touch sitch a poor, pitiful, shrivelled-up package o' bones an' half-tanned leather. Moreover, I'm goin' to be indebted to 'ee! Ha! ha!" (he laughed bitterly, and with a dash of wild humour in the tone), "to travel under yer care, an' eat yer accursed bread, and—and—oh! there ain't no sitch thing as shame left in my corpus. I'm a low mean-spirited boastful idiot, that's wot *I* am, an' I don't care the fag-end of a hunk o' gingerbread who knows it."

After this explosion the sorely tried mariner brought his right hand down on his thigh with a tremendous crack, turned about and walked away to cool himself.

CHAPTER TWENTY ONE

PROGRESS OF THE SLAVE-RUN—THE DEADLY SWAMP, AND THE UNEXPECTED RESCUE

We will now leap over a short period of time—about two or three weeks—during which the sable procession had been winding its weary way over hill and dale, plain and swamp.

During that comparatively brief period, Harold and Disco had seen so much cruelty and suffering that they both felt a strange tendency to believe that the whole must be the wild imaginings of a horrible dream. Perhaps weakness, resulting from illness, might have had something to do with this peculiar feeling of unbelief, for both had been subject to a second, though slight, attack of fever. Nevertheless, coupled with their scepticism was a contradictory and dreadful certainty that they were not dreaming, but that what they witnessed was absolute verity.

It is probable that if they had been in their ordinary health and vigour they would have made a violent attempt to rescue the slaves, even at the cost of their own lives. But severe and prolonged illness often unhinges the mind as well as the body, and renders the spirit all but impotent.

One sultry evening the sad procession came to a long stretch

R. M. Ballantyne

of swamp, and prepared to cross it. Although already thinned by death, the slave-gang was large. It numbered several hundreds, and was led by Marizano; Yoosoof having started some days in advance in charge of a similar gang.

Harold and Disco were by that time in the habit of walking together in front of the gang, chiefly for the purpose of avoiding the sight of cruelties and woes which they were powerless to prevent or assuage. On reaching the edge of the swamp, however, they felt so utterly wearied and dis-spirited that they sat down on a bank to rest, intending to let the slave-gang go into the swamp before them and then follow in rear. Antonio and Jumbo also remained with them.

"You should go on in front," said Marizano significantly, on observing their intention.

"Tell him we'll remain where we are," said Disco sternly to Antonio.

Marizano shrugged his shoulders and left them.

The leading men of the slave-gang were ordered to advance, as soon as the armed guard had commenced the toilsome march over ground into which they sank knee-deep at every step.

The first man of the gang hesitated and heaved a deep sigh as though his heart failed him at the prospect—and well it might, for, although young, he was not robust, and over-driving, coupled with the weight and the chafing of the goree, had worn him to a skeleton.

It was not the policy of the slave-traders to take much care of their Black Ivory. They procured it so cheaply that it was easier and more profitable to lose or cast away some of it, than to put off time in resting and recruiting the weak.

The moment it was observed, therefore, that the leading man hesitated, one of the drivers gave him a slash across his naked back with a heavy whip which at once drew blood. Poor wretch; he could ill bear further loss of the precious stream of life, for it had already been deeply drained from him by the slave-stick. The chafing of that instrument of torture had not only worn the skin off his shoulders, but had cut into the quivering flesh, so that blood constantly dropped in small quantities from it.

No cry burst from the man's lips on receiving the cruel blow, but he turned his eyes on his captors with a look that seemed to implore for mercy. As well might he have looked for mercy at the hands of Satan. The lash again fell on him with stinging force. He made a feeble effort to advance, staggered, and fell to the ground, dragging down the man to whom he was coupled with such violence as almost to break his neck. The lash was again about to be applied to make him rise, but Disco and Harold rose simultaneously and rushed at the driver, with what intent they scarcely knew; but four armed half-castes stepped between them and the slave.

"You had better not interfere," said Marizano, who stood close by.

"Out of the way!" cried Harold fiercely, in the strength of his passion hurling aside the man who opposed him.

"You shan't give him another cut," said Disco between his teeth, as he seized the driver by the throat.

"We don't intend to do so," said Marizano coolly, while the driver released himself from poor Disco's weakened grasp, "he won't need any more."

The Englishmen required no explanation of these words. A glance told them that the man was dying.

"Cut him out," said Marizano.

One of his men immediately brought a saw and cut the fork of the stick which still held the living to the dying man, and which, being riveted on them, could not otherwise be removed.

Harold and Disco lifted him up as soon as he was free, and carrying him a short distance aside to a soft part of the bank, laid him gently down.

The dying slave looked as if he were surprised at such unwonted tenderness. There was even a slight smile on his lips for a few moments, but it quickly passed away with the fast ebbing tide of life.

"Go fetch some water," said Harold. "His lips are dry."

Disco rose and ran to fill a small cocoa-nut-shell which he carried at his girdle as a drinking-cup. Returning with it he moistened the man's lips and poured a little of the cool water on the raw sores on each side of his neck.

They were so much engrossed with their occupation that neither of them observed that the slave-gang had commenced to pass through the swamp, until the sharp cry of a child drew their attention to it for a moment; but, knowing that they could do no good, they endeavoured to shut their eyes and ears to everything save the duty they had in hand.

By degrees the greater part of the long line had got into the swamp and were slowly toiling through it under the stimulus of the lash. Some, like the poor fellow who first fell, had sunk under their accumulated trials, and after a fruitless effort on the part of the slavers to drive them forward, had been kicked aside into the jungle, there to die, or to be torn in pieces by that ever-watchful scavenger of the wilderness, the hyena. These were chiefly women, who having become mothers not long before were unable to carry their infants and keep up with the gang. Others, under the intense dread of flagellation, made the attempt, and staggered on a short distance, only to fall and be left behind in the pestilential swamp, where rank reeds and grass closed over them and formed a ready grave.

The difficulties of the swamp were, however, felt most severely by the children, who, from little creatures of not much more than five years of age to well-grown boys and girls, were mingled with and chained to the adults along the line. Their comparatively short legs were not well adapted for such ground, and not a few of them perished there; but although the losses here were terribly numerous in one sense, they after all bore but a small proportion to those whose native vigour carried them through in safety.

Among the men there were some whose strength of frame and fierce expression indicated untameable spirits—men who might have been, probably were, heroes among their fellows. It was for men of this stamp that the *goree*, or slave-stick, had been invented, and most effectually did that instrument serve its purpose. Samson himself would have been a mere child in it.

There were men in the gang quite as bold, if not as strong, as Samson. One of these, a very tall and powerful negro, on drawing near to the place where Marizano stood super-intending the passage, turned suddenly aside, and, although coupled by the neck to a fellow-slave, and securely bound at the wrists with a cord, which was evidently cutting into his

R. M. Ballantyne

swelled flesh, made a desperate kick at the half-caste leader.

Although the slave failed to reach him, Marizano was so enraged that he drew a hatchet from his belt and instantly dashed out the man's brains. He fell dead without even a groan. Terrified by this, the rest passed on more rapidly, and there was no further check till a woman in the line, with an infant on her back, stumbled, and, falling down, appeared unable to rise.

"Get up!" shouted Marizano, whose rage had rather been increased than abated by the murder he had just committed.

The woman rose and attempted to advance, but seemed ready to fall again. Seeing this, Marizano plucked the infant from her back, dashed it against a tree, and flung its quivering body into the jungle, while a terrible application of the lash sent the mother shrieking into the swamp. [See Livingstone's *Zambesi and its Tributaries*, page 857; and for a record of cruelties too horrible to be set down in a book like this, we refer the reader to McLeod's *Travels in Eastern Africa*, volume two page 26. Also to the Appendix of Captain Sulivan's *Dhow-Chasing in Zanzibar Waters*, which contains copious and interesting extracts from evidence taken before the Select Committee of the House of Commons.]

Harold and Disco did not witness this, though they heard the shriek of despair, for at the moment the negro they were tending was breathing his last. When his eyes had closed and the spirit had been set free, they rose, and, purposely refraining from looking back, hurried away from the dreadful scene, intending to plunge into the swamp at some distance from the place, and push on until they should regain the head of the column.

"Better if we'd never fallen behind, sir," said Disco, in a

deep, tremulous voice.

"True," replied Harold. "We should have been spared these sights, and the pain of knowing that we cannot prevent this appalling misery and cruelty."

"But surely it is to be prevented *somehow*," cried Disco, almost fiercely. "Many a war that has cost mints o' money has been carried on for causes that ain't worth mentionin' in the same breath with *this*!"

As Harold knew not what to say, and was toiling knee-deep in the swamp at the moment he made no reply.

After marching about half an hour he stopped abruptly and said, with a heavy sigh,—"I hope we haven't missed our way?"

"Hope not sir, but it looks like as if we had."

"I've bin so took up thinkin' o' that accursed traffic in human bein's that I've lost my reckonin'. Howsever, we can't be far out, an', with the sun to guide us, we'll—"

He was stopped by a loud halloo in the woods, on the belt of the swamp.

It was repeated in a few seconds, and Antonio, who, with Jumbo, had followed his master, cried in an excited tone—

"Me knows dat sound!"

"Wot may it be, Tony?" asked Disco.

There was neither time nor need for an answer, for at that moment a ringing cry, something like a bad imitation of a

British cheer, was heard, and a band of men sprang out of the woods and ran at full speed towards our Englishmen.

"Why, Zombo!" exclaimed Disco, wildly.

"Oliveira!" cried Harold.

"Masiko! Songolo!" shouted Antonio and Jumbo.

"An' Jose, Nakoda, Chimbolo, Mabruki!—the whole bun' of 'em," cried Disco, as one after another these worthies emerged from the wood and rushed in a state of frantic excitement towards their friends—"Hooray!"

"Hooroo-hay!" replied the runners.

In another minute our adventurous party of travellers was re-united, and for some time nothing but wild excitement, congratulations, queries that got no replies, and replies that ran tilt at irrelevant queries, with confusion worse confounded by explosions of unbounded and irrepressible laughter not unmingled with tears, was the order of the hour.

"But wat! yoos ill?" cried Zombo suddenly, looking into Disco's face with an anxious expression.

"Well, I ain't 'xac'ly ill, nor I ain't 'xac'ly well neither, but I'm hearty all the same, and werry glad to see your black face, Zombo."

"Ho! hooroo-hay! so's me for see you," cried the excitable Zombo; "but come, not good for talkee in de knees to watter. Fall in boy, ho! sholler 'ums—queek mash!"

That Zombo had assumed command of his party was made evident by the pat way in which he trolled off the words of command formerly taught to him by Harold, as well as by the prompt obedience that was accorded to his orders. He led the party out of the swamp, and, on reaching a dry spot, halted, in order to make further inquiries and answer questions.

"How did you find us, Zombo?" asked Harold, throwing himself wearily on the ground.

"*Yoos* ill," said Zombo, holding up a finger by way of rebuke.

"So I am, though not so ill as I look. But come, answer me. How came you to discover us? You could not have found us by mere chance in this wilderness?"

"Chanz; wat am chanz?" asked the Makololo.

There was some difficulty in getting Antonio to explain the word, from the circumstance of himself being ignorant of it, therefore Harold put the question in a more direct form.

"Oh! ve comes here look for yoo, 'cause peepils d'reck 'ums—show de way. Ve's been veeks, monts, oh! *days* look for yoo. Travil far—g'rong road—turin bak—try agin—fin' yoo now—hooroo-hay!"

"You may say that, indeed. I'd have it in my heart," said Disco, "to give three good rousin' British cheers if it warn't for the thoughts o' that black-hearted villain, Marizano, an' his poor, miserable slaves."

"Marizano!" shouted Chimbolo, glaring at Harold.

"Marizano!" echoed Zombo, glaring at Disco.

Harold now explained to his friends that the slave-hunter was close at hand—a piece of news which visibly excited them,—and described the cruelties of which he had recently been a witness. Zombo showed his teeth like a savage mastiff, and grasped his musket as though he longed to use it, but he uttered no word until the narrative reached that point in which the death of the poor captive was described. Then he suddenly started forward and said something to his followers in the native tongue, which caused each to fling down the small bundle that was strapped to his shoulders.

"Yoo stop here," he cried, earnestly, as he turned to Harold and Disco. "Ve's com bak soon. Ho! boys, sholler 'ums! queek mash!"

No trained band of Britons ever obeyed with more ready alacrity. No attention was paid to Harold's questions. The "queek mash" carried them out of sight in a few minutes, and when the Englishmen, who had run after them a few paces, halted, under the conviction that in their weak condition they might as well endeavour to keep up with race-horses as with their old friends, they found that Antonio alone remained to keep them company.

"Where's Jumbo?" inquired Harold.

"Gon' 'way wid oders," replied the interpreter.

Examining the bundles of their friends, they found that their contents were powder, ball, and food. It was therefore resolved that a fire should be kindled, and food prepared, to be ready for their friends on their return.

"I'm not so sure about their return," said Harold gravely. "They will have to fight against fearful odds if they find the slavers. Foolish fellows; I wish they had not rushed away so madly without consulting us."

The day passed; night came and passed also, and another day dawned, but there was no appearance of Zombo and his men, until the sun had been up for some hours. Then they came back, wending their way slowly—very slowly—through the woods, with the whole of the slave-gang, men, women, and children, at their heels!

"Where is Marizano?" inquired Harold, almost breathless with surprise.

"Dead!" said Zombo.

"Dead?"

"Ay, dead, couldn't be deader."

"And his armed followers?"

"Dead, too—some ob ums. Ve got at um in de night. Shotted Marizano all to hatoms. Shotted mos' ob um follerers too. De res' all scatter like leaves in de wind. Me giv' up now," added Zombo, handing his musket to Harold. "Boys! orrer ums! mees Capitin not no more. Now, Capitin Harol', yoos once more look afer us, an' take care ob all ums peepil."

Having thus demitted his charge, the faithful Zombo stepped back and left our hero in the unenviable position of a half broken-down man with the responsibility of conducting an expedition, and disposing of a large gang of slaves in some unknown part of equatorial Africa!

Leaving him there, we will proceed at once to the coast and follow, for a time, the fortunes of that archvillain, Yoosoof.

CHAPTER TWENTY TWO

DESCRIBES "BLACK IVORY" AT SEA

Having started for the coast with a large gang of slaves a short time before Marizano, as we have already said, and having left the Englishmen to the care of the half-caste, chiefly because he did not desire their company, although he had no objection to the ransom, Yoosoof proceeded over the same track which we have already described in part, leaving a bloody trail behind him.

It is a fearful track, of about 500 miles in length, that which lies between the head of Lake Nyassa and the sea-coast at Kilwa. We have no intention of dragging the reader over it to witness the cruelties and murders that were perpetrated by the slavers, or the agonies endured by the slaves. Livingstone speaks of it as a land of death, of desolation, and dead men's bones. And no wonder, for it is one of the main arteries through which the blood of Africa flows, like the water of natural rivers, to the sea. The slave-gangs are perpetually passing eastward through it—perpetually dropping four-fifths of their numbers on it as they go. Dr Livingstone estimates that, in some cases, not more than *one-tenth* of the slaves captured reach the sea-coast alive. It is therefore rather under than over-stating the case to say that out of every hundred starting from the interior, *eighty* perish on the road.

Yoosoof left with several thousands of strong and healthy men, women, and children—most of them being children—he arrived at Kilwa with only eight hundred. The rest had sunk by the way, either from exhaustion or cruel treatment, or both. The loss was great; but as regards the trader it could not be called severe, because the whole gang of slaves cost him little—some of them even nothing!—and the remaining eight hundred would fetch a good price. They were miserably thin, indeed, and exhibited on their poor, worn, and travel-stained bodies the evidence of many a cruel castigation; but Yoosoof knew that a little rest and good feeding at Kilwa would restore them to some degree of marketable value, and at Zanzibar he was pretty sure of obtaining, in round numbers, about 10 pounds a head for them, while in the Arabian and Persian ports he could obtain much more, if he chose to pass beyond the treaty-protected water at Lamoo, and run the risk of being captured by British cruisers. It is "piracy" to carry slaves north of Lamoo. South of that point for hundreds of miles, robbery, rapine, murder, cruelty, such as devils could not excel if they were to try, is a "domestic institution" with which Britons are pledged not to interfere!

Since the above was written Sir Bartle Frere has returned from his mission, and we are told that a treaty has been signed by the Sultan of Zanzibar putting an end to this domestic slavery. We have not yet seen the terms of this treaty, and must go to press before it appears. We have reason to rejoice and be thankful, however, that such an advantage has been gained. But let not the reader imagine that this settles the question of East African slavery. Portugal still holds to the "domestic institution" in her colonies, and has decreed that it shall not expire till the year 1878. Decreed, in fact, that the horrors which we have attempted to depict shall continue for five years longer! And let it be noted, that the export slave-trade cannot be stopped as long

R. M. Ballantyne

as domestic slavery is permitted. Besides this, there is a continual drain of human beings from Africa through Egypt. Sir Samuel Baker's mission is a blow aimed at that; but nothing, that we know of, is being done in regard to Portuguese wickedness. If the people of this country could only realise the frightful state of things that exists in the African Portuguese territory, and knew how many thousand bodies shall be racked with torture, and souls be launched into eternity during these five years, they would indignantly insist that Portugal should be *compelled* to stop it *at once*. If it is righteous to constrain the Sultan of Zanzibar, is it not equally so to compel the King of Portugal?

The arch robber and murderer, Yoosoof—smooth and oily of face, tongue, and manner though he was—possessed a bold spirit and a grasping heart. The domestic institution did not suit him. Rather than sneak along his villainous course under its protecting "pass," he resolved to bid defiance to laws, treaties, and men-of-war to boot—as many hundreds of his compeers have done and do—and make a bold dash to the north with his eight hundred specimens of Black Ivory.

Accordingly, full of his purpose, one afternoon he sauntered up to the barracoons in which his "cattle" were being rested and fed-up.

Moosa, his chief driver, was busy among them with the lash, for, like other cattle, they had a tendency to rebel, at least a few of them had; the most of them were by that time reduced to the callous condition which had struck Harold and Disco so much on the occasion of their visits to the slave-market of Zanzibar.

Moosa was engaged, when Yoosoof entered, in whipping most unmercifully a small boy whose piercing shrieks had no influence whatever on his tormentor. Close beside them a large strong-boned man lay stretched on the ground. He had just been felled with a heavy stick by Moosa for interfering. He had raised himself on one elbow, while with his right hand he wiped away the blood that oozed from the wound in his head, and appeared to struggle to recover himself from the stunning blow.

"What has he been doing?" asked Yoosoof carelessly, in Portuguese.

"Oh, the old story, rebelling," said Moosa, savagely hurling the boy into the midst of a group of cowering children, amongst whom he instantly shrank as much as possible out of sight. "That brute," pointing to the prostrate man, "was a chief, it appears, in his own country, and has not yet got all the spirit lashed out of him. But it can't last much longer; either the spirit or the life must go. He has carried that little whelp the last part of the way on his back, and now objects to part with him,—got fond of him, I fancy. If you had taken my advice you would have cast them both to the hyenas long ago."

"You are a bad judge of human flesh, Moosa," said Yoosoof, quietly; "more than once you have allowed your passion to rob me of a valuable piece of goods. This man will fetch a good price in Persia, and so will his son. I know that the child is his son, though the fool thinks no one knows that but himself, and rather prides himself on the clever way in which he has continued to keep his whelp beside him on the journey down. Bah! what can one expect from such cattle? Don't separate them, Moosa. They will thrive better together. If we only get them to market in good condition, then we can sell them in separate lots without risking loss of value from pining."

In a somewhat sulky tone, for he was not pleased to be found fault with by his chief, the slave-driver ordered out the boy,

R. M. Ballantyne

who was little more than five years old, though the careworn expression of his thin face seemed to indicate a much more advanced age.

Trembling with alarm, for he expected a repetition of the punishment, yet not daring to disobey, the child came slowly out from the midst of his hapless companions, and advanced. The man who had partly recovered rose to a sitting position, and regarded Moosa and the Arab with a look of hatred so intense that it is quite certain he would have sprung at them, if the heavy slave-stick had not rendered such an act impossible.

"Go, you little whelp," said Moosa, pointing to the fallen chief, and at the same time giving the child a cut with the whip.

With a cry of mingled pain and delight poor Obo, for it was he, rushed into his father's open arms, and laid his sobbing head on his breast. He could not nestle into his neck as, in the days of old, he had been wont to do,—the rough goree effectually prevented that.

Kambira bent his head over the child and remained perfectly still. He did not dare to move, lest any action, however inoffensive, might induce Moosa to change his mind and separate them again.

Poor Kambira! How different from the hearty, bold, kindly chief to whom we introduced the reader in his own wilderness home! His colossal frame was now gaunt in the extreme, and so thin that every rib stood out as though it would burst the skin, and every joint seemed hideously large, while from head to foot his skin was crossed and recrossed with terrible weals, and scarred with open sores, telling of the horrible cruelties to which he had been subjected in the vain attempt to tame his untameable spirit. There can be no question that, if he had been left to the tender mercies of such Portuguese half-caste scoundrels as Moosa or Marizano, he would have been brained with an axe or whipped to death long ago. But Yoosoof was more cool and calculating in his cruelty; he had more respect for his pocket than for the gratification of his angry feelings. Therefore Kambira had reached the coast alive.

Little had the simple chief imagined what awaited him on that coast, and on his way to it, when, in the fulness of his heart, he had stated to Harold Seadrift his determination to proceed thither in search of Azinte. Experience had now crushed hope, and taught him to despair. There was but one gleam of light in his otherwise black sky, and that was the presence of his boy. Life had still one charm in it as long as he could lay hold of Obo's little hand and hoist him, not quite so easily as of yore, on his broad shoulders. Yoosoof was sufficiently a judge of human character to be aware that if he separated these two, Kambira would become more dangerous to approach than the fiercest monster in the African wilderness.

"We must sail to-night and take our chance," said Yoosoof, turning away from his captives; "the time allowed for our trade is past and I shall run straight north without delay."

The Arab here referred to the fact that the period of the year allowed by treaty for the "lawful slave-trade" of the Zanzibar dominions had come to an end. That period extended over several months, and during its course passes from the Sultan secured "domestic slavers" against the British cruisers. After its expiration no export of slaves was permitted anywhere; nevertheless a very large export was carried on, despite non-permission and cruisers. Yoosoof meant to run the blockade and take his chance.

"How many dhows have you got?" asked Yoosoof.

"Three," replied Moosa.

"That will do," returned the Arab after a few minutes' thought; "it will be a tight fit at first, perhaps, but a few days at sea will rectify that. Even in the most healthy season and favourable conditions we must unfortunately count on a good many losses. We shall sail to-morrow."

The morrow came, and three dhows left the harbour of Kilwa, hoisted their lateen sails, and steered northwards.

They were densely crowded with slaves. Even to the eye of a superficial observer this would have been patent, for the upper deck of each was so closely packed with black men, women, and children, that a square inch of it could not anywhere be seen.

They were packed very systematically, in order to secure economical stowage. Each human being sat on his haunches with his thighs against his breast, and his knees touching his chin. They were all ranged thus in rows, shoulder to shoulder, and back to shin, so that the deck was covered with a solid phalanx of human flesh. Change of posture was not provided for: *it was not possible*. There was no awning over the upper deck. The tropical sun poured its rays on the heads of the slaves all day. The dews fell on them all night. The voyage might last for days or weeks, but there was no relief to the wretched multitude. For no purpose whatever could they move from their terrible position, save for the one purpose of being thrown overboard when dead.

But we have only spoken of the upper deck of these dhows. Beneath this there was a temporary bamboo deck, with just space sufficient to admit of men being seated in the position above referred to. This was also crowded, but it was not the "Black Hole" of the vessel. That was lower still. Seated on the stone ballast beneath the bamboo deck there was yet another layer of humanity, whose condition can neither be described nor conceived. Without air, without light, without room to move, without hope; with insufferable stench, with hunger and thirst, with heat unbearable, with agony of body and soul, with dread anticipations of the future, and despairing memories of the past, they sat for days and nights together—fed with just enough of uncooked rice and water to keep soul and body together.

Not enough in all cases, however, for many succumbed, especially among the women and children.

Down in the lowest, filthiest, and darkest corner of this foul hold sat Kambira, with little Obo crushed against his shins. It may be supposed that there was a touch of mercy in this arrangement. Let not the reader suppose so. Yoosoof knew that if Kambira was to be got to market alive, Obo must go along with him. Moosa also knew that if the strong-minded chief was to be subdued at all, it would only be by the most terrible means. Hence his position in the dhow.

There was a man seated alongside of Kambira who for some time had appeared to be ill. He could not be seen, for the place was quite dark, save when a man came down with a lantern daily to serve out rice and water; but Kambira knew that he was very ill from his groans and the quiverings of his body. One night these groans ceased, and the man leaned heavily on the chief—not very heavily, however, he was too closely wedged in all round to admit of that. Soon afterwards he became very cold, and Kambira knew that he was dead. All that night and the greater part of next day the dead man sat propped up by his living comrades. When the daily visitor came down, attention was drawn to the body and it

R. M. Ballantyne

was removed.

Moosa, who was in charge of this dhow (Yoosoof having command of another), gave orders to have the slaves in the hold examined, and it was discovered that three others were dead and two dying. The dead were thrown overboard; the dying were left till they died, and then followed their released comrades.

But now a worse evil befell that dhow. Smallpox broke out among the slaves.

It was a terrible emergency, but Moosa was quite equal to it. Ordering the infected, and suspected, slaves to be brought on deck, he examined them. In this operation he was assisted and accompanied by two powerful armed men. There were passengers on board the dhow, chiefly Arabs, and a crew, as well as slaves. The passengers and crew together numbered about thirty-four, all of whom were armed to the teeth. To these this inspection was of great importance, for it was their interest to get rid of the deadly disease as fast as possible.

The first slave inspected, a youth of about fifteen, was in an advanced stage of the disease, in fact, dying. A glance was sufficient and at a nod from Moosa, the two powerful men seized him and hurled him into the sea. The poor creature was too far gone even to struggle for life. He sank like a stone. Several children followed. They were unquestionably smitten with the disease, and were at once thrown overboard. Whether the passengers felt pity or no we cannot say. They expressed none, but looked on in silence.

So far the work was easy, but when men and women were brought up on whom the disease had not certainly taken effect, Moosa was divided between the desire to check the progress of the evil, and the desire to save valuable property.

The property itself also caused some trouble in a few instances, for when it became obvious to one or two of the stronger slave-girls and men what was going to be done with them, they made a hard struggle for their lives, and the two strong men were under the necessity of using a knife, now and then, to facilitate the accomplishment of their purpose. But such cases were rare. Most of the victims were callously submissive; it might not be beyond the truth, in some cases, to say willingly submissive.

Each day this scene was enacted, for Moosa was a very determined man, and full forty human beings were thus murdered, but the disease was not stayed. The effort to check it was therefore given up, and the slaves were left to recover or die where they sat. See account of capture of dhow by Captain Robert B. Cay, of H.M.S. "Vulture," in the *Times of India*, 1872.

While this was going on in the vessel commanded by Moosa, the other two dhows under Yoosoof and a man named Suliman had been lost sight of. But this was a matter of little moment, as they were all bound for the same Persian port, and were pretty sure, British cruisers permitting, to meet there at last. Meanwhile the dhow ran short of water, and Moosa did not like to venture at that time to make the land, lest he should be caught by one of the hated cruisers or their boats. He preferred to let the wretched slaves take their chance of dying of thirst—hoping, however, to lose only a few of the weakest, as water could be procured a little farther north with greater security.

Thus the horrible work of disease, death, and murder went on, until an event occurred which entirely changed the aspect of affairs on board the dhow.

Early one morning, Moosa directed the head of his vessel

R. M. Ballantyne

towards the land with the intention of procuring the much needed water. At the same hour and place two cutters belonging to H.M.S. 'Firefly,' armed with gun and rocket, twenty men, and an interpreter, crept out under sail with the fishing boats from a neighbouring village. They were under the command of Lieutenants Small and Lindsay respectively. For some days they had been there keeping vigilant watch, but had seen no dhows, and that morning were proceeding out rather depressed by the influence of "hope deferred," when a sail was observed in the offing—or, rather, a mast, for the sail of the dhow had been lowered—the owners intending to wait until the tide should enable them to cross the bar.

"Out oars and give way, lads," was the immediate order; for it was necessary to get up all speed on the boats if the dhow was to be reached before she had time to hoist her huge sail.

"I hope the haze will last," earnestly muttered Lieutenant Small in the first cutter.

"Oh that they may keep on sleeping for five minutes more," excitedly whispered Lieutenant Lindsay in the second cutter.

These hopes were coupled with orders to have the gun and rocket in readiness.

But the haze would not last to oblige Mr Small, neither would the Arabs keep on sleeping to please Mr Lindsay. On the contrary, the haze dissipated, and the Arabs observed and recognised their enemies when within about half a mile. With wonderful celerity they hoisted sail and stood out to sea in the full-swing of the monsoon.

There was no little probability that the boats would fail to overhaul a vessel with so large a sail, therefore other means were instantly resorted to.

"Fire!" said Mr Small.

"Fire!" cried Mr Lindsay.

Bang went the gun, whiz went the rocket, almost at the same moment. A rapid rifle-fire was also opened on the slaver— shot, rocket, and ball bespattered the sea and scattered foam in the air, but did no harm to the dhow, a heavy sea and a strong wind preventing accuracy of aim.

"Give it them as fast as you can," was now the order; and well was the order obeyed, for blue-jackets are notoriously smart men in action, and the gun, the rocket, and the rifles kept up a smart iron storm for upwards of two hours, during which time the exciting chase lasted.

At last Jackson, the linguist who was in the stern of Lindsay's boat, mortally wounded the steersman of the dhow with a rifle-ball at a distance of about six hundred yards. Not long afterwards the rocket-cutter, being less heavily weighted than her consort, crept ahead, and when within about a hundred and fifty yards of the slaver, let fly a well-directed rocket. It carried away the parrell which secured the yard of the dhow to the mast and brought the sail down instantly on the deck.

"Hurra!" burst irresistibly from the blue-jackets.

The Arabs were doubly overwhelmed, for besides getting the sail down on their heads, they were astonished and stunned by the shriek, smoke, and flame of the war-rocket. The gun-cutter coming up at the moment the two boats ranged alongside of the slaver, and boarded together.

R. M. Ballantyne

As we have said, the crew and passengers, numbering thirty-four, were armed to the teeth, and they had stood by the halyards during the chase with drawn *creases*, swearing to kill any one who should attempt to shorten sail. These now appeared for a moment as though they meditated resistance, but the irresistible dash of the sailors seemed to change their minds, for they submitted without striking a blow, though many of them were very reluctant to give up their swords and knives.

Fortunately the 'Firefly' arrived in search of her boats that evening, and the slaves were transferred to her deck. But who shall describe the harrowing scene! The dhow seemed a very nest of black ants, it was so crowded, and the sailors, who had to perform the duty of removing the slaves, were nearly suffocated by the horrible stench. Few of the slaves could straighten themselves after their long confinement. Indeed some of them were unable to stand for days afterwards, and many died on board the 'Firefly' before they reached a harbour of refuge and freedom. Those taken from the hold were in the worst condition, especially the children, many of whom were in the most loathsome stages of smallpox, and scrofula of every description. They were so emaciated and weak that many had to be carried on board, and lifted for every movement.

Kambira, although able to stand, was doubled up like an old man, and poor little Obo trembled and staggered when he attempted to follow his father, to whom he still clung as to his last and only refuge.

To convey these poor wretches to a place where they could be cared for was now Captain Romer's chief anxiety. First however, he landed the crew and passengers, with the exception of Moosa and three of his men. The filthy dhow was then scuttled and sunk, after which the 'Firefly' steamed away for Aden, that being the nearest port where the rescued slaves could be landed and set free.

R. M. Ballantyne

CHAPTER TWENTY THREE

THE REMEDY

Reader, we will turn aside at this point to preach you a lay sermon, if you will lend an attentive ear. It shall be brief, and straight to the point. Our text is,—Prevention and Cure.

There are at least three great channels by which the life-blood of Africa is drained. One trends to the east through the Zanzibar dominions, another to the south-east through the Portuguese dependencies, and a third to the north through Egypt. If the slave-trade is to be effectually checked, the flow through these three channels must be stopped. It is vain to rest content with the stoppage of one leak in our ship if two other leaks are left open.

Happily, in regard to the first of these channels, Sir Bartle Frere has been successful in making a grand stride in the way of prevention. If the Sultan of Zanzibar holds to his treaty engagements, "domestic slavery" in his dominions is at an end. Nevertheless, our fleet will be required just as much as ever to prevent the unauthorised, piratical, slave-trade, and this, after all, is but one-third of the preventive work we have to do. Domestic slavery remains untouched in the Portuguese dependencies, and Portugal has decreed that it shall remain untouched until the year 1878! It is well that we should be thoroughly impressed with the fact that so long as slavery in any form is tolerated, the internal—we may say infernal—miseries and horrors which we have attempted to depict will continue to blight the land and brutalise its people. Besides this, justice demands that the same constraint which we lay on the Sultan of Zanzibar should be applied to the King of Portugal. We ought to insist that *his* "domestic slavery" shall cease at *once*. Still further, as Sir Bartle Frere himself has recommended, we should urge upon our Government the appointment of efficient consular establishments in the Portuguese dependencies, as well as vigilance in securing the observance of the treaties signed by the Sultans of Zanzibar and Muscat.

A recent telegram from Sir Samuel Baker assures us that a great step has been made in the way of checking the tide of slavery in the third—the Egyptian—channel, and Sir Bartle Frere bears testimony to the desire of the Khedive that slavery should be put down in his dominions. For this we have reason to be thankful; and the appearance of affairs in that quarter is hopeful, but our hope is mingled with anxiety, because mankind is terribly prone to go to sleep on hopeful appearances. Our nature is such, that our only chance of success lies, under God, in resolving ceaselessly to energise until our ends be accomplished. We must see to it that the Khedive of Egypt acts in accordance with his professions, and for this end efficient consular agency is as needful in the north-east as in the south-east.

So much for prevention, but prevention is not cure. In order to accomplish this two things are necessary. There must be points or centres of refuge for the oppressed on the *mainland* of Africa, and there must be the introduction of the Bible. The first is essential to the second. Where anarchy, murder, injustice, and tyranny are rampant and triumphant, the advance of the missionary is either terribly slow or altogether

R. M. Ballantyne

impossible. The life-giving, soul-softening Word of God, is the only remedy for the woes of mankind, and, therefore, the only cure for Africa. To introduce it effectually, and along with it civilisation and all the blessings that flow therefrom, it is indispensable that Great Britain should obtain, by treaty or by purchase, one or more small pieces of land, there to establish free Christian negro settlements, and there, with force sufficient to defend them from the savages, and worse than savages,—the Arab and Portuguese half-caste barbarians and lawless men who infest the land—hold out the hand of friendship to all natives who choose to claim her protection from the man-stealer, and offer to teach them the blessed truths of Christianity and the arts of civilisation. Many of the men who are best fitted to give an opinion on the point agree in holding that some such centre, or centres, on the mainland are essential to the permanent cure of slavery, although they differ a little as to the best localities for them. Take, for instance, Darra Salaam on the coast, the Manganja highlands near the river Shire, and Kartoum on the Nile. Three such centres would, if established, begin at once to dry up the slave-trade at its three fountain-heads, while our cruisers would check it on the coast. In these centres of light and freedom the negroes might see exemplified the blessings of Christianity and civilisation, and, thence, trained native missionaries might radiate into all parts of the vast continent armed only with the Word of God, the shield of Faith, and the sword of the Spirit in order to preach the glad tidings of salvation through Jesus Christ our Lord.

In brief, the great points on which we ought as a nation, to insist, are the *immediate* abolition of the slave-trade in Portuguese dependencies; the scrupulous fulfilment of treaty obligations by the Sultans of Zanzibar and Muscat, the Shah of Persia, and the Khedive of Egypt; the establishment by our Government of efficient consular agencies where such are required; the acquisition of territory on the mainland for the purposes already mentioned, and the united action of all Christians in our land to raise funds and send men to preach the Gospel to the negro. So doing we shall, with God's blessing, put an end to the Eastern slave-trade, save equatorial Africa, and materially increase the commerce, the riches, and the happiness of the world.

R. M. Ballantyne

CHAPTER TWENTY FOUR

TELLS OF SAD SIGHTS, AND SUDDEN EVENTS, AND UNEXPECTED MEETINGS

In the course of time, our hero, Harold Seadrift, and his faithful ally, Disco Lillihammer, after innumerable adventures which we are unwillingly obliged to pass over in silence, returned to the coast and, in the course of their wanderings in search of a vessel which should convey them to Zanzibar, found themselves at last in the town of Governor Letotti. Being English travellers, they were received as guests by the Governor, and Harold was introduced to Senhorina Maraquita.

Passing through the market-place one day, they observed a crowd round the flag-staff in the centre of the square, and, following the irresistible tendency of human nature in such circumstances, ran to see what was going on.

They found that a slave was about to be publicly whipped by soldiers. The unhappy man was suspended by the wrists from the flag-staff, and a single cord of coir round his waist afforded him additional support.

"Come away, we can do no good here," said Harold, in a low, sorrowful tone, which was drowned in the shriek of the victim, as the first lash fell on his naked shoulders.

"Pra'ps he's a criminal," suggested Disco, as he hurried away, endeavouring to comfort himself with the thought that the man probably deserved punishment. "It's not the whippin' I think so much of," he added; "that is the only thing as will do for some characters, but it's the awful cruelties that goes along with it."

Returning through the same square about an hour later, having almost forgotten about the slave by that time, they were horrified to observe that the wretched man was still hanging there.

Hastening towards him, they found that he was gasping for breath. His veins were bursting, and his flesh was deeply lacerated by the cords with which he was suspended. He turned his head as the Englishmen approached, and spoke a few words which they did not understand; but the appealing look of his bloodshot eyes spoke a language that required no interpreter.

At an earlier period in their career in Africa, both Harold and Disco would have acted on their first impulse, and cut the man down; but experience had taught them that this style of interference, while it put their own lives in jeopardy, had sometimes the effect of increasing the punishment and sufferings of those whom they sought to befriend.

Acting on a wiser plan, they resolved to appeal to Governor Letotti in his behalf. They therefore ran to his residence, where Maraquita, who conversed with Harold in French, informed them that her father was in the "Geresa," or public palaver house. To that building they hastened, and found that it was in the very square they had left. But Senhor Letotti was not there. He had observed the Englishmen coming, and, having a shrewd guess what their errand was, had disappeared and hid himself. His chief-officer informed them that he had left the town early in the morning, and would not return till the afternoon.

Harold felt quite sure that this was a falsehood, but of course was obliged to accept it as truth.

"Is there no one to act for the Governor in his absence?" he asked, anxiously.

No, there was no one; but after a few minutes the chief-officer appeared to be overcome by Harold's earnest entreaties, and said that he could take upon himself to act, that he would suspend the punishment till the Governor's return, when Harold might prefer his petition to him in person.

Accordingly, the slave was taken down. In the afternoon Harold saw the Governor, and explained that he did not wish to interfere with his province as a magistrate, but that what he had witnessed was so shocking that he availed himself of his privilege as a guest to pray that the man's punishment might be mitigated.

Governor Letotti's health had failed him of late, and he had suffered some severe disappointments in money matters, so that his wonted amiability had been considerably reduced. He objected, at first, to interfere with the course of justice; but finally gave a reluctant consent, and the man was pardoned. Afterwards, however, when our travellers were absent from the town for a day, the wretched slave was again tied up, and the full amount of his punishment inflicted; in other words, he was flogged to death. [For the incident on which this is founded we are indebted to the Reverend Doctor Ryan, late Bishop of the Mauritius.]

This incident had such an effect on the mind of Harold, that he resolved no longer to accept the hospitality of Governor Letotti. He had some difficulty, however, in persuading himself to carry his resolve into effect, for the Governor, although harsh in his dealing with the slave, had been exceedingly kind and amiable to himself; but an unexpected event occurred which put an end to his difficulties. This was the illness and sudden death of his host.

Poor, disconsolate Maraquita, in the first passion of her grief, fled to the residence of the only female friend she had in the town, and refused firmly to return home. Thus it came to pass that Harold's intercourse with the Senhorina was cut short at its commencement, and thus he missed the opportunity of learning something of the fortunes of Azinte; for it is certain that, if they had conversed much together, as would probably have been the case had her father lived, some mention of the slave-girl's name could not fail to have been made, and their mutual knowledge of her to have been elicited and interchanged.

In those days there was no regular communication between one point and another of the east coast of Africa and the neighbouring islands. Travellers had frequently to wait long for a chance; and when they got one were often glad to take advantage of it without being fastidious as to its character. Soon after the events above narrated, a small trading schooner touched at the port. It was bound for the Seychelles, intending to return by Zanzibar and Madagascar, and proceed to the Cape. Harold would rather have gone direct to Zanzibar, but, having plenty of time on his hands, as well as means, he was content to avail himself of the opportunity, and took passage in the schooner for himself, Disco, and Jumbo. That sable and faithful friend was the only one of his companions who was willing to follow him anywhere on the face of the earth. The others received their pay and their discharge with smiling faces, and scattered to their several homes—Antonio departing to complete his interrupted honeymoon.

Just before leaving, Harold sought and obtained permission to visit Maraquita, to bid her good-bye. The poor child was terribly overwhelmed by the death of her father, and could not speak of him without giving way to passionate grief. She told Harold that she meant to leave the coast by the first opportunity that should offer, and proceed to the Cape of Good Hope, where, in some part of the interior, lived an old aunt, the only relative she now had on earth, who, she knew, would be glad to receive her. Our hero did his best to comfort the poor girl, and expressed deep sympathy with her, but felt that his power to console was very small indeed. After a brief interview he bade her farewell.

The voyage which our travellers now commenced was likely to be of considerable duration, for the Seychelles Islands lie a long way to the eastward of Africa, but as we have said, time was of no importance to Harold, and he was not sorry to have an opportunity of visiting a group of islands which are of some celebrity in connexion with the East African slave-trade. Thus, all unknown to himself or Disco, as well as to Maraquita, who would have been intensely interested had she known the fact, he was led towards the new abode of our sable heroine Azinte.

But alas! for Kambira and Obo,—they were being conveyed, also, of course, unknown to themselves or to any one else, further and further away from one whom they would have given their heart's blood to meet with and embrace, and it seemed as if there were not a chance of any gleam of light bridging over the ever widening gulf that lay between them, for although Lieutenant Lindsay knew that Azinte had been left at the Seychelles, he had not the remotest idea that Kambira was Azinte's husband, and among several hundreds of freed slaves the second lieutenant of the 'Firefly' was not likely to single out, and hold converse with a chief whose language he did not understand, and who, as far as appearances went, was almost as miserable, sickly, and degraded as were the rest of the unhappy beings by whom he was surrounded.

Providence, however, turned the tide of affairs in favour of Kambira and his son. On reaching Zanzibar Captain Romer had learned from the commander of another cruiser that Aden was at that time somewhat overwhelmed with freed slaves, a considerable number of captures having been recently made about the neighbourhood of that great rendezvous of slavers, the island of Socotra.

The captain therefore changed his mind, and once more very unwillingly directed his course towards the distant Seychelles.

On the way thither many of the poor negroes died, but many began to recover strength under the influence of kind treatment and generous diet. Among these latter was Kambira. His erect gait and manly look soon began to return, and his ribs, so to speak, to disappear. It was otherwise with poor Obo. The severity of the treatment to which he had been exposed was almost too much for so young a frame. He lost appetite and slowly declined, notwithstanding the doctor's utmost care.

This state of things continuing until the 'Firefly' arrived at the Seychelles, Obo was at once conveyed to the hospital which we have referred to as having been established there.

Azinte chanced to be absent in the neighbouring town on some errand connected with her duties as nurse, when her boy was laid on his bed beside a number of similar sufferers. It was a sad sight to behold these little ones. Out of the

R. M. Ballantyne

original eighty-three children who had been placed there forty-seven had died in three weeks, and the remnant were still in a pitiable condition. While on their beds of pain, tossing about in their delirium, the minds of these little ones frequently ran back to their forest homes, and while some, in spirit, laughed and romped once more around their huts, thousands of miles away on the banks of some African river, others called aloud in their sufferings for the dearest of all earthly beings to them—their mothers. Some of them also whispered the name of Jesus, for the missionary had been careful to tell them the story of our loving Lord, while tending their poor bodies.

Obo had fevered slightly, and in the restless half-slumber into which he fell on being put to bed, he, too, called earnestly for his mother. In *his* case, poor child, the call was not in vain.

Lieutenant Lindsay and the doctor of the ship, with Kambira, had accompanied Obo to the hospital.

"Now, Lindsay," said the doctor, when the child had been made as comfortable as circumstances would admit of, "this man must not be left here, for he will be useless, and it is of the utmost consequence that the child should have some days of absolute repose. What shall we do with him?"

"Take him on board again," said Lindsay. "I daresay we shall find him employment for a short time."

"If you will allow me to take charge of him," interposed the missionary, who was standing by them at the time, "I can easily find him employment in the neighbourhood, so that he can come occasionally to see his child when we think it safe to allow him."

"That will be the better plan," said the doctor, "for as long as—"

A short sharp cry near the door of the room cut the sentence short.

All eyes were turned in that direction and they beheld Azinte gazing wildly at them, and standing as if transformed to stone.

The instant Kambira saw his wife he leaped up as if he had received an electric shock, bounded forward like a panther, uttered a shout that did full credit to the chief of a warlike African tribe, and seized Azinte in his arms.

No wonder that thirty-six little black heads leaped from thirty-six little white pillows, and displayed all the whites of seventy-two eyes that were anything but little, when this astonishing scene took place!

But Kambira quickly recovered himself, and, grasping Azinte by the arm, led her gently towards the bed which had just been occupied, and pointed to the little one that slumbered uneasily there. Strangely enough, just at the moment little Obo again whispered the word "mother."

Poor Azinte's eyes seemed ready to start from their sockets. She stretched out her arms and tried to rush towards her child, but Kambira held her back.

"Obo is very sick," he said, "you must touch him tenderly."

The chief looked into his wife's eyes, saw that she understood him, and let her go.

Azinte crept softly to the bed, knelt down beside it and put her arms so softly round Obo that she scarcely moved him, yet she gradually drew him towards her until his head rested on her swelling bosom, and she pressed her lips tenderly upon his brow. It was an old familiar attitude which seemed to pierce the slumbers of the child with a pleasant reminiscence, and dissipate his malady, for he heaved a deep sigh of contentment and sank into profound repose.

"Good!" said the doctor, in a low tone, with a significant nod to Lindsay, when an interpreter had explained what had been already guessed by all present, that Kambira and Azinte were man and wife; "Obo has a better chance now of recovery than I had anticipated; for joy goes a long way towards effecting a cure. Come, we will leave them together."

Kambira was naturally anxious to remain, but like all commanding spirits, he had long ago learned that cardinal virtue, "obedience to whom obedience is due." When it was explained to him that it would be for Obo's advantage to be left alone with his mother for a time, he arose, bowed his head, and meekly followed his friends out of the room.

Exactly one week from that date little Obo had recovered so much of his former health that he was permitted to go out into the air, and, a few days later, Lieutenant Lindsay resolved to take him, and his father and mother, on board the 'Firefly,' by way of a little ploy. In pursuance of this plan he set off from the hospital in company with Kambira, followed at a short distance by Azinte and Obo.

Poor Lindsay! his heart was heavy, while he did his best to convey in dumb show his congratulations to Kambira, for he saw in this unexpected re-union an insurmountable difficulty in the way of taking Azinte back to her former mistress—not that he had ever seen the remotest chance of his being able to achieve that desirable end before this difficulty arose, but love is at times insanely hopeful, just as at other times—and with equally little reason—it is madly despairing.

He had just made some complicated signs with hands, mouth, and eyebrows, and had succeeded in rendering himself altogether incomprehensible to his sable companion, when, on rounding a turn of the path that led to the harbour, he found himself suddenly face to face with Harold Seadrift, Disco Lillihammer, and their follower, Jumbo, all of whom had landed from a schooner, which, about an hour before, had cast anchor in the bay.

"Mr Lindsay!" "Mr Seadrift!" exclaimed each to the other simultaneously, for the reader will remember that they had met once before when our heroes were rescued from Yoosoof by the "Firefly."

"Kambira!" shouted Disco.

"Azinte!" cried Harold, as our sable heroine came into view.

"Obo!" roared the stricken mariner.

Jumbo could only vent his feelings in an appalling yell and an impromptu war-dance round the party, in which he was joined by Disco, who performed a hornpipe with Obo in his arms, to the intense delight of that convalescent youngster.

Thus laughing, questioning, shouting, and dancing, they all effervesced towards the shore like a band of lunatics just escaped from Bedlam!

R. M. Ballantyne

CHAPTER TWENTY FIVE

THE LAST

"How comes it," said Lieutenant Lindsay to Harold, on the first favourable opportunity that occurred after the meeting described in the last chapter; "how comes it that you and Kambira know each other so well?"

"I might reply by asking," said Harold, with a smile, "how comes it that you are so well acquainted with Azinte? but, before putting that question, I will give a satisfactory answer to your own."

Hereupon he gave a brief outline of those events, already narrated in full to the reader, which bore on his first meeting with the slave-girl, and his subsequent sojourn with her husband.

"After leaving the interior," continued our hero, "and returning to the coast, I visited various towns in order to observe the state of the slaves in the Portuguese settlements, and, truly, what I saw was most deplorable—demoralisation and cruelty, and the obstruction of lawful trade, prevailed everywhere. The settlements are to my mind a very pandemonium on earth. Every one seemed to me more or less affected by the accursed atmosphere that prevails. Of course there must be some exceptions. I met with one, at the last town I visited, in the person of Governor Letotti."

"Letotti!" exclaimed Lindsay, stopping abruptly.

"Yes!" said Harold, in some surprise at the lieutenant's manner, "and a most amiable man he was—"

"Was!—was! What do you mean? Is—is he dead?" exclaimed Lindsay, turning pale.

"He died suddenly just before I left," said Harold.

"And Maraquita—I mean his daughter—what of her?" asked the lieutenant, turning as red as he had previously turned pale.

Harold noted the change, and a gleam of light seemed to break upon him as he replied:—

"Poor girl, she was overwhelmed at first by the heavy blow. I had to quit the place almost immediately after the event."

"Did you know her well?" asked Lindsay, with an uneasy glance at his companion's handsome face.

"No; I had just been introduced to her shortly before her father's death, and have scarcely exchanged a dozen sentences with her. It is said that her father died in debt, but of course in regard to that I know nothing certainly. At parting, she told me that she meant to leave the coast and go to stay with a relative at the Cape."

The poor lieutenant's look on hearing this was so peculiar, not to say alarming, that Harold could not help referring to it, and Lindsay was so much overwhelmed by such unexpected news, and, withal, so strongly attracted by Harold's sympathetic manner, that he straightway made a confidant of him, told him of his love for Maraquita, of Maraquita's love for Azinte, of the utter impossibility of his being able to take Azinte back to her old mistress, now that she had found her husband and child, even if it had been admissible for a lieutenant in the British navy to return freed negroes again into slavery, and wound up with bitter lamentations as to his unhappy fate, and expressions of poignant regret that fighting and other desperate means, congenial and easy to his disposition, were not available in the circumstances. After which explosion he subsided, felt ashamed of having thus committed himself, and looked rather foolish.

But Harold quickly put him at his ease. He entered on the subject with earnest gravity.

"It strikes me, Lindsay," he said thoughtfully, after the lieutenant had finished, "that I can aid you in this affair; but you must not ask me how at present. Give me a few hours to think over it, and then I shall have matured my plans."

Of course the lieutenant hailed with heartfelt gratitude the gleam of hope held out to him, and thus the friends parted for a time.

That same afternoon Harold sat under a palm-tree in company with Disco, Jumbo, Kambira, Azinte, and Obo.

"How would you like to go with me to the Cape of Good Hope, Kambira?" asked Harold abruptly.

"Whar dat?" asked the chief through Jumbo.

"Far away to the south of Africa," answered Harold. "You know that you can never go back to your own land now, unless you want to be again enslaved."

"Him say him no' want to go back," interpreted Jumbo; "got all him care for now—Azinte and Obo."

"Then do you agree to go with me?" said Harold.

To this Kambira replied heartily that he did.

"W'y, wot do 'ee mean for to do with 'em?" asked Disco, in some surprise.

"I will get them comfortably settled there," replied Harold. "My father has a business friend in Cape Town who will easily manage to put me in the way of doing it. Besides, I have a particular reason for wishing to take Azinte there.— Ask her, Jumbo, if she remembers a young lady named Senhorina Maraquita Letotti."

To this Azinte replied that she did, and the way in which her eyes sparkled proved that she remembered her with intense pleasure.

"Well, tell her," rejoined Harold, "that Maraquita has grieved very much at losing her, and is *very* anxious to get her back again—not as a slave, but as a friend, for no slavery is allowed in English settlements anywhere, and I am sure that Maraquita hates slavery as much as I do, though she is not English, so I intend to take her and Kambira and Obo to the Cape, where Maraquita is living—or will be living soon."

"Ye don't stick at trifles, sir," said Disco, whose eyes, on hearing this, assumed a thoughtful, almost a troubled look.

"My plan does not seem to please you," said Harold.

R. M. Ballantyne

"Please me, sir, w'y shouldn't it please me? In course you knows best; I was only a little puzzled, that's all."

Disco said no more, but he thought a good deal, for he had noted the beauty and sprightliness of Maraquita, and the admiration with which Harold had first beheld her; and it seemed to him that this rather powerful method of attempting to gratify the Portuguese girl was proof positive that Harold had lost his heart to her.

Harold guessed what was running in Disco's mind, but did not care to undeceive him, as, in so doing, he might run some risk of betraying the trust reposed in him by Lindsay.

The captain of the schooner, being bound for the Cape after visiting Zanzibar, was willing to take these additional passengers, and the anxious lieutenant was induced to postpone total and irrevocable despair, although, Maraquita being poor, and he being poor, and promotion in the service being very slow, he had little reason to believe his prospects much brighter than they were before,—poor fellow!

* * * * *

Time passed on rapid wing—as time is notoriously prone to do—and the fortunes of our *dramatis personae* varied somewhat.

Captain Romer continued to roam the Eastern seas, along with brother captains, and spent his labour and strength in rescuing a few hundreds of captives from among the hundreds of thousands that were continually flowing out of unhappy Africa. Yoosoof and Moosa continued to throw a boat-load or two of damaged "cattle" in the way of the British cruisers, as a decoy, and succeeded on the whole pretty well in running full cargoes of valuable Black Ivory to the northern markets. The Sultan of Zanzibar continued to assure the British Consul that he heartily sympathised with England in her desire to abolish slavery, and to allow his officials, for a "consideration," to prosecute the slave-trade to any extent they pleased! Portugal continued to assure England of her sympathy and co-operation in the good work of repression, and her subjects on the east coast of Africa continued to export thousands of slaves under the protection of the Portuguese and French flags, styling them *free engages*. British-Indian subjects—the Banyans of Zanzibar,—continued to furnish the sinews of war which kept the gigantic trade in human flesh going on merrily. Murders, etcetera, continued to be perpetrated, tribes to be plundered, and hearts to be broken—of course "legally" and "domestically," as well as piratically—during this rapid flight of time.

But nearly everything in this life has its bright lights and half-tints, as well as its deep shadows. During the same flight of time, humane individuals have continued to urge on the good cause of the total abolition of slavery, and Christian missionaries have continued, despite the difficulties of slave-trade, climate, and human apathy, to sow here and there on the coasts the precious seed of Gospel truth, which we trust shall yet be sown broad-cast by native hands, throughout the length and breadth of that mighty land.

To come more closely to the subjects of our tale:

Chimbolo, with his recovered wife and child, sought safety from the slavers in the far interior, and continued to think with pleasure and gratitude of the two Englishmen who hated slavery, and who had gone to Africa just in the nick of time to rescue that unhappy slave who had been almost flogged to death, and was on the point of being drowned in the Zambesi in a sack. Mokompa, also, continued to poetise, as in days gone by, having made a safe retreat with Chimbolo, and, among other things, enshrined all the deeds of the two white men in native verse. Yambo continued to extol play, admire, and propagate the life-sized jumping-jack to such an extent that, unless his career has been cut short by the slavers, we fully expect to find that creature a "domestic institution" when the slave-trade has been crushed, and Africa opened up—as in the end it is certain to be.

During the progress and continuance of all these things, you may be sure our hero was not idle. He sailed, as proposed, with Kambira, Azinte, Obo, Disco, and Jumbo for Zanzibar, touched at the town over which poor Senhor Francisco Alfonso Toledo Bignoso Letotti had ruled, found that the Senhorina had taken her departure; followed, as Disco said, in her wake; reached the Cape, hunted her up, found her out and presented to her, with Lieutenant Lindsay's compliments, the African chief Kambira, his wife Azinte, and his son Obo!

Poor Maraquita, being of a passionately affectionate and romantic disposition, went nearly mad with joy, and bestowed so many grateful glances and smiles on Harold that Disco's suspicions were confirmed, and that bold mariner wished her, Maraquita, "at the bottom of the sea!" for Disco disliked foreigners, and could not bear the thought of his friend being caught by one of them.

Maraquita introduced Harold to her aunt, a middle-aged, leather-skinned, excessively dark-eyed daughter of Portugal. She also introduced him to a bosom friend, at that time on a visit to her aunt. The bosom friend was an auburn-haired, fair-skinned, cheerful-spirited English girl. Before her, Harold Seadrift at once, without an instant's warning, fell flat down, figuratively speaking of course, and remained so— stricken through the heart!

The exigencies of our tale require, at this point, that we should draw our outline with a bold and rapid pencil.

Disco Lillihammer was stunned, and so was Jumbo, when Harold, some weeks after their arrival at the Cape, informed them that he was engaged to be married to Alice Gray, only daughter of the late Sir Eustace Gray, who had been M.P. for some county in England, which he had forgotten the name of, Alice not having been able to recall it, as her father had died when she was four years old, leaving her a fortune of next-to-nothing a year, and a sweet temper.

Being incapable of further stunning, Disco was rather revived than otherwise, and his dark shadow was resuscitated, when Harold added that Kambira had become Maraquita's head-gardener, Azinte cook to the establishment, and Obo page-in-waiting—more probably page-in-mischief—to the young Senhorina. But both Disco and Jumbo had a relapse from which they were long of recovering, when Harold went on to say that he meant to sail for England by the next mail, take Jumbo with him as valet, make proposals to his father to establish a branch of their house at the Cape, come back to manage the branch, marry Alice, and reside in the neighbourhood of the Senhorina Maraquita Letotti's dwelling.

"You means wot you say, I s'pose?" asked Disco.

"Of course I do," said Harold.

"An' yer goin' to take Jumbo as yer walley?"

"Yes."

"H'm; I'll go too as yer keeper."

"My what?"

"Yer keeper—yer strait-veskit buckler, for if you ain't a loonatic ye ought to be."

But Disco did not go to England in that capacity. He remained at the Cape to assist Kambira, at the express command of Maraquita; and continued there until Harold returned, bringing Lieutenant Lindsay with him as a partner in the business; until Harold was married and required a gardener for his own domain; until the Senhorina became Mrs Lindsay; until a large and thriving band of little Cape colonists found it necessary to have a general story-teller and adventure-recounter with a nautical turn of mind; until, in short, he found it convenient to go to England himself for the gal of his heart who had been photographed there years before, and could be rubbed off neither by sickness, sunstroke, nor adversity.

When Disco had returned to the colony with the original of the said photograph, and had fairly settled down on his own farm, then it was that he was wont at eventide to assemble the little colonists round him, light his pipe, and, through its hazy influence, recount his experiences, and deliver his opinions on the slave-trade of East Africa. Sometimes he was pathetic, sometimes humorous, but, however jocular he might be on other subjects, he invariably became very grave and very earnest when he touched on the latter theme.

"There's only one way to cure it," he was wont to say, "and that is, to bring the Portuguese and Arabs to their marrow-bones; put the fleet on the east coast in better workin' order; have consuls everywhere, with orders to keep their weather-eyes open to the slave-dealers; start two or three British settlements—ports o' refuge—on the mainland; hoist the Union Jack, and, last but not least, send 'em the Bible."

We earnestly commend the substance of Disco's opinions to

the reader, for there is urgent need for action. There is death where life should be; ashes instead of beauty; desolation in place of fertility, and, even while we write, terrible activity in the horrible traffic in—"Black Ivory."

THE END

R. M. Ballantyne

Choose from Thousands of 1stWorldLibrary Classics By

A. M. Barnard
Ada Leverson
Adolphus William Ward
Aesop
Agatha Christie
Alexander Aaronsohn
Alexander Kielland
Alexandre Dumas
Alfred Gatty
Alfred Ollivant
Alice Duer Miller
Alice Turner Curtis
Alice Dunbar
Allen Chapman
Alleyne Ireland
Ambrose Bierce
Amelia E. Barr
Amory H. Bradford
Andrew Lang
Andrew McFarland Davis
Andy Adams
Angela Brazil
Anna Alice Chapin
Anna Sewell
Annie Besant
Annie Hamilton Donnell
Annie Payson Call
Annie Roe Carr
Annonaymous
Anton Chekhov
Archibald Lee Fletcher
Arnold Bennett
Arthur C. Benson
Arthur Conan Doyle
Arthur M. Winfield
Arthur Ransome
Arthur Schnitzler
Arthur Train
Atticus
B.H. Baden-Powell
B. M. Bower
B. C. Chatterjee
Baroness Emmuska Orczy
Baroness Orczy
Basil King
Bayard Taylor
Ben Macomber
Bertha Muzzy Bower
Bjornstjerne Bjornson

Booth Tarkington
Boyd Cable
Bram Stoker
C. Collodi
C. E. Orr
C. M. Ingleby
Carolyn Wells
Catherine Parr Traill
Charles A. Eastman
Charles Amory Beach
Charles Dickens
Charles Dudley Warner
Charles Farrar Browne
Charles Ives
Charles Kingsley
Charles Klein
Charles Hanson Towne
Charles Lathrop Pack
Charles Romyn Dake
Charles Whibley
Charles Willing Beale
Charlotte M. Braeme
Charlotte M. Yonge
Charlotte Perkins Stetson
Clair W. Hayes
Clarence Day Jr.
Clarence E. Mulford
Clemence Housman
Confucius
Coningsby Dawson
Cornelis DeWitt Wilcox
Cyril Burleigh
D. H. Lawrence
Daniel Defoe
David Garnett
Dinah Craik
Don Carlos Janes
Donald Keyhoe
Dorothy Kilner
Dougan Clark
Douglas Fairbanks
E. Nesbit
E. P. Roe
E. Phillips Oppenheim
E. S. Brooks
Earl Barnes
Edgar Rice Burroughs
Edith Van Dyne
Edith Wharton

Edward Everett Hale
Edward J. O'Biren
Edward S. Ellis
Edwin L. Arnold
Eleanor Atkins
Eleanor Hallowell Abbott
Eliot Gregory
Elizabeth Gaskell
Elizabeth McCracken
Elizabeth Von Arnim
Ellem Key
Emerson Hough
Emilie F. Carlen
Emily Bronte
Emily Dickinson
Enid Bagnold
Enilor Macartney Lane
Erasmus W. Jones
Ernie Howard Pie
Ethel May Dell
Ethel Turner
Ethel Watts Mumford
Eugene Sue
Eugenie Foa
Eugene Wood
Eustace Hale Ball
Evelyn Everett-green
Everard Cotes
F. H. Cheley
F. J. Cross
F. Marion Crawford
Fannie E. Newberry
Federick Austin Ogg
Ferdinand Ossendowski
Fergus Hume
Florence A. Kilpatrick
Fremont B. Deering
Francis Bacon
Francis Darwin
Frances Hodgson Burnett
Frances Parkinson Keyes
Frank Gee Patchin
Frank Harris
Frank Jewett Mather
Frank L. Packard
Frank V. Webster
Frederic Stewart Isham
Frederick Trevor Hill
Frederick Winslow Taylor

Friedrich Kerst
Friedrich Nietzsche
Fyodor Dostoyevsky
G.A. Henty
G.K. Chesterton
Gabrielle E. Jackson
Garrett P. Serviss
Gaston Leroux
George A. Warren
George Ade
Geroge Bernard Shaw
George Cary Eggleston
George Durston
George Ebers
George Eliot
George Gissing
George MacDonald
George Meredith
George Orwell
George Sylvester Viereck
George Tucker
George W. Cable
George Wharton James
Gertrude Atherton
Gordon Casserly
Grace E. King
Grace Gallatin
Grace Greenwood
Grant Allen
Guillermo A. Sherwell
Gulielma Zollinger
Gustav Flaubert
H. A. Cody
H. B. Irving
H.C. Bailey
H. G. Wells
H. H. Munro
H. Irving Hancock
H. R. Naylor
H. Rider Haggard
H. W. C. Davis
Haldeman Julius
Hall Caine
Hamilton Wright Mabie
Hans Christian Andersen
Harold Avery
Harold McGrath
Harriet Beecher Stowe
Harry Castlemon
Harry Coghill
Harry Houidini

Hayden Carruth
Helent Hunt Jackson
Helen Nicolay
Hendrik Conscience
Hendy David Thoreau
Henri Barbusse
Henrik Ibsen
Henry Adams
Henry Ford
Henry Frost
Henry James
Henry Jones Ford
Henry Seton Merriman
Henry W Longfellow
Herbert A. Giles
Herbert Carter
Herbert N. Casson
Herman Hesse
Hildegard G. Frey
Homer
Honore De Balzac
Horace B. Day
Horace Walpole
Horatio Alger Jr.
Howard Pyle
Howard R. Garis
Hugh Lofting
Hugh Walpole
Humphry Ward
Ian Maclaren
Inez Haynes Gillmore
Irving Bacheller
Isabel Cecilia Williams
Isabel Hornibrook
Israel Abrahams
Ivan Turgenev
J.G.Austin
J. Henri Fabre
J. M. Barrie
J. M. Walsh
J. Macdonald Oxley
J. R. Miller
J. S. Fletcher
J. S. Knowles
J. Storer Clouston
J. W. Duffield
Jack London
Jacob Abbott
James Allen
James Andrews
James Baldwin

James Branch Cabell
James DeMille
James Joyce
James Lane Allen
James Lane Allen
James Oliver Curwood
James Oppenheim
James Otis
James R. Driscoll
Jane Abbott
Jane Austen
Jane L. Stewart
Janet Aldridge
Jens Peter Jacobsen
Jerome K. Jerome
Jessie Graham Flower
John Buchan
John Burroughs
John Cournos
John F. Kennedy
John Gay
John Glasworthy
John Habberton
John Joy Bell
John Kendrick Bangs
John Milton
John Philip Sousa
John Taintor Foote
Jonas Lauritz Idemil Lie
Jonathan Swift
Joseph A. Altsheler
Joseph Carey
Joseph Conrad
Joseph E. Badger Jr
Joseph Hergesheimer
Joseph Jacobs
Jules Vernes
Julian Hawthrone
Julie A Lippmann
Justin Huntly McCarthy
Kakuzo Okakura
Karle Wilson Baker
Kate Chopin
Kenneth Grahame
Kenneth McGaffey
Kate Langley Bosher
Kate Langley Bosher
Katherine Cecil Thurston
Katherine Stokes
L. A. Abbot
L. T. Meade

L. Frank Baum
Latta Griswold
Laura Dent Crane
Laura Lee Hope
Laurence Housman
Lawrence Beasley
Leo Tolstoy
Leonid Andreyev
Lewis Carroll
Lewis Sperry Chafer
Lilian Bell
Lloyd Osbourne
Louis Hughes
Louis Joseph Vance
Louis Tracy
Louisa May Alcott
Lucy Fitch Perkins
Lucy Maud Montgomery
Luther Benson
Lydia Miller Middleton
Lyndon Orr
M. Corvus
M. H. Adams
Margaret E. Sangster
Margret Howth
Margaret Vandercook
Margaret W. Hungerford
Margret Penrose
Maria Edgeworth
Maria Thompson Daviess
Mariano Azuela
Marion Polk Angellotti
Mark Overton
Mark Twain
Mary Austin
Mary Catherine Crowley
Mary Cole
Mary Hastings Bradley
Mary Roberts Rinehart
Mary Rowlandson
M. Wollstonecraft Shelley
Maud Lindsay
Max Beerbohm
Myra Kelly
Nathaniel Hawthrone
Nicolo Machiavelli
O. F. Walton
Oscar Wilde

Owen Johnson
P.G. Wodehouse
Paul and Mabel Thorne
Paul G. Tomlinson
Paul Severing
Percy Brebner
Percy Keese Fitzhugh
Peter B. Kyne
Plato
Quincy Allen
R. Derby Holmes
R. L. Stevenson
R. S. Ball
Rabindranath Tagore
Rahul Alvares
Ralph Bonehill
Ralph Henry Barbour
Ralph Victor
Ralph Waldo Emmerson
Rene Descartes
Ray Cummings
Rex Beach
Rex E. Beach
Richard Harding Davis
Richard Jefferies
Richard Le Gallienne
Robert Barr
Robert Frost
Robert Gordon Anderson
Robert L. Drake
Robert Lansing
Robert Lynd
Robert Michael Ballantyne
Robert W. Chambers
Rosa Nouchette Carey
Rudyard Kipling
Saint Augustine
Samuel B. Allison
Samuel Hopkins Adams
Sarah Bernhardt
Sarah C. Hallowell
Selma Lagerlof
Sherwood Anderson
Sigmund Freud
Standish O'Grady
Stanley Weyman
Stella Benson
Stella M. Francis

Stephen Crane
Stewart Edward White
Stijn Streuvels
Swami Abhedananda
Swami Parmananda
T. S. Ackland
T. S. Arthur
The Princess Der Ling
Thomas A. Janvier
Thomas A Kempis
Thomas Anderton
Thomas Bailey Aldrich
Thomas Bulfinch
Thomas De Quincey
Thomas Dixon
Thomas H. Huxley
Thomas Hardy
Thomas More
Thornton W. Burgess
U. S. Grant
Upton Sinclair
Valentine Williams
Various Authors
Vaughan Kester
Victor Appleton
Victor G. Durham
Victoria Cross
Virginia Woolf
Wadsworth Camp
Walter Camp
Walter Scott
Washington Irving
Wilbur Lawton
Wilkie Collins
Willa Cather
Willard F. Baker
William Dean Howells
William le Queux
W. Makepeace Thackeray
William W. Walter
William Shakespeare
Winston Churchill
Yei Theodora Ozaki
Yogi Ramacharaka
Young E. Allison
Zane Grey